D0467430

TEXANS

ALSO BY RON STRICKLAND:

Shank's Mare: A Compendium of Remarkable Walks
River Pigs and Cayuses
*Vermonters: Oral Histories from Down Country to the Northeast
 Kingdom*
Pacific Northwest Trail Guide
*Whistlepunks and Geoducks: Oral Histories from the Pacific
 Northwest*

Oral Histories

from the

Lone Star

State

TEXANS

RON
STRICKLAND

PARAGON HOUSE
NEW YORK

PUBLISHED IN THE UNITED STATES BY
PARAGON HOUSE
90 FIFTH AVENUE
NEW YORK, NY 10011

THE RUSTY BRADLEY STORY IN "A LITTLE ORNERY STREAK" IS FROM
BRIDLEWISE AND OTHERWISE, VOL. II, AND REPRINTED BY PERMISSION OF
RUSTY BRADLEY.

MANUFACTURED IN THE UNITED STATES OF AMERICA

LIBRARY OF CONGRESS CATALOGING-IN-PUBLICATION DATA
STRICKLAND, RON.
TEXANS: ORAL HISTORIES FROM THE LONE STAR STATE/RON
   STRICKLAND.—1ST ED.
    P. CM.
   INCLUDES INDEX.
   ISBN 1-55778-038-2 : $24.95
  1. TEXAS—BIOGRAPHY. 2. ORAL BIOGRAPHY. I. TITLE.
CT262.S87 1991
920.0764—DC20   91-4469
                                             CIP

10 9 8 7 6 5 4 3 2

There was no trail to follow, but Leigh knew the waterings, and as for keeping our course all we had to do was to head towards the north star and bear a fraction to the right. From Palo Duro Canyon to Dodge City we did not see a soul; but deer and antelopes, prairie dogs, prairie chickens, coyotes, and wild turkeys were visible by the thousands with now and then a lonesome buffalo. I had a profound attachment for the canyons and plains and all this wild life. As we trailed along day by day with only the sounds of the tramping cattle, of the swish of grass beneath my horse's feet, and of the creak of saddle leather to disturb the silence, I felt that attachment. But something stronger than the plains and the canyons was pulling me back to the brush and prairies of the Nueces River country. Whether I stayed on the Plains, however, or drifted west into the mountains, or rode until I smelled the salt in the bayous off Matagorda Bay, my freedom would not be hampered by crowding population. From the Canadian Rockies to the Platte, from the Platte to Dodge on the Arkansas, from Dodge to the Gulf of Mexico, the land was free and open and it belonged to the cowboy. I was free too and, therefore, I was happy.

J. Frank Dobie,
A Vaquero of the Brush Country

I am often asked why I, a true-born Texan, moved east, and as good an answer as any is that I got tired of dealing creatively with the kind of mental and emotive inarticulateness that I found in Texas. The move off the land is now virtually completed, and that was the great subject that Texas offered writers of my generation. The one basic subject it offers us now is loneliness.

Larry McMurtry,
The Atlantic, 1975

The first thing that I remember as a child is that I was standing in front of a huge TV and I saw this man land on the moon.

Michael Dell, President,
Dell Computer Corp., 1990

CONTENTS

ACKNOWLEDGMENTS

Frank "Chips" Alexander (Dallas); Paula Allen (Galveston); Roger Allen (San Angelo); AMTRAK; Jim Braud, Crawfish Racing Commissioner (Port Neches); Susan Brown (Houston); Dan Bus, editor, Del Rio Guide; Mimi Campbell (Dallas); Gail Cooper (Oakland, Calif.); Antje Fedderke (West Germany); Carol Follett (El Paso); Judith A. Graham (Westford, Mass.); Jud Singleton Gray (San Angelo); A. J. Judice (Bridge City); Jane Knapak, Uvalde *Leader-News;* Buster Lehnis (Early); Sally and Frank Light (formerly of the American consulate at Juárez, Mexico); Campbell and Lynn Loughmiller (Whitehouse); Jack McGuire (Fredericksburg); James McNutt (San Antonio); Bonnie and Bill Miller (Houston); Charlotte Baker Montgomery (Nacogdoches); Lucille and Martin Nerger (Houston); Old Chicken Farm Art Center (San Angelo); Jan Olson (Renton, Wash.); Genora Burkholder Prewit, curator, West of the Pecos Museum (Pecos); John Robert Prude (Fort Davis); Tumbleweed Smith (Big Spring); Willie Sofka, manager, Christie's Beachcomber Restaurant (Galveston); George Smiley (Alpine); Burnley Snyder (Seattle, Wash.); Suzanne Stubblefield (Houston); Garland Weeks (Loveland, Colo.); Robert Whistler, former chief naturalist, Padre Island National Seashore (Corpus Christi).

INTRODUCTION

Texans is a collection of miniautobiographies the common thread of which is Lone Star identity. *Texans* is about that kernel of regional self which has evolved from the Wild West through the twentieth century's flight from the land and into the twenty-first century's steps into space. I won't offer a definition of Texan-ness except to remind you of the stranger who asked an old-timer about his origins. The old man replied, "Son, don't ever ask a man where he's from. If he's from Texas, he'll tell ya. And if he isn't, there's no use in making him ashamed of himself."

Texans is nearly four dozen telling something important about their own lives. I have selected these stories both for their inherent interest and for their value as a cumulative portrait of the state. If you already know Texas well, these tales will enrich your understanding. If you are a newcomer, hang on for the ride!

Let me warn you that I am partial to several themes crucial to the future of Texas and the nation. First, *education* has been constantly in the news whether as (1) no-pass/no-Play athletic eligibility rules, (2) student boycotts of inadequately funded classrooms, or (3) legislative and constitutional formulas for school funding. This compost pile of despair and bitterness will heat up throughout the 1990s and into the twenty-first century until finally politicians will be held accountable for the failure of vision that has characterized Texas education. Solons such as Rae Files Still who led the way for change will be remembered as heroes.

I have met many complacent dunces in Texas, some of whom have college degrees. And I could add my two bits to the national

chorus of those eager to deride the Texas penchant for materialism and status-seeking. After all, a quest for knowledge is certainly
not part of the Texas legacy!

Or is it? I have included, among others, the story of a cotton-
pulling lad, Gordon Wood, who determined at an early age to
escape stoop labor through schooling. Education was and is the
key to the hopes of people like Octavio Garcia, who overcame
prejudice to bring medicine to the neglected people of the Rio
Grande Valley. Education literally took Alan Bean from Fort
Worth to the moon.

A second theme here is that Texas's *natural environment* is in-
creasingly out of kilter. For instance, the lowly fire ant is a threat
to the four-and-a-half-billion-dollar supercollider south of Dallas
in Ellis County. More important, the "biohazard" ants, besides
munching electrical cables, are radically altering the environment
as they advance across the state. Tom Powell of the Delta P Ranch
in Giddings raises exotic deer but he has been fighting a losing
battle against the marauders. "The whole landscape on my range
has changed," he says. "The fire ants are devastating the young
deer, who are taught by Mother Nature to lay there and not move
when their mother goes to feed. The ants get all over them, get in
their eyes, and it's too damn late. They get infected or blinded."

It is not only the land that has been changing. I often hear
old-timers say that they remember when Texas was a less homoge-
nized place where the accents were as colorful as the sunsets and
where cultural groups were as separate as Texas's two hundred
fifty-four counties. So another theme is *personal geography* and how
people are imbued with love of place. Because Texas places are no
mere coordinates on a map. This geography is down home! It's
Texas Ranger Dan Westbrook corralling a fugitive on the Rio
Grande, coach Gordon Wood marshaling Brownwood football
squads, legislator Rae Files Still making Ellis County stump
speeches, and outlaw Joe Newton robbing trains Old West-style
across the whole map. And Hallie Stillwell traveling to West Texas
by covered wagon.

In 1924 would-be folklorist J. Frank Dobie wrote to a friend: "I
wish that I could take a year off to do nothing but collect legends
and write them down. I can smell a legend as far as a buzzard can

smell a dead cow, and the moment I cross Red River my nostrils are a-quiver with the delectable odor of legends of my own soil." One of those legends concerns covered wagons. Nowadays prairie schooners are as legendary to most Americans as Columbus's ships. Wagon wheels have become mere lawn decorations. That's why I asked Hallie Stillwell (born in 1897) about her first lesson in personal geography.

In 1910 Hallie and her sister drove a covered wagon as part of their family's migration from New Mexico to Brewster County, the southwest Texas province always trumpeted as being larger than Connecticut. To her it was not a romantic undertaking, the way many of us would think of it today, but merely "a necessity" to enable her to go to school. Texas was full of people like Hallie's family. In some ways it still is. Hallie says of her father, Alvin Guy Crawford, "He was a pioneer and a venturesome sort of person, always looking for a greener pasture. My father had lived in different places. But he was kind of a natural pioneer. And when New Mexico was opened up for settlement along about 1907, he decided to go out there and take up some land."[1]

Hallie's father spent three years proving up on a homestead, raising beans, but decided in 1910 to emigrate with his six kids to Alpine, Texas, because he heard of a good new school. Twelve-year-old Hallie wore a plain, homemade dress and was eager to get to Texas.

So we lit out for Alpine. Our speed depended on the terrain but we might go twenty to twenty-five miles a day on those iron-rimmed, wooden wheels. You'd just bump along all day. It took us twenty-four days to come from where we lived in the Estancia Valley, New Mexico. I don't know how my father found the way. But he did. We just went from place to place, cross-country. He knew which direction he was goin' and that's how we came. He didn't have a compass and he hadn't been there before. He'd talk to different people and when we'd stop along the way, he'd inquire about what was ahead, where there'd be water, and where we could likely stay.

---

[1] J. Frank Dobie memorialized such Texans in *A Vaquero of the Brush Country*, based upon Hallie's father's lifelong friend John Young.

That brings up the theme of *mentors*. Hallie Stillwell's first hero was her father, a self-educated merchant whose level-headedness influenced her eventual management of her own ranch and store. Hallie's next mentor (on whom she had a crush), school principal J. Frank Dobie, later became famous as a Texas folk historian. Partly because of his influence Hallie went on to become a teacher herself.

One of today's Dallas teenagers demonstrated the same thirst for education when I met him near his public housing project. "I like to draw houses and figure out how they will look after they are built," said sixteen-year-old Herman Nieto. Herman wanted to attend a junior college on his way to becoming an architect. I wonder how likely it is that someone from projects known locally as Roach City can achieve that goal. Herman Nieto is a personable kid, a Texan whose ticket up is education. Perhaps what he needs most is a mentor.

In this book folks often discuss mentors, those personal heroes who help us choose our life's trail. For instance, the great Texas essayist and raconteur John Henry Faulk successfully defended himself in the early 1960s against being blacklisted by political zealots after he had defended other writers from attack. Much later he recalled a man whose example had led him in this direction. John Henry had grown up in such a strict Travis County Methodist family that he had not known until he was sixteen years old that "people ever had any kind of social gatherings unconnected with the Methodist Church." Summer revival meetings were a central focus of John Henry's boyhood, but one summer a "sweet old man" opened the boy's eyes to another perspective:

I had a friend, old Grandpa Bible, who was a hunting companion of mine. And he didn't go to church. He didn't believe in organized religion. And I'll never forget, he was having Sunday dinner with us, and the preacher, Brother Culpepper, was there eating his share of the fried chicken. And he looked over at Grandpa Bible and said, "Brother Bible, I'm quite surprised that I haven't seen you in services during the whole course of this revival meeting."

And Grandpa Bible looked up without missing a beat and said,

"You'd be a blamed sight more surprised if you ever seen me there. I don't believe in goin' to church."

Mama looked embarrassed and Daddy looked embarrassed. Brother Culpepper looked shocked. He said, "I can't believe a man of your stature would say a thing like that in front of these little children."

Grandpa Bible looked him right in the eye and said, "Let me tell you something. As I understand this here country and the constitution of the United States, it guarantees you a right to preach any gospel you want to preach and it guarantees me the right not to have to listen to it."

Well, Brother Culpepper allowed as how he was going to pray for Grandpa Bible and Grandpa Bible would see the error of that shocking, terrible thinking but for some reason or other Grandpa Bible was always a hero to me after that. And the more I reflect on it, the more I understand that perhaps Grandpa Bible understood the constitution better than Brother Culpepper did.[2]

Besides mentors, another theme of *Texans* is *change.* Texas in the boom-to-bust, high-tech 1980s changed even faster than it had in the 1880s, when the open range had faded away. Now in the 1990s we continue to watch the transition from a rural to an urban Texas, from an Anglo majority to greater pluralism, from farm/oil dependance to greater diversity. The 1980s collapse of much of Texas's savings and loan industry brought with it the greatest region-to-region transfer of wealth in American history, Congress's savings and loan bailout. Change is occurring so rapidly that Texan-ness is fast evolving. Recently a Korean named Sam Lee immigrated from Los Angeles looking for opportunity in El Paso—where Spanish explorers had sought wealth and fame four centuries earlier. Soon Sam Lee's store near the bridge to Juarez was one of many Korean-owned shops, selling everything from Mexican knickknacks to Korean ginseng.

The hopes and dreams of all the Sam Lees make up Texas.

I still find it very romantic. Abilene-born A. C. Greene recalls

---

[2]Broadcast on National Public Radio during the late 1970s.

that in his West Texas boyhood people still often traveled by team and wagon. "It was exciting, but not at all uncommon," he says, "to see a covered wagon or two pulling out South First early in the morning, headed for New Mexico or some remote, far West Texas ranch."[3]

That is the kind of thrill I have sought in Texas. Almost always it occurs unexpectedly, as when Bones Nobles played his fifty-year-old cowbones for me at his Beaumont home. Afterward he began to tell how he had grown up as a young pine-gum gatherer in segregated East Texas. His strongly remembered emotions affected me like the sight of those westering wagons had thrilled A. C. Greene.

The full diversity of Texans often takes me by surprise as I travel the state. I often make heady jumps from one Texas to another, as on the Memorial Day I went from interviewing an Arlington motorcycle gang to talking with the Aggie banker/owner of the Dallas Cowboys. The leather-jacketed outlaws were convinced that the straight world envied them their "freedom." The banker, surrounded by his A&M memorabilia, was sure that God was an Aggie.

I treasure everyone's stories. Memory, experience, and the narrative urge are the raw materials novelists, poets, entertainers, and balladeers carve and burnish into rich gems of invention. I believe that at its best nothing can surpass the warmth and drama of a single voice speaking directly to us of the things that matter. The campfire flickers on the rapt faces. The radio reader charms and gladdens through the limpid pulses of the air. A pastor delivers a sermon full of passion and life. A parent invents a fable for the falling-asleep child. Our impersonal age cries out for this balm, the healing touch of words, the storyteller's art.

This book seeks Texan-ness in the tales of natives, immigrants, and even exiles. *Texans* is less a history than a collection of reminiscences, some of which may need a grain of salt. After all, who could believe barbecue king Clem Mikeska when he says that 4-H kids never cry when their prize steers are led away for someone's din-

---

[3]A. C. Greene, *A Personal Country* (College Station: Texas A & M, 1979), pp. 319–320.

ner? And did Wyatt Moore really poach all those Caddo Lake fish and make all that moonshine? And what about all those tall tales about Texas weather?

I hope you will approach *Texans* the same way I do out among the feedlots, stock tanks, dry creeks, hardscrabble hills, Piney Woods, and city streets! I go as a listener, reining in my preconceptions, eager to hear the richness of many voices and cultures.

Take time to read the stories aloud to yourself and to your family, friends, and neighbors. Look for the grins, pauses, smiles, and tears that are not printed on the page but are part of the story just the same.

Take Johnny Lindroos, for instance, of Galveston. Like so many American ports Galveston is but a shadow of its old maritime self. The city has been tastefully resurrected as a tourist mecca, but the shipping moved to Houston decades ago. There is still one tall ship, however, the *Elissa,* an iron-hulled bark. She serves now as a museum, cruise ship, and school for sailors. She served me by delivering a cargo of echoes of the old Galveston, the old Texas.

Capt. Johnny Lindroos (born in 1889) relished his daily bellringing role at the Beachcomber Restaurant's ship's bell to signal the noon hour. But I sensed as I talked with him at our table heaped high with delicacies that Johnny would have been happier sailing before the mast, with plain hardtack and hard lot. So I took him out to see the *Elissa.* At the age of ninety-seven he was slow to climb the gangplank and was much more frail than he had seemed in the restaurant.

But once the old sea dog stood again among the marlinspikes, lines, hatches, and other shipboard gear he seemed like a different man. In fact, Captain Lindroos told me in no uncertain terms when I wanted to go up to the great wooden wheel that an ordinary seaman couldn't go up on the poop deck. "That's right," he said forcefully, "the helmsman is the only one that could go up there."

Everything around us brought forth tales of shipboard life. Even the grain of the deck planking reminded Johnny of holystoning and caulking. As I listened to the old salt it was easy to imagine our sails billowing and our ship standing out into the roads where the captain would chart our course for the Horn. Before long I had the illusion that we and our cotton cargo had left Galveston astern and that we were settling down to our watches and tales. Johnny said that once when he had been furling a sail up on the royal, astraddle the foot rope, clinging by belly and elbows to the yard, he had slipped just at the moment the sail had ballooned him into empty space. "What saved me was that foot stirrup. I fell but I hung upside down from that rope."

Accidents, sails, storms, cargoes, exotic ports of call—of course, this is only one Texas world among many. What is a Texan? He or she is history, geography, weather, literature, customs, and a core of pithy experience. *Texans* is about the dreams of youth and the memories of age, all of which improve with the telling. So come with me to the piney woods and the trans-Pecos and the Gulf of Mexico, to the great cities and the great distances. Share with me the wit and wisdom of my favorite Texans.

TEXANS

"SHOELACE JIM" ESPY: "I LIKE A GOOD USIN' HORSE"

Fort Davis, TX

Born 1910

The eyes were what I noticed first about the big cat. Alien, wild eyes that looked me over as if I were just a piece of meat.

The rancher poked a stick through the metal cage to rouse the mountain lion to action. A roar engulfed us and a tawny paw struck out ferociously. I had to remind myself that this trapped cougar could not bound across the four feet that separated us.

I had surprised a mountain lion a decade earlier on a wilderness trail near the Canadian border in northwest Montana. I had never forgotten its thick, ropelike tail as it bounded away into the brush.

My gut reaction to this caged cat was embarrassment, the kind of avert-the-eyes unease you'd feel in the presence of someone brought low by fate. Yet I was mesmerized by those unblinking eyes and by that tawny, powerful body. Here was an athlete at the height of his powers. Muscles, bones, and senses perfectly adapted to the Davis Mountains of trans-Pecos Texas.

I did not share these thoughts with captor Jim Espy. Like most ranchers, he had no sympathy for varmints:

Lions will kill the big sheep or goats. The coyotes will kill ewes and small ones. Eagles will kill the baby lambs and baby goats by diving down and catching them by the neck.

I had not come to the Espy ranch to discuss predator control or cougar conservation. I had heard of Jim as a noted calf roper and

The lace-up shoes or "brogans" in which Jim Espy always roped earned him the nickname "Shoelace Jim."

horse breeder, so I was pleased when he proudly showed me some of his three hundred trophies and photos of his champions.

But when we got to talking about the West Texas ranch life of Jim's youth, I got the strong impression that not only the big cats were at risk in today's Texas. Jim complained forcefully that it would be impossible for someone like his father to break into ranching today. The limitless horizons have been carved up. Only oilmen able to pay a premium price for arid land could piece together a vast spread now the way J. W. Espy had. "A lot of ranches have been bought by the oil people," said Jim sadly. "That's fine. They are good people and they've got the money. We ranchers never have the money."

Leaving the mountain lion snarling in its cage, Jim and I walked up to the house. The cat continued to scream for a long time after we had gone.

I AM OPERATING THREE RANCHES with a total of about eighty-five sections of land. This place here on the edge of Fort Davis is the center of our business. We have ranches each direction from Fort Davis. We leave here every morning and go to a ranch.

Ranching is different than it used to be. We load our horses and go thirty miles and work and come back here to our place in town each night.

We had thirty thousand sheep at one time and fifteen to twenty thousand goats but the varmints killed them out. Lions, coyotes, and eagles ate all the lambs and kids, so we are in the straight cow business now.

We went out of the sheep business first on account of the eagles. They put a law on the eagle that it was a federal offense to try to control them. As long as it was just county law we could get along fine but the federal law, you don't fool with that. They set you back there and forget you. So we finally had to get out of the sheep business.

Then the mountain lions started killing our animals. Only my boy and another man killing them. They finally beat us.

We can run about twenty-five cows to a section. There are six hundred and forty acres in a section. We figure about twenty-five head to a section of our own cattle or cattle we pasture for other people.

They had a lot of farming area at Pecos. My brother and I had two sections of farmland over there. They didn't pass a groundwater conservation law and everybody was drillin' wherever they wanted to and they poked it off. They lowered the water table so bad that we sold out. We never did move away from Fort Davis; we have been here all our lives.

Our father, J. W. Espy, was thirty years old when he established here in the Davis Mountains.

He got to buying land and he had four good ranches when he died in 1972 at age ninety-six.

My brother Clay was older than I am. My father let us have one of his little ranches and he set us up with a few sheep when I was eighteen.

My dad was my teacher. He never did worry about anything. "It will work out all right." Just like rain, "It will work out all right. The Lord will take care of it."

As my father got older, he spent the last twenty-five to thirty years of his life in California buying and selling cattle. I operated all of his ranches and took care of mine, too, for forty-five years. He came back to check on things real often, even when he was over ninety years old.

In California he was a real goer, I'll tell you that. Over the telephone he would buy a thousand steers, learn their size, weight, age, and everything. Then he would describe them to so-and-so and the first thing you would know he had sold those cattle and made a nice profit out of it. He told them exactly what they were and the buyers often said that the cattle were better than what he had said they were. That makes your business pretty sound. That makes your word better.

My mom and dad used to say, "We don't have a very good contract. We just wrote it down on cigarette paper."

In other words, people just took each other's word. This day and time you can't do that.

In my father's day he had just common horses. This day and time you get hot-blooded horses, thoroughbreds, quarter horses. A quarter horse with a little thoroughbred makes a longer gait and better travelin' horse. That's the kind we usually use on the ranch.

I like a good ranch horse. What I mean by a good ranch horse, he's got a good saddle gait, he travels good, he's not rough, he's gentle, you can throw whatever you want to on him and he'll carry it. A usin' horse, in other words.

I used to rope a whole lot when I was young. In fact, I held the World's Calf Roping for a short time years ago in the early 1940s. I'd rope a calf and tie him down in nine seconds. Now they have it cut down to eight seconds. That is just the difference in the breed of horses. Better cowboys that train more than we did.

I had a lot of nice trophies in my day. One time in 1940 they matched me at a calf roping with Preston Fowlkes to rope twenty calves each without stopping. How come that come about, we were practicin' over here at Fort Davis in what we called arena roping. We were over there roping one day when Mannie and Edwin Fowlkes came by. Mannie kept a-hollerin' that he would rope his brother Preston Fowlkes with anybody in the world in thirty days in Pecos, Texas, twenty calf maximum, three thousand dollars.

He just kept a-hollerin'.

So I roped a calf and came back by this fella Herbert Colton that owns the O 6 Ranch. Well, Herbert Colton called me over to the fence and he said, "What does that Fowlkes boy keep a-hollering?"

I said, "He'll rope Preston with anybody in the world for three thousand dollars."

Herbert said, "What do you think about it, Jim?"

I said, "Heck, there's a carload of cowboys who can beat Preston." I said, "Wait just a minute, I'll go get my brother." Clay was over to the chutes. I called him over and I said, "Clay, Herbert wants to know about ropin' Preston Fowlkes."

My brother said the same thing, there's a carload of boys who could beat Fowlkes. Preston was just a young boy, a good boy, and a friend.

Herbert said, "Who do you think, Clay, ought to rope him?"

"Oh," he said, "it don't make any difference."

Herbert spoke up and said, "I would just as soon have Jim." Herbert said, "How much do you all want of the three thousand?"

I said, "I'll take five hundred."

My brother said he would take five hundred. Mr. Colton said, "Well, we'll just write out a check for three thousand dollars." So he went over there and matched the ropin'.

That whole month was real exciting.

The Fowlkeses moved to Pecos trying to get Preston acclimated. You know, it is awful hot down there. They kept bringing horses in there every day for him to work them. I stayed right here and I roped ten calves in the mornin' and ten calves in the afternoon. I stayed right here. When I went down there I was in shape; they had partied every night, and Preston wasn't in very good shape.

Anyway I roped nineteen calves on one horse. I had my brother's horse for a second if something happened to mine. My brother kept wanting me to rope on his horse and I said, "O.K., I'll rope the last calf, Clay, but I won't jerk a rope down on him." Clay's horse, if a rope caught his hind leg, he went crazy.

It was the hottest day of the year, one hundred ten or fifteen degrees and everyone was looking for a patch of shade.

When our times were added up for roping twenty calves each, I had beat Preston Fowlkes by over a minute and I had won a little money besides.

Yes, I have had a lot of experience with good horses. It goes along with the ranch business. You get to likin' horses and you breed 'em and if you are lucky, you get a horse that is a winner.

With a lot of ranch boys, it just comes natural and we have had our share of winners but a lot of boys don't have the time to learn how to handle horses. It is expensive and lots of work to it.

Nowadays we have rodeos all over the world and contestants can win thousands of dollars in a year.

Back in the thirties the pot wasn't very big and money wasn't the big attraction like it is today. We mostly rodeoed for the fun of it.

And we did have fun! We used to have a dice game right there by the chute where they were roping. And as soon as the official roping was over we would go to match ropings. You would match somebody for a fifty-dollar pot and the first thing you knew other boys got in and we had a two- or three-hundred-dollar purse.

That unofficial competition was more fun. Now it is all business. They don't have match ropings like we used to have.

A cowboy this day and time is liable to rope here tonight and tomorrow night in California. He will ride somebody else's horse up there for a percent of his winnings. But in the 1930s we used to know everybody and we were just a big family and had a lot of fun doing it.

It is all business now, though.

And young people today don't want to stay on the ranch and work like we used to. Now they just want to go out at eight o'clock in the morning and come back at night in a pick-up. It's hard to run a ranch this way.

It used to be that for all my dad's ranches and my ranch we had about fifty men. Now we keep about one or two men on each ranch and we can get a crew of about seven or eight men overnight to work a half day or whatever we need.

Today a man can load his horses, do whatever needs to be done, and return home till the next day.

In this area we have quit neighboring, helping our neighbor with branding and such. These are just our own boys that we use. Years ago we used to neighbor a lot. We sure did! But after we began to use these pick-ups and trailers, we haven't neighbored like we used to because we can get more done in a shorter time.

We had a better time then. We would go to a ranch and spend an afternoon and maybe a night, helping that neighbor with whatever job he had to do. Then he would return the favor.

Now we run up to a place, jump out of the pick-up, go inside and drink a cup of coffee, eat a bite, do some work, and then back into the pick-up with a "I'll see you later."

We are livin' too fast. I liked the old days best.

HULING USSERY:

STAMPEDE!

Carlsbad, NM

Born 1898

In 1882 Huling Ussery's father John Green Ussery settled on the Chico Ranch, about fifteen miles south of Pine Springs, Texas, in the Delaware Mountains. He had come from Live Oak County in South Texas to seek his fortune in the newly opening West. "The first time that he was there in eighty-two," says Huling, "the fire of the Indians was still hot."

Ever since his 1870s and 1880s heyday, the American cowboy has been viewed by the world as a romantic figure. His courage, independence, and stoicism have been extolled by a century of dime novels and Hollywood oaters. Huling Ussery grew up on classic cattle spreads and at the age of fourteen helped five other drovers and a horse wrangler and a cook herd five hundred beeves from the Guadalupe Mountains almost to Lubbock, Texas. Was it actually romantic? I expected Huling to make a disclaimer about the hundred-degree heat and the choking dust and the voracious flies and the long hours. But he said "For a month we saw something new every day. Met new people, everything. That cattle drive *was* romantic."

THE LAND HAS CHANGED AND the cattleman has had to change, too. With the present set-up like it is now, it would be impossible to return to the old way of life. You couldn't do it.

I didn't see anything wrong with those days. It's all with people, though, even today. Some people work hard and some people don't.

When I was fourteen years old, 1912, our neighbor bought five

hundred head of steers over in Old Mexico, kept the cattle at his ranch in the Guadalupe Mountains that winter, and then wanted to take them farther north to the grass near Lubbock for the summer. So he hired me to help drive those five hundred steers from his ranch to that place that he was going to pasture. He paid me two dollars a day and I mounted myself with seven horses. I had my own bed, of course, and chuck. Stood guard around those five hundred cattle a third of the night, every night.

In 1912, they were just starting to fence. There's maybe ten times as much fencing there now as there was then. Our first night out, the first place that had pasture, there was one man on one side of a fence saying "Shove them on in, boys." But there was an old peg-legged man on the other side of that fence with a Winchester layin' across the saddle. He said "Keep them out, boy. Keep them out."

We went on and I never did know whether they were neighbors. We didn't stop there.

But that night before we got away from there we had a stampede. The stampede started just like that! The cattle broke and run when they saw flashes of electricity coming from that barbed-wire fence. Barbed wire, if you get it banging, there will be flashes of lightning come from it.

The first thing I knew, I was started after them. Then my horse wouldn't go any farther. He turned back. When daylight came, I had about forty-five head of cattle that I was holding out of the five hundred.

We didn't have any more trouble from then on. I was gone thirty-one days. I made sixty-two dollars.

BUCK JACKSON:
PECOS RODEO ANNOUNCER
Pecos, TX
Born 1908

West Texas tradition has it that the world's first rodeo took place in Pecos, Texas, July 4, 1883. Ever since then the Glorious Fourth in Pecos has been associated with bronc and bull riding, calf roping, and other cowboy fun.

My favorite rodeo hand is Buck Jackson, even though he never competed much at all. But Buck has been announcing at the Pecos Rodeo since 1928, originally on horseback with a megaphone in an arena formed by a circle of the audience's Model Ts and other ranch vehicles. Rodeo has become big business, but Foghorn Jackson is a link with a time not so long ago when the contestants were not professionals but plain old working cowhands.

Buck Jackson took me on a maintenance tour of stock tanks at his ranch near Orla, Texas, where he runs about six hundred head of cattle. Some inquisitive whitefaces moseyed up to see what we were doing out in that flat, thirsty, sun-baked patch of mesquite. Probably some of them were among the two hundred eighty Jackson cattle that Buck's wranglers had branded three days earlier.

I could see that my host's mind was on keeping the water flowing, fences mended, and the cattle gaining weight. "You can go write a book," Buck told me, "but I got to wait to get these cattle cleaned, sold, and delivered before I can do anything."

With all the responsibility of one hundred sections to attend to, didn't Buck prefer the old carefree days when he was merely a thirty-five-dollar-a-month cowboy?

"I'll take now!" he exclaimed. "In those good old days, riding a horse all day was pretty hard on you."

No harder I guessed than being Reeves County's only sheriff—which Buck Jackson had been for eight years in the 1940s. I had heard a lot about Judge Roy Bean's "only law west of the Pecos River" kangaroo court at Langtry, so I asked Buck to tell me about the confrontations of his lawman days.

We used to have a lot of trouble with drunks at the Pecos Rodeo when they had a day show and people would get full of beer out in the hot sun. One time these two old boys from out of town got too much beer and got in a fight over nothing. Probably a dollar bill. They were fighting and they rolled clear down those steps to the bottom of the stands. I had to get out of the announcer booth, go over to the grandstand, and take them to jail.

Someone come and bailed them out pretty soon and they went home happy. A little bit skinned up.

Yeah, I was pretty tough on drunks but nobody ever did whip me. They threatened to, but they never did get me.

When I went out of office, that was when they were going to whip me.

Never did any of them get around to it.

I am going to leave the last word about Buck Jackson to Buck Newsome, former United States border patrolman and frequent Pecos visitor. He recalled in his 1975 book *Shod with Iron* that

Twenty-five years ago, Pecos, Texas, was a dusty cowtown, and has been so since back in the eighties. In summer it is hot as the hinges of hell. In winter as cold as a witch's tit. In spring as windy as a Washinton politician, but always has been full of good people. Buck Jackson, a good cowman and ex-sheriff, who can talk your right arm off and whisper in the hole. . . .

I CAME OUT HERE TO Pecos from Fort Worth in 1925 looking for a job as a cowboy.

I worked on the same big ranch for ten years. Collier Ranch. It had chuck wagons, a lot of cowboys.

Collier did O.K. but a lot of those big ranchers were going broke when I come here. Never did get back on their feet financially.

If you were a kid like me, you got thirty-five dollars a month and board. Not very good wages but that was what all the ranchers were paying. If you were real good, you got fifty dollars. If you broke some horses on the side, you would get sixty.

Most everybody paid thirty-five dollars a month. Now I am payin' fifty dollars *a day* to cowboys!

I was a blank, ignorant, when I started out. Yeah, I got bawled out many a time for making a bad break, making a mistake. I would have a horse runnin' through the cattle and I would get eat out good. Once I tied my horse to the chuck-wagon grocery box on the back end. I tied my horse to the lid, I got rimmed out for that pretty good because it would have pulled the chuck-wagon box right off into the dirt, groceries and all.

You need to be jack-of-all-trades when you work on a ranch. The biggest job is the windmill, to keep water pumping. You can do without grass easier than you can do without water. You got to have water. Stock tanks are sure to go dry so you must depend on your windmills.

Mending fences.

You learn more on the ground on a ranch than you do on a horse. That's why everybody's got a pick-up now.

I worked for a lot of different people. They were good to me. They had to be or they would have killed me I was so crazy.

Pot Wadley was good to me. He took me in as a partner and sold out to me on credit. He treated me just like my father.

Pot was an old-timer who had gone up the trail around Amarillo as a young fella. He weighed about a hundred and ten pounds. He run a livery stable here in the early days. He had horses and mules and buggies and wagons that he rented out. People came in and would rent a buggy then instead of a car like U-Haul.

Pot was one of the finest men I ever knew. I would be cowboyin' today at thirty-five dollars a month if it hadn't been for him. Fine guy, he was!

He called me Littleton. He just nicknamed me that. I don't know why.

I started out announcing on horseback at the Pecos Rodeo in 1928. They called me Foghorn after Foghorn Clancy who announced for years and years with a megaphone.

I announced a-horseback in twenty-eight, twenty-nine, thirty, but in 1931 we got a loudspeaker. From then on we used a loud-speaker all the time.

In 1928 our rodeo arena was a circle of Model-T Fords, Chevrolets, and old Buicks. People set in them and watched. I would ride around the arena about twice and give them what John Jones, what Jackson did, and I would go back up to the chutes and there would be another one coming out. After he roped his calf and they got his time, why I would ride around the arena again and give it out twice.

Had that ole megaphone in my hand and swallowed that ole dirt and it would go down in my belly and it would be sore for about a week after the rodeo was over.

Then we graduated to the loudspeaker. The Gulf Oil Company used to furnish them for years. Then the Budweiser beer furnished them until finally the rodeo bought their own equipment.

The rodeo was very different in those days. Back then you couldn't hardly get anybody to judge. But now it's very strict rules and you can't even complain to the judges like you can to a baseball umpire. The judges can throw you out and take away your membership in the Professional Rodeo Cowboy Association.

Nowadays the rodeo is a business. It has to be because we have several *hundred* entrants here and it takes a lot of bookkeeping to put on such a big rodeo. We bring in a rodeo producer who has a contract for the stock and he has a bookkeeper and we furnish one, too.

A guy could be in Louisiana and maybe he is going to ride tomorrow night. He phones in and asks "When am I up?" Our secretary has got to look it up and be able to tell him "You're up in the slack at twelve o'clock."

After the rodeo is over at night they call it a slack. Say there is ten entered and you only have room for eight during the show. Them other two are in the slack. Extry.

So this Louisiana man can plan ahead to ride at twelve o'clock midnight during the slack. If he ain't there, he gets fined.

Most ropers like to draw so they are in the slack. Not as many people yellin' and havin' a fit out there. That makes the horse get excited.

Usually in the slack it's just the cowboys and their wives that are there. It makes it a whole lot easier to win if you rope durin' the slack.

Sometimes the slack is at night after the show is over and sometimes it is the next morning. The show starts on Wednesday and we will start ropin' and ridin' at eight o'clock Monday morning. That gets rid of several hundred contestants.

There will be over a hundred steer ropers, over a hundred calf ropers, and you can't get but about forty of them in the show. So there's a lot of them goin' home before the rodeo starts and before they know if they won.

I know a boy, Ray Wharton, one year he roped first. His time stood up during the whole four-day rodeo. He had been home a week before he found out that he had won.

Riders now are professional athletes but there were good riders even back when I was a kid like Ron Roach, Jonas De Armon, Chief Corrells, Hugh Strickland, Blackie Russell. They were mean son-of-a-bucks but they were good riders. Oh, man, they were rough! They would fight you all night.

Chief Corrells and Blackie Russell were good friends of mine and good riders. Lou Roberts, Oklahoma Curly. . . .

Hugh Strickland was from Denton, Texas. Mabel Strickland was his wife. She was a beauty! She rode broncs, too. Back in those days women rode broncs but they don't any more. I don't know why not. They just played out. I really don't know but those bronc-riding women were the prettiest women I ever saw in my life!

Back there when I was just a kid, it was more Wild West show rodeos. There was one hundred and one Wild West shows. Miller Brothers, Hackberry Slim, everyone would go to these little towns and put on Wild West shows.

Rodeo is a perfection now. It is organized just like a union now. The Professional Cowboy Association out of Colorado Springs, they have several thousand members. They can blackball your rodeo if you don't comply to their rules and regulations. They are as strong as these Teamsters.

The first strike the rodeo cowboys had was in 1936, when old Colonel Johnson had a Wild West show. He as the rodeo producer wasn't even putting all the money the cowboys had put up back into the purse. He was taking some of it to himself and they wouldn't have nothin'. That's when they struck.

They were called the Cowboys' Turtle Association—CTA—for a long time. The reason they called it turtle was because it was slow getting organized.

Anyway they started the Professional Cowboy Association in 1936.

There wasn't no professional rodeo cowboys then. The ropers were ranchers who owned horses, trailers, saddles, ropes, and cattle to practice on. You got to have money to be a roper. Very few straight cowboys make ropers. Sometimes a rich man or a rancher will sponsor somebody but that doesn't happen often. Most ropers are ranchers or their sons.

I knew most of them and I teased them when they were in the arena competing. I used to tell a fella that he had to catch the calf before he could tie it. "You got to catch 'em before you hang 'em."

Back when I rode around the arena with that megaphone, every once in a while a calf or a horse would get out between the cars. Then we would have to go out and drag it back.

Before the rodeo we used to bring range cows and calves to town from somebody's ranch. We separated the cows from their calves at the corrals when we were ready to rope. We kept the mama cows opposite the chute and when the calves ran over to their mammies, they would run like the devil. Some would get started off in the wrong direction, but most of them would go straight to their mammy. You had better hurry if you were goin' to catch him before he got there.

In calf roping we have two men. One comes down on one side of the rope and one on the other. One man grabs the calf's tail and the roper picks up the calf's hind feet with the rope. While one man holds the calf's tail, the heeler flops the animal over easy by pulling the rear legs out from under it with the rope.

I pull on the tail and you pull on the rope and the calf goes over on his side.

Then one man grabs the front feet and one grabs the hind feet. Here come the branding man and the vaccine and the calf is up and gone.

I used to heel a good deal.

I was born in Texas. I don't want to live anywhere but West Texas. I come here as a runaway kid in 1925 and I worked for thirty-five dollars a month on the ranch that I own now.*

Pecos has been good to me.

---

*Pecos Rodeo announcer Buck Jackson cowboyed on the Ross ranch in the 1920s and eventually bought it.

CALLIE ROSS BEVILL: "MAMO WAS MY HERO!"
Pecos, TX
Born 1908

Though Callie Ross's father died when she was only seven years old, her childhood was very family-oriented. Not only did she idolize her mother but she also doted on her brother Bill. "He and I were the last ones to marry and leave home. I felt like I had really done something if I could please that particular brother and could perform all right. He would give me a nudge and say "That's O.K., Sis!"

Callie Ross was a lucky girl. Her West Texas youth was complete with cowboy brothers, beloved pony, and even her own cattle brand. Ranch life suited tomboy Callie to a T even though her ranch's only air conditioning was the method that had come with the patent on the place. "We opened up," says Callie, "and let the wind blow through. Every morning we would brush it out with a broom." She and her mother continued to cook on a wood-fired range even after the arrival of power and natural gas when she was fourteen years old.

Callie Ross says that she was different from most West Texas ranch girls.

I had a lot of friends whose parents were also ranchers and they thought I was quite strange because I enjoyed staying every summer out at our ranch instead of staying in town and going to the parties and things of that sort. But I just really enjoyed the country. I guess that was the tomboy in me.

Tomboy or not, Callie's mother was a Southern lady whose idea of femininity did not include suntans. As a child little Callie was

Callie Ross Bevill's
mother riding Sterling
in the Fourth of July
parade in Pecos.

supposed to wear a protective bonnet, arm guards of black stocking legs, and a chamois face mask.

My mother was a beautiful horsewoman. She wore what she called a chamois mask to protect her from sunburn. She and her friend that lived eight or ten miles south of us, they would make their masks religiously every summer. They would take a big chamois like we would use for our cars now and they would mold it to their faces by taking tucks and darts where necessary. Mother said it was quite comfortable. She would perspire and then as she rode, it was cooling to her face.

I didn't feel the same way about it. She made me one and I was supposed to wear it but I really didn't. It was in my pocket because I didn't want to be teased.

I HAD A SISTER AND three brothers that were older than I and we all would head for the ranch as soon as the Pecos school year was over. As soon as school was out, we would take off and go to the ranch and spend the summer. Oh, I wish everybody could grow up in the country! It is a good, wholesome life.

The roads were such that you didn't come back and forth a lot.

In a wagon, a hack, or a buggy the fifty-four-mile trip took all day. But by the time I came along we had gotten a car and we could make the trip in three or four hours (barring no flat tires or car trouble!).

I had my own horse. A tiny Spanish dun named Pat. He had a golden mane and tail and he was a smart little fella.

At the beginning of the summer the cowboys would know that the family was coming and they would have Pat in the corral for me. I think he was as glad to see me as I was him. We would meet and he would come and put his head right down in my face. It was always a real happy time for us to be together.

I had a lot of fun with Pat but I couldn't go out riding by myself. Any time that my brothers had time for me to tag along with them, I would. Otherwise, if they had work to do and I couldn't go along and keep up, I stayed home and I rode the fence.

Do you know what it means to ride the fence? That's when a cowboy was sent out to ride these fences which were miles in length to see if there were any breaks in the fence. So my mother would send me to ride the fence, but it was the *yard* fence. I never got outside of the yard.

I kept that yard fence in apple-pie shape all the time!

Pat had been trained for a child. I guess I was about four when I got him. I was up in high school before he died. That was a sad day. It was like losing a member of the family. I cried!

Pat enjoyed eating the mesquite beans. We would be riding down the trails and I'd reach over. . . . I figured that I would just save him all that I could so I would break off the mesquite beans; then he'd turn his nose around and I would stick beans in his mouth. He had a hard time crunching them with the bit in his mouth.

I was not the best cowgirl in the world, but I did quite a bit of it. Soon after his children were born, my father would give us each a brand and start us a little line of calves. The new brand usually carried the initials of the child. My sister and my oldest brother had a brand together for their little jag of cattle. It was called *and X.* Then Bill and George, my next two brothers, had *W J bar.*

When I came along about five years later, I got one all by myself. My brand was *C T bar.*

At branding time we each one got to bring our own cows and calves to the corral. The cowboys would round up all the cattle in the pasture, throwing them into one huge herd. After the cattle were quiet and settled down, one man rode through the herd cutting out unbranded calves and their mammas until all unbranded calves were cut out and grouped by brands. These individual groups were corralled in separate pens. That is when I got to take, with a little help, my bunch of stock and put them in the pen so that later on they would be branded. I felt real important from the round-up grounds down to the house, where we penned my stock.

I didn't brand them myself. No, no, no. I did a lot of things but my mother frowned on girls in the branding pen! When I was a little girl my mother really fixed me up, but I didn't like it a bit because I was more of a tomboy and dressing up just wasn't that exciting. It surely wasn't! Now I would give anything to have that heavy cloth riding skirt she made me!

My mother didn't like to see me sunburn at all! I always had to wear a big-brimmed hat or a bonnet. Somehow or other it would get off my head by the time I got over the hill.

It always managed to get it back up on my head as I come back home.

I didn't have cowboy boots. I had some high-topped lace-up boots that I wore most of the time because they were more comfortable and less expensive.

I would put that kind of a garb on of a morning when I got up and wear it all day.

Anytime I could help, I was ready to. For instance, we had a pretty deep water well at headquarters, and when it was necessary to pull the windmill's sucker rods or put new leathers on the cylinder, my job was to drive the car or truck. It was too heavy to pull any other way. So that was my chore, to drive back and forth pulling a rope so that the boys could pull the plunger rods out one by one until they got down to the bottom to get the cylinder off to put in new leathers. The sand would grind away at those washers and the boys would have to replace them. When they got everything out of the well and had replaced the worn-out parts, then we had to put it all down into the well again.

Of course, I wasn't supposed to *climb* the windmill. But I used to climb the windmill ladder with my brothers and slide rapidly down a cable on part of a block-and-tackle deal to that old dirt tank! That and jumpin' out of the barn windows and things like helpin' to ride the milk-pen calves. We weren't supposed to do that either, but once in a while it was fun to rodeo at their expense.

We usually had Jerseys who were able to help raise an orphan doggie as well as her own. After the boys had milked the cows of a morning, the cows were put out into the pasture but the calves would be kept in the pen so that they wouldn't steal the milk through the day. We could play with them, practice roping them and that sort of thing. I was never good at roping. I couldn't even catch a fencepost that stood still for me.

Of course, we killed our own beef. I never liked to be within hearing distance of the killing, but the procedure was always kind of interesting. They would usually string the old calf up in the windmill tower and that's where the boys would dress the beef. Then cover it and leave it hang overnight to cool before they would bring it into the house. Because of lack of refrigeration in the summertime, one rancher would kill a beef and send a quarter over to a neighbor. When that was all gone, the next time a neighbor would butcher.

Before we had any kind of electricity, we just depended on coal-oil lamps and a wood stove. Of course, our cooked meals were breakfast and dinner, what folks now think of as lunch. We just ate scraps at suppertime—especially in summer when the cooking heat was not welcome!

I helped my mother with a lot of the cooking. We ate lots of frijole beans. Just a little ole brown, speckled pinto. We bought them at the store but my mother had a little garden for tomatoes, peppers, onions, and fresh things for salads. A few vegetables. Yes, when we would go to the ranch, we would buy a case of English peas, a case of tomatoes, a case of corn, a side of bacon, a hundred-pound sack of flour, a hundred-pound sack of sugar, and Arbuckle's whole-bean coffee, dry onions, and potatoes.

We had little hot chilies that my mother made into a relish that everybody just loved. We called it "cowboy chili." It was always something fresh when maybe we wouldn't have access to a lot of fresh vegetables. She would chop up an onion with some green chili peppers, season it with salt, pepper, sugar and add a can of tomatoes. It made a delightful relish. I still make that when I have frijole beans and cornbread. They go together like old friends.

Oh yes, I liked to make a cake every once in a while. That was my department. My brother Bill liked a "sad cake," one that had fallen. He did a jig in the kitchen just to try to make the cake fall!

My mother frequently made cobblers, cookies, and pies for the cowboys. She would always have just the right ingredients for a pie though it might be a butter roll or vinegar pie. We used to have peach trees growin' all around the old dirt tank and we had lots of fruit. So she kept them supplied with peaches and cobblers.

We never went hungry. We had lots of milk and ice tea. Pecos was fifty-four miles from the ranch. Sometimes we would bring out a three-hundred-pound block of ice to make ice cream. Much would melt on the way, even though it had been wrapped in heavy tarps. It was a special time, because everybody was most willin' to crank the ice-cream freezer to get some ice cream. By the time it was gettin' hard we would take turns cranking. Somebody would come and sit on the ice-cream freezer to hold it down while the other turned it, thinking that the faster they turned it, the faster and sooner the ice cream would freeze.

We were busy cooking every day but there were times of the year when you were especially busy, when the neighbors would come in and you would gather your cattle to brand or to sell. There was a lot of exchange of neighbor help. They would come when you needed help and then you would go when your neighbor needed help.

When a cook and the chuck wagon went out, on the back of that chuck wagon would be the chuck box with the tin pans, tin cups, old forks, knives, and spoons. The cook would do his cooking outside.

We had a big family. There were five children. If you had to carry the water through a sandy waterin' lot, the distance of about a block in length, up to the house, you were kind of conservative with your water. You saved it and everybody bathed in the same water and you hoped that you would get a chance at it first while the water was still kind of clean. I remember that we used to take turns washing in an old number-three wash tub because we didn't have water to the house for quite a while. Finally in the late twenties they built a tower beside the windmill and put a tank up on that for a little bit of pressure and then they ran a line from there up to the house and we had an indoor bathroom!

Later we had a big ole iron water tank that was about six feet tall and about fifty feet across. Water was piped to the stock troughs from this holding tank. Mother would send the boys to the tank to get clean.

We lost Papa in 1915. I grew up with his antics and his life more as a secondhand memory, things that people would tell me about him, more than I could remember on my own.

My middle brother, whose name was Bill, ran the ranch with Mama after Papa's death.

I could cowgirl well enough to please Bill!

After Papa died Mama became quite involved in the business world. She hadn't known *anything* about the cattle business. She used to ask my father to tell her something about it and he would say "You just don't worry about that. You take care of the house and the family and I'll take care of the business."

I felt like my mother was the most wonderful woman in all of the world. Callie Felts was her maiden name. Her father was a Civil War veteran and her mother a lovely pioneer woman, so she was built of real solid stuff. She never lost control of the situation, but she was always a perfect lady and everybody loved her. She was known as Mamo after my sister's children came along.

Mamo was a true Texan, born in Springtown, a little place out from Fort Worth. She was born in 1872, married in 1892, and she died in 1955. She was eighty-three when she passed away.

After 1915, there was a pretty bad depression and the years were awfully hard. A lot of cattlemen out here went under. There was my little mother; she had not known anything about the cattle business but she managed to keep everything goin' and held it together and rode right on through that storm like nobody's business.

I always thought that was really something special, especially when so many of the well-known, influential cattlemen who were her peers had gone under and just lost everything. Mamo managed to keep us together as a family as well as her business. She is my hero, my heroine! She was a hero and a heroine all combined.

ELMER KELTON: WEST TEXAS NOVELIST
San Angelo, TX
Born 1926

Since 1948 Elmer Kelton has been a livestock and farm reporter, beginning with the *Standard Times* in San Angelo. At least on paper, he has seen more sheep, cattle, and goats than many a cowboy. Elmer is not a rancher or a good hand with stock. A boy growing up on a West Texas ranch, he never had the knack for it. When it came to throwing a rope over a dogie's neck, he was about as blind as a one-eyed mule in a root cellar.

Yet an early desire to be a writer and a boyhood at the tail end of the horse era made a novelist out of Elmer Kelton. His books *The Day the Cowboys Quit* (1971) and *The Time It Never Rained* (1973) are full of expressions peculiar to the cattle business like *hoolihan.* Elmer uses West Texas expressions and dialect in his novels like a camp cook would use salt in his beans, just enough to flavor but not too much to distract.

Elmer Kelton's work deserves a much wider audience. He has achieved critical acclaim among Western writers and readers, but I am rooting for him to achieve a national success.

Texas has been an overwhelmingly urban state for several decades, but the rural myths persist. Novelist Kelton writes about the changes that have overtaken the country people of West Texas. "Where are you going to stop the clock?" he says. "Are you going to be like the Amish and stop everything in the mid-1800s or are you going to change with the times? I find that I want to stop the clock. The older I get, the less I want to change."

I GREW UP AROUND A lot of old men who had been cowboys back in the open-range days. A few of them had been up all the Western cattle trails. I had this heritage handed down to me. After supper in the summertime, they would sit out on the bunkhouse porch and reminisce, tell stories. Dad and I would always go over and sit in with the cowpunchers. They would get to telling stories about people, and I would just listen. I can't remember a lot of the specific stories, but the flavor and the spirit of those stories stayed with me. They have been the background for a lot of what I have written, particularly a book called *The Good Old Boys* [1978], which was kind of an amalgamation of a lot of those old stories kind of bound together with my imagination.

Oh yeah, you can still find good storytelling. It isn't as prevalent as it was in the earlier days because people have a lot more opportunities besides sitting around visiting with their neighbors at night. Television, first of all, and people are a lot more mobile today. They can get up and go somewhere. When I was a kid growing up, we didn't go anywhere that much unless it was to visit neighbors and talk or play Forty-two. How many people play Forty-two nowadays? That was a domino game that my parents loved to play. I'll bet they played it three nights and sometimes four nights a week with the people who lived on the ranch.

I was born on the Scharbauer Cattle Company Ranch out in

Andrews County. My grandfather was a ranch foreman and my father was a cowpuncher for the company. My folks lived out in a line camp, and I was born there, in Horse Camp.

Despite all my father's best efforts to train me, I was never any good as a cowboy. I just always seemed to have two left hands when it came to working with horses and cattle. Partly I think it was because I grew up around a bunch of real good cowhands, and I just didn't seem to have the knack. So I guess I got an inferiority complex pretty early because I couldn't match what the other people were doing. A lot of the kids who were my age just seemed to have the knack. I had three younger brothers, and all of them were good cowboys compared to me. Another thing, too, was starting school as early as I did. My mother taught me to read at five so when I turned seven I went to town to go to school. They put me in the third grade, which left me as the runt in all the classes that I was in growing up. I didn't fit in with the other boys in athletics and things like that because I was too small. So I guess I took to the books as a refuge from that. Besides, I wanted to be a writer. That was my whole purpose even when I was in grade school.

Writing itself is very hard work. I can't say that I always enjoy it while I am doing it. It takes a lot out of you, but I enjoy having written it. I get a satisfaction out of having told a story, out of defining my characters, personifying ideas, and possibly delivering a message that I want to deliver. I am not at all averse at slipping a little message into these stories, even if first of all they have to entertain. If I can enlighten the reader a little bit, teach him a little bit about history, teach him a little bit about people I know—that is sort of a bonus and a challenge, and I like to do it.

I like to emphasize tolerance of different attitudes and of different kinds of people. Intolerance is why we are having all the fighting and trouble in the Mideast, intolerance of one group of people to another. We have it in Ireland, South Africa. It is a universal problem. In my stories it is usually either the black or Hispanic and his relationship with the white or Anglo. But that only stands for the bigger problem we have worldwide. I try to make my stories universal so that they will appeal to a person who is looking for something more than just a Western adventure.

For instance, *The Man Who Rode Midnight* is contemporary, about an old rancher on a place that has grown too small for today's economics. Also, they are trying to take it away from him to build a lake to help the economy of the town. He doesn't want to give it up but obviously he is going to have to. So the book more or less is about how he gradually comes around to the adjustment and how he tries to find some common ground with a grandson who has been brought up in Dallas and doesn't know or care anything about ranch life. Through the course of the summer a relationship solidifies between the old man and the young boy, a student. At the same time the old man is undergoing the stress of losing his ranch.

The old man in his youth had been a bronc rider and a minor celebrity. Midnight was a famous bucking horse back in the early thirties. Very few people rode Midnight. But this man had. Now, though, most people don't remember what he did when he was young and he is just an old man standing in the way of progress.

The way I write, I let the characters and the conflict between characters more or less make the plot through natural conflicts of interest. Like in *The Man Who Rode Midnight* I have the old man who wants to resist change. He has had this place all these years and he doesn't want to give it up. He is in opposition to all the people who want to build a lake. They are promoting change and he is resisting it. I have a natural conflict there; I don't have to have a bunch of white hats and black hats. I just have a natural conflict between people who naturally believe that they are right.

Why does a man like my hero want to continue on as a West Texas rancher instead of doing something easier? Basically he looks at it as a way of life as much as a way of making a living. It's a tradition. It's something that most people who are in the business were brought up doing as children. Most people who are ranching today, the bona-fide rancher (not the cattleman who has done it as an investment or a hobby, but the bona-fide cattleman, sheepman, or all-around ranchman) has been brought up in that. That has been his way of life since he was born. It is something that he holds onto because he likes it as a way of life. It is sometimes an awful poor way to make a living. But it is still a good life. That's why people hang on to it.

John Graves, who to me is one of the best Texas writers, we were talking one time about our backgrounds. He said most writers are basically misfits in their own society. There is something about them that sets them apart from everybody else around them.

I guess that happened to me, too, as a kid growing up. I didn't quite fit in and I was sort of the odd man out.

But compared to some modern novelists of the West, I have tended to look for the most positive. If Larry McMurtry and I were both taken out to a barnyard, he would see the manure and I would see the pony and we would both be right.

It is a question of interpretation and selection of material.

My version doesn't sell like Larry's.

The Time It Never Rained is set more or less here in the Concho Valley. I made it vague enough that you can make it where you want it to be, but in my own mind when I wrote it, I set it more or less in the Eldorado area. I used Eldorado physically because it was a good combination of farming land and ranch land and because it was in this general area. I used the Sonora wool warehouse. I used the Concho County courthouse.

There again, my main character, Charlie Flagg, I used as an embodiment of an old-time ethic which you find especially among the older generation of ranchers in this country. Very independent-minded, proud of their independence, and proud of fighting their own battles, standing on their own feet, reluctant to get tied down by government programs.

These people don't want to be on the government teat because there are all these strings attached to that teat. There is an old dread here of the pauper's oath that goes back several generations to earlier hard times, when you had to declare yourself a pauper with no means of supporting yourself to be able to get government grants of food. This feeling has been passed on, that you take something away from your manhood if you put yourself on the dole.

The majority of the younger generation don't understand rural Texas. But a lot of the people living in those Texas cities came from small towns, and you find worlds of them just yearning to get back to that. They spent all of their youth trying to get an education so that they could get out of the country. All of their adult lives were spent trying to earn enough money so that they can go back to the country to retire. They are at cross-purposes with themselves.

People find something that looks like paradise away from the city. But they take most of the problems of the city with them. Give them ten years and they will have seventy-five percent of the problems there that they ran away from when they left Fort Worth or Dallas.

You can see the same thing in communities around Austin and San Antonio. Wimberley is a little town outside Austin about twenty-five miles. It has become a pseudo-rustic big draw for the people from the city, and yet it is not Wimberley as it would have been thirty years ago. It is something totally different. Kind of a fictional place.

Texas itself has tried to live up to the image that has been created for it. Tried to live up to that whether it is the real image or not. Texas is such a broad and diverse country. It has so many distinct areas that are all different from each other and the people in those areas tend to be somewhat different from each other, too. When I go somewhere else, I always feel like I am a little different. I know my accent is different. I go to Western writers' meetings and sometimes I am asked to get up and speak and I always sense immediately that my accent is different. I'm very much aware of that. You can be from Ohio and go somewhere and you don't stand out. But if you come from Texas, there is something about it. . . . Maybe it is favorable or unfavorable, but they do tend to put you in a special niche because you are a Texan.

This is true in Europe. Everywhere you go over there, everybody knows where Texas is. They know where Dallas is. They have all seen the TV show or they have seen the Westerns. If you were from Michigan or someplace, possibly that wouldn't be quite so strong. You would be an American, not a Michigander. If you, a Texan, go overseas, you are a Texan as much as you are an American.

Well, Texans aren't anything like the *Dallas* TV show; most Texans don't have a lot of money. But there is always this old image of Texas, created by the braggarts among us, about Texas being bigger, richer, better, nicer, meaner, and all this. . . . This old booster image has given us a bad name along with a certain identity of our own. It has been a two-way sword. I think to a large extent Texans are trying to live that down. I know that I am. I don't mean to be apologetic about Texas, but I think there is a real Texas and a false Texas, and I do everything I can in my stories to show the Texas that I know and the people that I know. I want to get as far away from that other image as I can. Most of my stories are basically about common people, the little people, not the big movers and shakers.

Of course, one of the hazards of becoming regarded as a professional writer is that lots of other people think they would like to be one, too, and they think I have all the answers they need. Several times a year I get letters, calls, or visits from people who have come up with what they think is the "perfect plot" for a book. They'll want to tell me the story, have me write and polish it, and we'll split the proceeds, making both of us rich. They usually see not only a best-selling book but also a blockbuster Hollywood movie as well.

I always seek a graceful way to avoid these propositions. But I can't always avoid giving advice and counsel to well-meaning people who have written or want to write a book themselves. The best advice usually would be "Don't do it," but that seems callous and cold and could be taken as an attempt to discourage competition.

Once in a while somebody I've taken some time with actually comes up with a book that gets published, not because of anything I did but because the person had something worthwhile to begin with.

We used to have a jackleg veterinarian–horse trader here in San Angelo. Everybody called him Doc Green. He was a great talker, one of the best oral story-tellers I ever knew, but his credentials as a vet were spurious and the reliability of his statements about a horse he was trying to sell were open to considerable suspicion.

One day he approached me in a local hotel lobby and asked for advice on publishing a book. I was not even convinced that Doc could read, much less write, but I sat down with him and told him all I knew. I thought he was about the most unlikely candidate for an author I had ever known.

I was wrong, of course. Ben K. Green's first commercially published book, *Horse Tradin'*, was a tremendous success, not only with the book-buying public but also with critics. He published something on the order of a dozen books before he died.

I occasionally went to *him* for advice.

Most of his books are still in print and continue to sell. So, you never know.

I am still dubious about giving advice and I warn people that it is probably worth what it costs them, which is nothing. But I always worry that if I don't give them a little serious consideration, I may be turning away another Doc Green.

SLIM SINGLETON:
BLOWING WITH THE WIND
San Angelo, TX
Born 1908

Few things are more reassuring to a rancher than the creaking of a windmill. As Elmer Kelton wrote in *The Time It Never Rained*, "For a man who has often turned his face to the hot breath of drouth, the sight of a windmill tower—its big steel fan clanking patiently and pumping up water clear and cool—somehow reaches deep and touches something in his soul."

Until the late nineteenth century stock-watering in West Texas was a job for Mother Nature. But with the fencing of the open range and the realization that each step a cow walks to water decreases the animal's marketable weight came efforts to bring water to the herds. Rainwater reservoirs or tanks were built to catch runoff and wells were dug to tap underground supplies. Because there was no electricity ranchers turned to windmills.

The first models—such as Eclipse, Fairbury, Dempster, and Monitor—were made of wood, but by 1930 most mills were made of steel. The industry went through many technical and marketing refinements, with Axtell and Aeromotor being two of the most famous names.

Frank Joplin of Pecos, Texas, was a windmill drummer for forty-two years (1942–1984). He told me that he originally sold a ten-foot Aeromotor for six hundred dollars plus money for rods and cylinders and for materials to make a homemade tower.

The late Slim Singleton was the right man to be with in Southwest and West Texas if you were thirsty out in that desert and needed a drink right away. Slim had worked on oil wells in 1926 and 1927, when he switched over to the old wooden water rigs.

Slim beside his truck with his nephew Daley Gene and their
windmill dog Bull.

"They tore up too bad and they run too slow," he said. "A wood
mill was geared direct. Where you can use a ten-foot steel mill to
handle one load, you had to have about a fourteen- to sixteen-foot
in a wooden mill. Because you had more cost people didn't want
them and began to change from wood to steel pretty fast in the
1930s."

An "outdoor boy" from the piney woods of East Texas, Slim was
a large man who was lucky to have lived a long life fooling around
with wells and towers out back of yonder. Once he was working on
a booster pump when his foot slipped and got mangled in the
machinery. "Broke it all up till it looked like scrambled eggs," Slim
said. Alone at noon with a foot "painin' so bad that you don't know
whether you lived or died," he had to wait till after midnight for
help.

When I saw Slim many decades later, he was threatening to
retire because of "the bursitis, rheumabitis, and everything else."
For someone who had been sleeping out on the ground and eating
rough for much of his life, he was doing pretty well. "We lived on
goat meat, beans, taters, quail," he said. "I've eaten more quail!

Chicory coffee. Have you ever drunk any chicory coffee? It's purty good slop, that's all I can say for it."

Slim's conversation was full of the weights and widths and depths of the windmill business, but what fascinated me was his life-style as a cowboy of the air:

Windmills'll sometimes break in big storms. I was out there in most of them snowstorms. Don't think it don't get cold. You get up north of Sierra Blanca back in those Christmas Mountains, now that gets cold!

Slim Singleton was a nomad who blew with the wind across Southwest and West Texas for over half a century. Like his windmills, Slim was a reliable fellow, winter or summer, and even an inventor. When the Axtell Company's booster pumps proved inadequate, Slim created his own and installed several on the Spade Ranch near Sterling City. "They patented it and I began putting them all down along the Rio Grande," said Slim. "It was my idea but all I got out of it was just labor; that was back when you couldn't get a job."

Of course, maybe this tall piney woods fella may just have had the best job in West Texas! "I've got customers that I worked for for probably a good fifty-five years," said Slim happily. "They just call me and tell me where the windmill is that needs fixing. I've got keys. . . . I've got three hundred keys of ranch gates."

I WORKED FORTY-SOME COUNTIES. Alpine, Midland, Odessa, Big Spring, and down to Abilene. I did lots of work around Del Rio, Junction, Menard, and on back up. I put in new ones, repaired a lot of old ones, and worked on wells. Most of the time we just come back to camp, loaded up, and headed right back out to the next windmill.

In April of 1929 I worked for Axtell Steel Company in San Angelo repairing windmills and setting up new ones. After about eight years I started contracting with them for windmill work. I worked some around Uvalde, some around Junction, but most of it was from Del Rio to El Paso, the big stuff along the Rio Grande River.

Then in 1936 I crossed the river into Old Mexico. If you have ever been to Del Rio, you've seen those big, high Burro Mountains back there. I worked off and on out of Del Rio for eighteen years.

Dr. Brinkley was still hanging around Del Rio in those days, but he was getting pretty feeble. Bob Crosby was still living, too. His restaurant in Ciudad Acuña was my hangout. Mrs. Crosby and the wife were just like that [gesture of closeness]. When I was away, Mrs. Crosby let her stay until I could come get her.

I liked them good old days best because nobody cared what you ate, what you killed. And you had good, free air. You were not breathing this old dust and stuff.

We slept out on the ground. I helped get the rattlesnakes out of an ole boy's bed. That's a fact! Right down here on Houston Myers's ranch out of Del Rio about twenty miles where that road turns and goes up to. . . .

We had a bedroll and chuck box. We never used to go to town because there wasn't nuthin' to eat except at a little ole greasy-spoon cafe.

My brother and I would pull into Alpine at the first grocery store and get a chunk of what we called goose liver cheese with olives in it. It was good! And we would buy those little dromedary cakes in cans, get us a quart of milk, and sit alongside there. I tell you we would eat! Maybe get us a quart of San Antonio ice cream.

That's how I got the name Slim, because at one time I *was* slim. I weighed a hundred and sixty-five pounds when I was forty-five or forty-seven years old. I eat all the beans I could eat, taters, deer, goat, quail, and I couldn't gain no weight at all. One day a doctor said, "I'm going to tell ya something. This is off the book. Before you eat supper at night drink one or maybe two beers. Don't drink no more than that. See what that does for you." Well, I told him I could drink beer all right!

I made a little home brew and I started drinkin' that and I begin to put on a little extry weight. I built up then to over two hundred pounds. Before I quit I weighed two hundred and eighty-one pounds and I couldn't even bend over to tie my shoes.

You know, I never did diet. It just started fallin' off me. I hold it at two hundred fifteen or two-twenty.

My real name is Renzo P. Singleton. P is for Powell, my grand-dad Hefran Powell.

Renzo is French. My grandmother was one of these old Alabama gals. She went to school with some sweetheart over there and she wanted to name me after him.

I was born in Houston County right out of Grapeland at a little place called Percilla. I was raised up outdoors in East Texas in Anderson County and I don't know why, but if you put me in the house, I would only be there, like my dad used to say, "Long enough to get me a drink of water and take out across that mountain."

When I was thirteen years old I knew which way a nut went on a bolt. I went to work in a sawmill in the piney woods.

I used to fight school but I got through to the sixth grade. Then my dad decided he was going to make me real smart and he sent me off to San Antonio Business College. I had about as much use for that college as I did a bitin' dog.

I was fifteen years old when we come out here in 1923. I was used to them piney woods springs where you could fall down and just lap water up till you got full. But after we moved, I decided that Alpine has the best water in Texas and I must have drunk out of five hundred windmill wells in my life.

I started rawhiding windmills in the summer of 1928. I really done a lot of that. I helped my dad farm at Water Valley near San Angelo and then when we got the crop loaded by, I had about six weeks in there and that is when I went out rawhiding.

The bearing on those small windmills, with the straight up-and-down slide, now they were bad about wearing out if you didn't keep them greased. And the head on the old Eclipse, it had a special bearing in it. I jacked those wheels up a lot of times and put rawhide on them bearings and greased the moving parts with liquid soap. (That soap will outlast any oil you can put on.)

I'd go around to the feed store boss to get a green hide after he'd skinned a cow. I would soak them hides in water and cut strips about as big as my finger and just as long as I could get.

Old Rawhide Bill was out of Big Spring. My first summer I worked with him rawhiding those old wood windmills, those slats were hard to keep nails and bolts on. But Bill could do it with rawhide! He was a short fella that weighed about three hundred and fifty pounds. He could climb those wood towers but he couldn't get through the windmill manhole. He would have to climb over! It beat anything I ever seen.

He could take them slats, and arms, and stuff like that and some way he could put a rawhide cross on them that was just like sewing. They say that in thirty days you could take every bolt and nail out of those wheels and throw them away. That hide stayed there. I mean it got tight!

At the Spade Ranch we rawhided a bunch of them that summer of 1928. The next year we would take down a bunch of 'em to replace them with steel mills. There was no reason to take a wrench up there. You needed a hacksaw to cut that rawhide. I tell you, it held fast!

All along this Sugg country we rawhided a bunch of them that summer.

I was raised on a little cotton farm on Dove Creek near Knicker-bocker, Texas, near Angelo. The Depression came on and the next fat man that I was working with, Mr. Logan, he got a better job in Del Rio. I took his place and I moved on up and then I took on the big windmills. I'll show you a few pictures. I've got pictures of all these lies I tell. I can back them up.

Del Rio was our main headquarters when goin' into Old Mexico and up the river. In the Depression when it just got so you couldn't get a helper here in the U.S., they furnished helpers out of Old Mexico. There is only one way to speak Spanish with those Indians across the river. You do this and this and this [gesturing] and grunt real big. I got along with them real good.

I had four different breeds of them. I was supposed to have been the instructor, but you damned sure work when you are there. I had about forty men in my deal, ten, twelve, fourteen in a bunch. At night every bunch got in their own squat and they could talk to one another. Other Indians, they couldn't talk to them because they were just as far off of them as I was.

I really liked it over there in Old Mexico. One of the ranches that I was on was a thousand sections and I'd stay out there working on the windmills and wells for three months at a time. Then I'd come into Del Rio, looking forward to Ma Crosby's, eating good and drinking that Mexican beer.

We were trying to put a windmill on top of the bluff because in the summertime the wind blew up on the bluff but not down on the vega, where there was no wind and where the temperature was hitting about a hundred fifteen to twenty degrees. So we had to drill a twelve-hundred-foot hole on top of the bluff.

We were also trying to pump water from the Rio Grande up that sixteen-hundred-foot bluff to our camp. A vega is a sandbar or bottomland. The Rio Grande often flooded that sand vega so they put an engine on a huge rock above the flood level.

That bluff was sixteen hundred feet and that river was the only water in the country. We had rope ladders and we went down those rope ladders to keep from going around the trail, which would take you about twice or three times as long as it did down by rope ladder.

From where we camped on this bluff, late in the evening, we'd sit up above the river and watch two or three bandits coming across. I had thought about bandits a lot during my first trip into Old Mexico with Mr. Logan in 1936 working for Axtell Company. One night we made it to Fort Stockton by ten. The next day we sixty-miled it over to Marathon to the old Gage Hotel. Then to Alpine. The next morning freight wagons were leaving town with mule teams. They had men riding, all of them with pistols and rifles on their saddles. I was watching all those big ole Army wagons, each with a driver and a fella riding shotgun, six or eight wagons in the bunch and ten or twelve men riding out through the pastures. Unfenced, godforsaken country.

Well, I sidled up to Mr. Logan and I said, "Mr. Logan, what are all them wagons and guns and stuff?"

He said, "Ranchers down along the Rio Grande got to have guards or they can't get them groceries back to the ranch. Them Mexicans come across the river and take them groceries."

I didn't say nothing but I was thinking pretty heavy, though. I asked him which way we was goin'. He said, "Oh, we are goin' back in on the river."

I said, "The way them fellas are going with all them guns?"

"Yeah."

I thought to myself, "Ole boy, you sure played hell with things coming down here!"

Old man Knapp told me before I ever went in there, "Don't bother them bandits. All they want is goat to eat and horses to ride." I said, "Don't you worry, Mr. Knapp, I won't even speak to them." That's the way we got by. They never did bother us and we never bothered them.

RUSTY BRADLEY:

"A LITTLE

ORNERY STREAK"

Electra, TX

Born 1909

People often ask how I find the people I interview for my oral history books. The answer is simple: I quiz everyone I meet for potential interviewees.

That happened one day when I was in visiting at the Wichita Falls *Times-Record News.* Farm editor (and A&M graduate) Joe Brown had a tip for me. "Go see Rusty Bradley out at Electra," he said excitedly. When I asked why, he told me this story:

Rusty ranches about five thousand acres out by Kadane. The Kadane family found a bunch of oil out there and they just named it Kadane Corner.

One day Rusty came to town to visit with his banker. He's probably got millions in the bank, no tellin' how much, but he's still like a cowboy. Wore his old cowboy hat that he wears when he works on the windmills. Grease on the brim and all this. Rusty is a windmill-fixer, horsebreaker, stuff like that. Wore that hat and this ole denim jacket when the vice president of the bank took him upstairs to the exclusive Wichita Club to have coffee. While they were sitting there, a real slick-lookin' insurance salesman, you know with the French cuffs and big wide tie, come up and started visiting with the vice president. Rusty said he could see him lookin' over at him ever once in a while, wondering what he was doin' up at the Wichita Club. So Rusty just took his coffee cup, poured some in

his saucer, put both elbows on the table and then went to sipping.
When the insurance man left, the banker turned and said,
"Rusty, why in the hell did you do that?"
Rusty said, "What the heck! He expected me to do it."

JOE IS MUCH TOO KIND to me but I don't want him to change that story. Especially when he is around my banker, I want him to continue to blow that up a little.

Joe exaggerates my little oil income. There is some oil on the property but when you lease acreage to an oil company, they take seven-eighths of the oil and give you only one-eighth. We have a *small* royalty interest. I am just a wetback for the oilman who gave me a little interest in one lease. That is the only workin' interest that I have in the oil business.

Anyway, Joe doesn't get that story quite right. What happened, they got a real nice club up here, and I was having lunch with my attorney and one of the vice presidents of my bank. Well, there was a man that come to our table. . . . The man was *so* glad to see the attorney and the vice president of the bank but when they introduced him to me (I had on my Levis and brush jacket), God almighty, he didn't want to put his hand out! After we shook, you could tell that he wanted to rub his hand on his britches.

So I was drinkin' coffee. Well, I poured some of this coffee out in this saucer, then I picked it up, and I drank out of it.

God almighty, that man got every color in the world and he left in a hurry.

When he left, my attorney friend said, "Rusty, you little sorry son-of-a-bitch."

That is the story that Joe has always liked to tell. But, God, that man, he hated to recognize me as part of the human race. [Laughter] As soon as I set that saucer back down he was on his way! He didn't want any more action like that.

Actually, I've got kind of a little ornery streak in me. Just because I didn't have on a two-hundred-dollar suit, he felt like it was below his dignity to speak to me. This is why I done that.

That was one of the few times in my life time that I ever felt like a man deliberately put me down. I go dressed in the crudest of fashion and I don't have any problems. I can get into any eating place that I want to in Wichita Falls. I can go on business to other towns and I don't have any trouble even though I don't waste a hell of a lot of money on clothes.

You know Will Rogers said, "The cowboy gives fifty dollars for his hat, and fifty dollars for his boots, and from his hat to his boots he spends about four and a half."

I subscribe to that, too.

See these high-topped boots here? They are hand-made boots, that's what they are. They are more comfortable to wear in the summertime instead of chaps and I got to wearing them all year round.

These boots. . . . One autumn back in the late nineties, these two friends of mine, Joe Cole and Uncle Charlie Ancell, were in Seymour deliverin' their cattle. The price was pretty good and so they got to drinkin' a little bit. They went down to Mr. Bud Humphrey to order a pair of boots. He was known for miles as an outstanding bootmaker. They ordered these boots made fancy because they were drinkin' a little bit and the price of cattle had gone pretty good. They were tighter than bark on a log usually.

Bud had some reservations about the orders but two months later they were back down there and they were stone sober and there was a little drought on. The cattle didn't look near as shiny as they had when they had ordered those boots.

They put the new boots on and Bud asked, "How they fit?"

"Oh, Bud, they fit! They are beautiful. You are the best damned bootmaker in the whole world!"

They was a-walkin' up and down and Bud said, "Now you are sure they fit?"

"Bud, they are the best boots I ever saw and they couldn't fit any better."

At that little ole boot shop, Bud's boots generally were about twenty or twenty-five dollars. But Bud said, "Now, you know *these* boots cost thirty-two dollars."

Joe Cole just dropped down in the chair and kicked his foot up and said, "Bud, this damned instep is a-killin' me!"

So in our country around Electra we always said, when anything was too high, "It's too damned tight in the instep."

In Wichita County somebody in my family has been living on my ranch since 1887. My mother and I inherited some of it from her grandfather, J. H. Banta, and some that my father had bought.

Jack Bradley was my father. At the beginning of the century he was working on the XIT Ranch near Dalhart, Texas, for thirty-five dollars a month. Instead of spending that money, my father just put his check up and at the end of a two-year period he had twenty-three of them. He bought our first land up there not too far out of Amarillo. He sold that land and moved to Wichita County in 1906. This is the foundation of our little ranch right here near Electra, Texas.

I am very proud of my father. He was a very quiet, reserved man who had an awful lot of foresight and was very, very low-key. A very kind man. I never saw him in church over three or four times in my life but he was a most religious man. He had the morals that I think comply more with the teaching of Jesus Christ than anybody I ever knew. He didn't tell me what to do. He just set an example.

He was very disappointed in his son. I just didn't have what my father had when it come to integrity and moral fiber and all this stuff. He was a very deep thinker, my father.

When I was a young man and rode with my father checking the cattle, the range was virtually open. Today we have got a mesquite problem. The brush has become one of our big problems in this country.

The other big change here, of course, is the roads and vehicles. Before tractors, we used to do all our farming with horses. I drove a team myself, but we didn't do a lot of farming ourselves. We had people that lived on my father's place and rented. They were real fine people. They would rent this land and farm it and then my father would get a percent of the cotton or wheat. Dad got a portion and they did most of the farming.

In later years *we* used tractors and farmed wheat and oats.

In the spring of 1877 my grandmother came as a child from Missouri to Colorado and then to Texas in a wagon. Her name was Rella Banta. My ranch headquarters is about four miles from where they settled down in a log cabin with a rawhide roof. A little place called Beaver Creek.

They had to freight their lumber by wagon from Henrietta,

about thirty miles east of Wichita Falls. Sherman, about a week's journey from Wichita Falls by wagon, was where they had to go to buy their clothes and supplies. That is pretty rugged country.

My grandmother was a remarkable woman. She taught herself to read with a dictionary. She taught herself to read and write while she was taking care of her father's cattle and sheep.

I have a lot of respect for my grandmother.

The pioneer women like my grandmother had their babies way out in the country, with no doctor near!

One night my grandmother's mother awakened her to help her give birth to a stillborn baby. My grandmother had to bury the child in the yard.

My grandmother was a short woman but very active. If there was any fear in her, I didn't ever detect it. She could swim a horse across those streams when they were up. She branded cattle. She did everything there was to do on the ranch. She married Mr. Chilton; they had three young children when he died and she raised those children alone. She was just a remarkable woman.

I'm goin' to tell you a story about my grandmother. She is the first woman that taught me real discipline. My mother was sick a lot when I was small and I spent a lot of time with my grandmother. Once when I was a little bitty boy and we were walkin' along a tank dam, I was behind her and bawlin' as loud as a kid can bawl. My grandmother said, "If you don't quit bawlin' and shut up, I'm goin' to throw you in this tank."

My little stinking mind said to myself, "She wouldn't throw me in this tank." So God almighty, I kept a-bawlin' and the next thing I knew I was just like a rock flying out into that water.

I went down a couple of times.

My grandmother fished me out of there and you can damned well believe that I wasn't a-bawlin' anymore.

That was the first discipline that I had that I can really remember.

I loved that lady.

Texas's women made this country. That's where we got the culture. Them old boys didn't give a damn whether they had school or churches, the finer things in life. But them women did.

Mrs. Bradley is a damned sight more cultured than I am, no problem about that. She thinks I'm pretty crude and tells me.

Of course, she has been tellin' me that for fifty some-odd years. So I guess that it worked out all right. We have a real good relation. We disagree without being disagreeable.

We met at high school in Electra, Texas. I had trouble with my damned English. She was a Chaney and I was a Bradley so she always sat in front or behind me in all these classes.

I talked her into helpin' me with the damned English. She done so well, I just thought we ought to keep it up. So when I went to college, I come back and married her.

I have no regrets whatsoever.

She may have. Don't ask her that question.

[The following Rusty Bradley story is from *Bridlewise and Otherwise, Vol. II.*]

JEFF MCMURTRY IS A RANCHER of the old school, a little feller he is, but he has some pretty firm ideas as to just what might be wrong with the cow business and the country in general. He is sure about as sharp as they come, and I enjoy talking to Jeff. I hadn't seen him in a long time, so the other night I called him on the phone. In the course of a very nice visit he told me that in the latter part of the year nineteen hundred and seventy-three, he suffered a stroke, but he hastened to assure me that he was much better and was able to walk without his walker or his crutches. I told Jeff how sorry I was to hear this, and he made a statement that did my heart good. I think it well worth repeating. "Rusty," he says. "Hell, don't feel sorry for me. I have lived a good life, put together a little country and had the good fortune to marry a wonderful woman. We have raised what I think is a very fine family, and I have known some good men. I have two or three real good friends (this I question), and I have owned four or five real good horses in my lifetime. I have made a living in the cow business, and I have had the pleasure of feeling the sun, the rain, and the wind in my face. So don't feel sorry for me. I have had a very good life."

I just thought the above remarks were great because Jeff has lived through some very trying times in the cow business. He has weathered many a storm and many a drought. He has ridden some good horses, but like all the rest of old time cowmen, for every good horse he has ridden a hell of a lot of jug heads.

I got to thinking about Jeff's fine family, and quite naturally my thoughts turned to his son, Larry McMurtry, who has made a reputation for himself in the literary field. He has written several books that have become bestsellers, and has had the distinction of selling some of them to the movie folks who have made pictures of them, or at least made pictures based on the material in Larry's books.

One of these books was titled *The Last Picture Show.* The movie folks that bought the movie rights to the book thought it would be a good idea if they made the picture in and around Archer City, Texas, Larry's home town. They did just that—using local folks as much as possible, and by rebuilding the town a little they produced a picture that won nationwide recognition in the entertainment field. If memory serves me right, it was nominated for an Oscar or two. Whether it won the Oscars, I don't know.

Now the book and the picture had some words in them that have not been entirely accepted in some gatherings. As a result, the book as well as the picture drew its share of adverse publicity along with some very glowing and positive reviews.

Wichita Falls, Texas, a city of approximately one hundred thousand population, is only about thirty miles from Archer City. The people that made the movie thought that Wichita Falls would be a good place to have the premier showing of the film based on Larry McMurtry's book entitled *The Last Picture Show.*

You can well imagine how the home-town folks reacted to the show. Some thought it was great; some thought it was in rather poor taste. I think in one nearby town maybe the folks, or at least part of them, got up a petition to prevent its being shown in their village. Most of the reports that I read were highly favorable to the show.

But I must tell you about a discussion I had with an acquaintance of mine about this picture show. His name was, and is, John A. Kay.

Now with my limited mental capacity and my limited and profane vocabulary, I don't have too many acquaintances like John

Kay. John is a gentleman in every sense of the word—in speech, in action, and in his relations with the human race. He is a very intelligent person. I have heard several learned people say that Mr. Kay probably was blessed with as good a brain as anyone in the city of Wichita Falls. So you can readily see that I was a fortunate person to have the pleasure of a discussion of this show with John.

The following are John's remarks as near as I can recall them. We met on the streets of our county seat under the big clock on the bank building, and after a pleasant discussion about the price of cattle and the weather, John says, "Rusty, you know I've been reading all the reports on the movie *The Last Picture Show*, and I've been talking to some people about it. As most everyone has a different opinion, I decided yesterday afternoon that I would just go see the show myself and draw my own conclusions."

Now this was a perfectly normal thing for John to do for he has a scientific approach to all things. It was just natural that he wanted the facts as he saw them in order to reach his own conclusions. John continued:

"Rusty, I just closed the office about two o'clock and went to the theater. The show was pretty crowded, but I found a seat about halfway down the theater and in front of the screen. After my eyes had become accustomed to the dark, I looked to my right and in the next seat, you can imagine my surprise when I discovered a big dog. He had his hindquarters back against the seat, his front legs were in a rigid position, and his eyes were glued to the screen. His concentration and interest were so great I was unable to enjoy the show for watching this dog. He did not take his eyes off the screen. Only one time during the hour and a half I sat beside him did he move and that was to scratch his eye with his front paw. I assure you, Rusty, the rest of the time he was watching the show.

"At the conclusion of the feature they turned the lights on so we might depart in a little more comfort, and I discovered that the dog was in the company of a very attractive lady who was fast approaching, if she had not already arrived at, what is known as the middle age of life.

"Now, Rusty," he continued, "even though I had fears that I might be considered rude, I introduced myself to this attractive lady and engaged her in conversation. I asked her just how old the dog was, and it developed that he was five years of age. His ancestors were of the bird dog extraction with just a sliver of common mutt running through his veins. Then I said to this lady, 'Well, he most certainly did enjoy that show!' You know, Rusty, her reply rather surprised me. She said, 'Yes, Mr. Kay, he did enjoy the show very much. He thought it was great, but this is very surprising to me, *very* surprising, because he didn't like the book at all.' "

This is Mr. Kay's story, not mine, and if you are inclined to doubt it, just come by and we'll go see John, and you can question him yourself.

MARY RALPH LOWE:

OILWOMAN

Houston, TX

Born 1946

My first impression of Mary Ralph was that she was as colorful as her flame-red Thunderbird automobile. She had come to work in a yellow leotard and she and the women in the oil-exploration company she owns and manages were soon gyrating to aerobic dance records. Her office was tastefully decorated in a way that hinted at some of her many other interests: Houston Ballet and Museum of Fine Art; AIDS and the homeless; and new acquisitions for Washington's National Gallery. Obviously this was not the lair of some crusty old field geologist.

In macho Texas, CEO jobs have not usually been women's territory, but this mother of three lost no time in telling me that she was "sick of that question." The way she put it was that "Ginger Rogers did everything Fred Astaire did, only backwards and in high-heel shoes."

I wanted to learn about this socialite's wildcatter father, Ralph Lowe (1902–1965). Tapping into a Permian Basin fortune in the late 1940s and early 1950s, handsome Ralph Lowe always played his cards close to his chest like the ace poker player he was. A 1961 book about Texas's ultrarich, *The Super-Americans,* described him as a man who would gamble on anything. And, according to his long-time associate Don Looney, Mary Ralph's father had an uncanny nose for black gold. Despite the rush of landowners to his door with leases, he would never hurry his map ponderings. His string of successes rapidly pyramided his personal fortune from zero to thirty-four producing oil wells!

For such a born gambler, the oil patch must have been the

ultimate casino. He always had to be drilling at least one wildcat well.

He was the sort of Texan who would rather attend a dice or card game than a rodeo. People still remember the two-thousand-dollar baseball bet that he parlayed through ten games into two hundred eighty thousand dollars. Or the 1959 Kentucky Derby, when his Gallant Man lost by a nose because of jockey error by Bill Shoemaker.

Mary Ralph did not strike me as a gambler. In fact, during the 1980s oil depression she dug only a tenth of her usual number of wells. "We're sitting back pretty close," she said glumly. But maybe even her father would have sat that hand out at nine dollars a barrel!

As the 1990s begin, she is no friend of OPEC and its "stupid games," an environment far different from her father's time, when gumption and luck out in the mesquite were much more important than the doings of oil ministers and Arab dictators.

Ralph Lowe had many people who were loyal to him and if one of his "big family" quit, it upset him very much. "He had a lot of confidence in all of his people and all those people had confidence in him," says Don Looney. He adds that Mary Ralph reminds him of her father in more ways than just her good looks. "She's very honest," he says, "but she's a little more outgoing than her dad was. He was kinda laid back and he wouldn't say too much."

Mary Ralph is definitely ready to speak out on certain subjects.

"I think the independent is really about dead," she says. "I think bureaucracy has gotten us. And I think the large companies, the Exxons, the OPECs are hurting us as bad as anything. They obviously have more money. So they buy all the leases. They can afford to drill more than we can."

As I do everyone, I asked Midland-born Mary Ralph Lowe who had most inspired her.

MY DADDY, 'CAUSE I WAS the only child. Therefore the name Mary *Ralph*. His parents were dairy farmers in Missouri. He went to school a couple of years at Westminster Military and the Depression hit and he went back to Missouri and cared for thirty-seven cows and figured out that wasn't going to make any money.

Then he went to Wyoming and got a job in a machine shop. In 1928 he ended up in Wink, Texas, where the first oil boom in Texas other than Beaumont was. And he finally got enough money saved as a filling-station attendant that he bought a Texaco station. Then he pumped gas and repaired cars for several years.

But he loved to gamble and finally about 1938 he decided he'd take everything he had plus mother's wedding ring and an old bad-lookin' fox cape and sink it in one oil well.

And he hit thirty-four wells straight!

That's pretty lucky but in the Permian Basin, where he was around the Midland–Odessa area, there was so much oil that almost anywhere you drilled you'd hit it.

Actually, my father was a very strange character. He thought women were bad luck on oil wells. So he would take me out when he went to see a well but I wasn't allowed to approach a lease. And generally, more than not, he would forget me in the car, and I'd sleep there for a couple of days while he was waiting for a well to come in. Really!

My father was very ill with emphysema while I was at Briarcliff in New York. I came back and finished my education in Texas. He died when I was twenty years old.

There was no one else to continue the business other than me. I had the people that had worked for him in the past and I learned the business. Now there are very few of the old people still here that had worked for him.

I've got some pumpers that have been around a long, long time but the oldest one died last week. It cut my guts out that he died. And God bless, there was a lot of history there. A lot of everything goes into somebody that's helped you that long.

My father was one of the old Permian Basin wildcatters. The most honest person you could ever meet. I think probably his biggest asset was a lot of faith and a lot of spirit and a lot of guts.

Cause nobody had anything down here then. There were no Vanderbilts or Kennedys in this part of the world.

There were just guts. That's all there was.

JAKE SANDEFER:
A FUNNY BREED
Houston, TX
Born 1936

Is there a petroleum jackpot available for the taking in the 1990s the way there was earlier in this century? I put the question to Houston's J. D. Sandefer III,* a man who continued to put exploration deals together through the hard times of the 1980s. Jake Sandefer is a wildcatter and independent despite the pundits who chorus the demise of the little guy. If you believe Jake, and I wanted to, there is still a lot of wealth out there in the ground waiting to be discovered.

The key, he said, would be for me to put together the right deal, to find eager limited partners willing to pay our expenses and accord me a free twenty-five-percent share of the venture. That way, even if the bottom of my hole turned out to be lined with granite, I would have lost nothing. That sounded good but did I want to spend as much as two years working on a wildcat that failed? To hear Jake tell it, the oil-exploration business was even more risky than writing books.

"Drilling wells is the only business I know," said Jake. "I love it. As long as I can find partners that want to drill them, that is what I am going to do."

Jake Sandefer is known as a very confident man—as a wildcatter must be. He still gets excited when the latest drilling reports come

---

*Sandefer is a well-known name in West Texas because Jake's grandfather Jefferson Davis Sandefer (1868–1940) had been president for thirty-one years of the small Baptist college that grew into Hardin-Simmons University. Jake's father, also named Jake (1899–1975), was a respected Breckenridge oilman and raconteur.

in. "Sweating the wells is a very fun part," he says. "I go back and talk to the geologist and get excited."

There will be independents that will find a way to drill the deep wells. Back when I was just out of school I saw where Ralph Lowe was drilling a twenty-four-thousand-foot well in West Texas. Hell, the majors were drilling very few that deep back then.

He must have been something! He wasn't afraid to do it. Used to be that forty-five hundred foot was a deep well in my part of the country.

There is a lot of liability drilling deep wells. A lot of mechanical things can go wrong and you lose a lot of money.

But throughout our history independents have drilled eighty percent of these wildcat drills. I think there will always be wildcatters in the lower forty-eight states. They will find a way. They are a funny breed.

I THINK THE PEOPLE IN the oil business are a little bit different. The conversations, the oilfield talk, the comradeship, and the whole thing is an experience that is hard to leave. It is just a way of life.

Dad more or less bought production. He was what they call a stripper operator. A stripper well is a well that makes less than ten barrels a day. You have to keep expenses low. It's kind of like a mom-and-pop motel operation. A lot of owners look after their wells themselves. They are so marginal that if they produce a little too much water, they become uneconomical. But there are a lot of people that have made a lot of money on stripper wells. You got to have a bunch of them and you got to know how to operate them.

My father wildcatted some but he never really found anything real good. He was in a more low-reserve-type area in West Central Texas. Shallow fields. South Texas, North Texas, East Texas, nearly anywhere you go there has been deeper production found but very little in West Central Texas.

When I got out of the University of Oklahoma in 1949, Dad had more or less retired. He had a very small operation and I moved back to Breckenridge for a couple of years and started right out promotin' deals, raisin' money, and drillin' wells. Basically, I am in the same business he was but I have been more of a wildcatter and have used the outside sources for money more than my dad did.

I had had a little bit of money from my dad but not a lot. I definitely had to get out and do something. I had played football for the University of Oklahoma. I had a degree in business but not in geology, engineering, or something technical. I got back and saw what dad's situation was. He didn't have enough money or enough production to last me forever. I couldn't go to work as a geologist or an engineer so I had to get out and start promotin' deals.

In the early sixties I hadn't been out of school very long and I hadn't been doing very good when this geologist friend of my dad's in Abilene had three or four little shallow deals and it was going to cost fifteen thousand dollars to drill three twelve-hundred-foot Moutry sand tests in Callahan County. The Moutry was a very prolific pay zone in that area.

I got a newspaperman, a man on a radio station in Brownwood, and an insurance man in Wichita Falls, all of them friends of my dad, and I sold them interests in those three wells. One of those wells was beside a well that was producing but it had three dry holes three hundred feet apart. So we decided to drill a fourth well three hundred feet to the north of that one producing well.

I was living in Breckenridge at that time. One midnight my geologist friend called me from Abilene and said he was going to run a drill-stem test on this well but that he was not optimistic because the pay zone was twenty feet lower than the one well that we were offsetting. Twenty feet below what he had expected, which was not good because he thought it would be a salt water zone. He told me he was going to test it anyway because it had a show of oil, but things did not look good.

He called me the next day just before I left for Louisiana and he said he had gotten a very good test, a test that would be the same sensation that the old-timers would have had drilling into a gusher! They control it now. Oil doesn't flow over the top but we knew we had something good.

We drilled and made wells in a straight line for about two miles, just like a river channel. The field made over six hundred thousand barrels of oil!

That was what got me started. You have so much disappointment in this business, but the thrill of finding a good discovery is quite an experience!

We don't know to this day if that field that we found was connected to that one well that was already there. We cannot prove. . . . We found a field that was two miles long by offsetting a well that we thought would be in the same reservoir. But we might have opened a new field just by luck.

Most fields, funny things happen. You will be drilling for something in one zone and find another damned zone that totally surprises people.

We ended up with about thirty wells in that field. I was very excited. It was really a great, secure feeling because I didn't know if I was ever going to find *any* oil.

It is a scary feeling when you don't know what is coming next. A feeling that there is no security.

Oil and gas is a depleting asset and you have to continue to find it to stay in business. There are a few big fields that you find. A field that might last thirty or forty years, but there are few of those. You can't stand still. I have always been an enthusiastic and persistent person. I have been to the point where I could have quit a couple of times and had enough money to last. But I have continued to hire more people and put more money at risk and keep goin' to the challenge. I have always expanded my operation and put the money I had back in and just kept going.

In 1976 I was up in Abilene and had one of the nicest homes in West Texas, ten minutes from the country club, director of the biggest bank in town, and all the money I would ever need. But I wasn't satisfied.

What did I do but move to Houston and get a divorce, move into an apartment, and sign a note to decorate these offices, hire people, and start over again. Laid everything on the line.

Why? I don't know. I guess I wanted to see if I could come down here to Houston and play with the big boys.

Eighty-one was our first year with a whole new set of partners. Bigger-type operation and raising a different type of money. We've been moderately successful. I'm pretty optimistic today even though we have not found the reserves that I had hoped to. I am confident because we have continued to upgrade our geologists, our technology, our prospects.

When you lose partners, you got to continue to find new partners. We depend to a great extent on outside dollars. We do not have the money to drill these deep wells. We put our money in people and overhead, then go get the money to drill the wells. The equipment has changed but the substance of old-time wildcatting is there. You are out drilling a well, raising the money, and have the same high expectation of getting a big discovery.

In 1984 I was kind of down about our situation but now we have turned it around and I think that people that can stay in the business this time are going to have a bright future.

Yes, a person could come in today and do that! There *will* be people that keep doing it even though they would live longer doing something else. It is a nervewracking business. Most everything you do in this business is a failure. A geologist goes into the oil business and puts all his science, education, and technology into it but most of what he does for the rest of his life is to explain failure to somebody. Or a wildcatter is explaining a failure to partners because most wells are failures. No more than two percent of the wells that you drill will succeed. Only two out of a hundred are goin' to be real good. You will have a lot of marginal stuff that will make a little bit of money. Anybody goin' into this business better plan that only two out of a hundred will be real moneymakers.

I guess the Lord just made the stuff hard to find.

[I began this chapter wondering if I, too, could break into wildcatting. After reading Jake's father's *It's Been Fun,* what impresses me most is not the richness of his wells but the quality of his friendships. Here is how he remembered one of his pumpers, Henry Cosper.]

I HAVE MET A LOT of interesting characters in my life, but I can't think of any with a drier wit or who can get to the point quicker than Henry Cosper.

Henry has been in my employ, off and on, for more than twenty years, and he and his wife are a joy to be around. It's hard to get away when you drive up to the lease house because Mrs. Cosper is so cheerful.

Henry is a faithful employee who always has a smile, but he also has a mind—and a vernacular—of his own. And, as I said, when Henry wants to state his mind, he does it quick and simple and well.

One fall, my long-time superintendent and friend, T. S. Buckner, and another warm friend, Emmett Whiteside, and I met at Rising Star for our annual quail hunt. We were eager for the shooting because we had really taken the birds the year before.

We started early and went to a lease which usually paid off in quail—but found nothing. We went a few miles further to another lease I had—but no birds. We went a few miles more, this time to the place where the quail were just begging to be shot the fall before—with the same negative results.

Emmett suggested we go over to Uncle Bill's. It was more than twenty miles away but the year before, on Christmas Day, Emmett and his kin had gotten almost one hundred birds while they were waiting on the womenfolks to prepare dinner.

The results were the same everywhere we went. Finally, just before giving up entirely, I spotted one quail under a blue bush. I called for the gang to stop, and I announced a decision.

"Boys," I said, "we need meat for the table. I am going to shoot at those birds on the ground and you fellows can take 'em as they come up."

I fired. Not a bird rose.

We walked up to the bush and there were seven dead quail in it. That was our bag for the day—a day of extensive walking, driving, and frustration.

A few days later I got a letter from Henry Cosper about some trouble on the lease. He wrote, as he always did, with a pencil on tablet paper. He commenced the letter "Dear Potshot."

That was the only mention ever made again of that mighty hunt.

Several years ago we decided to get a little "intracompany" correspondence started so we could keep closer tab on how the oil business was running where we were operating.

I told all my pumpers I wanted them to write me a letter each Saturday night, provided I had not visited with them during that week so I would get it the following Monday morning. I said I wanted to know how much production they were getting, if anyone was drilling their area, what adjoining wells to us might be making—anything they heard of or saw I might need to know.

The first letter I got from Henry Cosper was short, but a real classic. Here is what he wrote, in its entirety:

J. D. Sandefer Corp
Breckenridge, Texas
Dear Corp:
There ain't no Trubble. Everything is alright. Everything is OK.
                    Love — Your Pumper Henry

Another time Henry wrote about some equipment problems on his lease. He was very fond of Bill Arnot, my son-in-law. The final line in Henry's letter said:

"How is old Bill, I ain't seen him since the peckerwoods et up the toilet."

In the early forties I had a lease up near Hamlin, in Jones County, which I sold to a friend and fellow townsman, Lester Clark. Henry Cosper's services as pumper went with the deal.

Not long after our transaction, Lester walked in my office looking all worn out. I asked him what in the world was the matter and he said, "That man of yours, Henry Cosper. He got me in trouble."

I asked how in the name of peace Henry could do anything that would get anybody in trouble. Then Clark told me the story.

He said that he had been out of the office for a full week, moving around the state, looking at properties, so he decided to come down at five o'clock in the morning and try to take care of the mail.

Right on top of the stack of a week's accumulation, Lester said he saw a post card from Henry which said, "No production yesterday. Myrtle died during the night."

Lester is the kind of man who can't sit still when he thinks he is needed. He said he read no further but grabbed his hat, jumped in the car, and headed for Hamlin.

"All the way up there I thought of what a wonderful lady and good mother Mrs. Cosper had been the few time I met her," Lester said. "I hated to think of her leaving all those children and good old Henry."

Lester said he arrived at the lease house just after daylight. Having made a fast trip on the empty highways, he walked upon the porch and knocked on the door softly.

"Mrs. Cosper greeted me with her usual smile and said, 'Well, good morning, Mr. Clark,' with a little bit of a question in her voice," Clark tells.

"I visited with her for a few minutes, making cautious inquiries about each of the little children, but everyone seemed in good shape."

"Finally I asked, 'Mrs. Cosper, where's Henry?' "

"He's down at No. 7," she replied. "Been down there since breakfast and most of yesterday."

Lester he thanked her and drove down to No. 7. Henry was all smiles as he looked up and saw his boss get out of the car.

"Well, Henry," Lester said, "what are you doing?"

Henry was splicing an old belt on the standard rig and said "Tryin' to fix this here."

Lester exchanged a few words and finally said, "Henry, who is 'Myrtle' you said died during the night?"

Without looking where he pointed, Henry shook his head and stuck out an arm.

"That ole gas engine right there," he said.

Henry came back to me after making Lester Clark a good hand for a few years. Henry likes to fish and each summer he drops me a note saying "When you gonna bring down all your friends and let's have a fish fry?"

One summer, after he had asked me twice and I hadn't visited him yet, he wrote, "I've got the fish; ain't you got the friends?"

BUM BRIGHT:
FROM A & M TO S & L'S
Dallas, TX
Born 1920

The Big Boys like the Hunts may go broke, attracting lots of headlines, but they always hang onto enough acres and baubles for their "broke" still to look downright desirable. Bum Bright lost properties, banks, and his controlling interest in the Dallas Cowboys in the 1980s recession but he has had the benefit of knowing how to start from scratch, if necessary. When he began in the oil business right after World War II, he was once down to his last twelve dollars!

Before meeting him in 1986, I assumed that Bum's nickname described that "broke" period before he had become a multimillionaire oilman/banker. The real explanation is that his parents thought their infant resembled "a little railroad bum" in appearance. In any case, names were a big thing in the go-go 1980s, when Bum and his family owned so many businesses that they named them in bunches like someone might name a litter of pups. Companies named after rocks, South-Sea islands, or types of spaghetti—all names having little or nothing to do with the subject of the enterprise. There *is* a lot in a name, of course, and some of the most famous in modern Texas emerged into the 1990s looking like road kills. Do you remember that news photo of bankrupt former governor John Connally at a black-tie auction, surrounded by his expensive possessions, as the gavel fell on his past life?

The case of Bum Bright interests me not because he is one of Texas's notorious savings and loan crooks (he isn't) but because he is an Aggie. Even if his companies shrivel like moon pies in the Dallas sun, Bum will always have Aggieness to fall back on. One teacher in particular inspires him even today. Perhaps that is why, Memorial Day 1986, surrounded by his World War II bayonet collection, Aggie memorabilia, and huge tapestry of King Arthur, Bum was hard at work evaluating college applications from Aggie wannabe's. He said he was looking for leadership potential. I know that I would not have wanted to have my application in that pile if I had been "simply a bookworm." It reminded me of what Bum said about the then coach and manager of the Dallas Cowboys:

Tom's leadership of the Cowboys on the field and Tex's leadership of the organization occurred from the inception of the team. I don't think Tom Landry or Tex Schramm patterned themselves after anybody. I think they are the pattern after which other people pattern themselves. *

Bum Bright's postwar pattern was to broker oilfield leases, keeping a sliver of the action on each deal. In 1972 he got into S & Ls as a hedge against inflation because he saw that "every time moneychangers touched money, they'd peel a little bit of it off."

I asked this go-getter to tell me who had inspired him the most about life's ups and downs.

A DETERMINATION TO ACCOMPLISH THE mission is a very, very important factor in the success of any business. I think it has been a significant factor in whatever success I've had. We do not turn up our toes and say we can't get it done. We find a way. In my lifetime I don't know how many times I have been confronted with a problem that I thought I could not solve. And then I would delay or put it off until I thought about old man Vance telling me that "This old world only pays off on results." And somehow I'd apply the effort, apply the time, apply the diligence, and find a way to get the job done.

When I was at A & M, I made pretty good grades. I had worked two years in the oilfield before I went to A & M. I started when I

---

*Bum Bright's distress sale of the Dallas Cowboys ended an era. Tom Landry, Cowboys coach for twenty-nine years, was summarily removed by Arkansas businessman Jerry Jones and replaced by Miami's Jimmy Johnson. In 1989 massive parades and farewells in Dallas were emotional tributes to football immortal Landry.

was seventeen in the oilfields roustaboutin'. Roughneckin'. And by the time I'd gotten to be a junior I had achieved some things on the campus. I was first sergeant of my outfit. And I was a little bit self-satisfied.

The head of our petroleum department was a man named Harold Vance and he seldom would condescend to know the name of anyone until they got to be a senior in the petroleum department. He had no contact with 'em. He taught only senior classes.

When I was a junior, I was in the hall in the petroleum building and he stopped me and said, "Harvey, will you come into my office a moment?" He knew who I was because I was one of his real comers as a student and as a campus leader.

So he took out a little three-by-five card and he wrote down the name of a book and he said "Would you go get this book for me?"

And I said "Yes, sir!" I had another class but I thought that here was a chance to get in good with the head of the petroleum department. So I cut my class, ran over to the library to get the book, and the lady came back and said "I'm sorry, the book's been checked out." And she gave me the due date and the name of the person who had checked it out. It was a Professor Jackson in the Academic Building.

I was very proud of myself for doing such a complete job for the head of the petroleum department. I said, "Mr. Vance, that book was checked out on this date by Professor A. M. Jackson and it's due back on this date. And the Dewey decimal number of that book is right here. And I sat back waitin' for him to pat me on the head and tell me what a good job I had done.

He said, "Well, son, you've wasted about fifteen minutes of your time and the same amount of my time. And have come back and reported to me why you couldn't get the job done that I sent you to do." He said, "Son, this old world only pays off on results. It doesn't pay off on why you couldn't get the job done. When you get out of school, you'll find hundreds of situations where you can make an excuse for not getting the job done. And you can make an excuse that sounds good and justifiable to your boss. And it may even sound justifiable and good to you. But, son, this old world doesn't pay off on why you can't get the job done. It only pays off on results. And you'll and when you go to work for a company. . . ."

I interrupted him. I said, "Mr. Vance, may I be excused?"
And he said yes.

I ran up to the Academic Building and I found that Professor Jackson had a class and I went into his class and told him I had to get that book.

He said, "I'm teaching a class."

I said, "Is it in your office?"

He said yes.

I said, "Give me your office key and I'll go get it."

He said, "No, I can't give you my key."

I said, "I've got to have it right now."

And he said, "Well, I'll go with ya and excuse myself from the class." He went and got the book and gave it to me.

I took it to Mr. Vance. And he sat back and kinda smiled. He said, "Son, did you learn anything?"

I said, "Yes, sir."

He said, "Don't you ever forget it as long as you live."

JOE NEWTON: TEXAS OUTLAW
Uvalde, TX
Born 1901

The usual bragging about the biggest and the best even extends to Texas's criminals. Even they are a source of local pride, going back to the time when lawlessness threatened public order during and after the Civil War. When Governor Coke re-established the Texas Rangers in 1874, Major L. H. McNelly brought calm to the border areas while Major John B. Jones's Frontier Battalion mopped up the West's assorted outlaws, bandits, and cattle thieves. Of course, Texas's most audacious recent criminals have been its savings-and-loan holdup men. Not the ones who walk in the front door wearing ski masks and passing tellers threatening notes. No, it is the owners and managers of some S & L's who have been stealing *billions* of our dollars while strutting their okra all up and down the state in Lear jets, executive suites, and hobby ranches.

Compared to those white-collar criminals, Joe Newton of Uvalde was as green as a pea from Portland. He was just a horse-crazy kid when his three older brothers roped him into the bank-robbery business. Stolen nitroglycerine from Oklahoma oilfields was his ticket to success, not phony bookkeeping.

"I never knew anybody that *liked* robbing banks," says Joe. "It was just a business deal to us."

The Newton Gang's last foray was a three-million-dollar train heist. One of Joe's brothers was accidentally shot, and when Joe took him to a doctor the jig was up. Joe served three years in Leavenworth and insists that he has kept right between the bar

ditches ever since and that the later ten years he did in the pen was
a bum rap for a bank robbery he never committed.

With so much cell time behind him, Joe finally returned to
Uvalde, where, he says, he should have stayed all along.

BEFORE I WAS BORN, MY great-great-grandfather, or somebody back
there, the insurance company, beat him out of the insurance and
ruined him. When I was a little kid they was a-talkin' about it. From
generation to generation everybody had it in for the insurance
company on account of what they had done to my grandfather.
Because of that we had it in our craw about insurance companies
being no good. As far as we was concerned, anything we did to the
company that insured banks shouldn't be against the law.

I was born in North Texas, Callahan County. We come down
here in 1907 in a covered wagon to Crystal City before there was
a Crystal City.

My father, he liked to travel around. He said he was always
lookin' for the land of honey palms and corn fritters.

Down here there was a world of old palms and the woodchucks
would dig a hole in there, huntin' bugs, and then make a nest.
Then the bees would come along and make their home in there.

That's where Uvalde got the honey palms.

Corn fritters are those flapjacks made out of cornmeal. You fried them and turned them over and they were very good with honey.

And Uvalde *is* a honey country. Everything here, every bush, tree, that I know of will bloom. The huajillo is supposed to make the best honey. Whitebrush blooms out with a little bitty bloom every time you get as much as a two-inch rain. It makes wonderful honey, too. The mesquites, folks make a lot of honey off the mesquite bloom.

I thought I had to be a cowboy. I mean a sure-'nuff cowboy. I wanted to rope, ride, and do all the cowboy things.

By the time I was seventeen, I was working on a hundred-square-mile ranch at Langtry. Our job, me and this other boy, was to ride the outlaw horses that the other boys wouldn't ride. The boss told me to "get the pitch out of them."

In the olden days the horse didn't buck. In my days when I was young, they was pitchin' horses. We didn't use the words *bucking horse.*

Anyway, I was breaking horses and living on the ranch.

When I was nineteen there come a flood, an eighteen-inch rain, that washed through every gap in that whole country. Water gaps where the fences cross the creek. There was just one creek after another out there because of the mountains. The big boss called from El Paso and said for us to come to the headquarter ranch and meet him there at a certain time. So we did and he went to cuttin' up the cow outfit and sending them to fix water gaps. Two or three go here, and two or three over there, all over that whole country.

When he got to me I told him I didn't want to fix any water gaps. When I had been hired, my boss had said "We don't want the cowboys doin' anything except riding them horses." I reminded the big boss of that. I said I wasn't mad at anybody or anything else like that, "but I don't build fence down in my home country. I never built any fence in my life and I never burnt any prairie except for my own stuff. I just don't do that." I said I would like to draw my time and cut out my horses.

He said "All right," even though that was so far out there there wasn't anything but a wagon road out there in those days, that he couldn't hire anybody else.

When I left, I had to tell the big boss how many horses I had.

That was the funniest thing. Like everybody else I was supposed to have six gentle cow horses and three broncs to ride. But I had gotten the ones that everybody else wouldn't ride. I had the bad horses and the rest of them just had ordinary horses.

I ended up with fifteen mounts. The big boss said "Where in the hell did you get so many horses? You are only supposed to have nine."

"Well, you wanted me to ride these pitchin' horses out here, and every time somebody didn't want one, I'd take it and when he quit pitchin' he was a gentle horse. Then they would take the gentle horse from me and I got another bad one."

So I had fifteen of them when I returned to Uvalde.

Then when I was nineteen, going on twenty, one of my brothers wrote me and wanted me to come up to Oklahoma. Had a job for me. I took my saddle, wore my boots, had my spurs in a tote sack that had my saddle in and everything. "What the hell you goin' to do with that saddle?" "Well, you said you had a good job and all I know how to do is work cows, ranch work, ride horses. So I brought my saddle."

He said "Throw that damned saddle away." I let him take my saddle and he gave it to somebody he knew. I don't know who.

When I got up there, my job from then on was bank-robbin'.

We also robbed six trains. We got on the plank of the passenger train in some town. Stayed there until the train got out of town and then we climbed over the coal tender and went down with the engineer and fireman and had them stop the train where we had someone waiting at a remote road. You didn't stop at a highway crossing because there would be too many people coming along.

The last train we robbed, we got three million dollars on it. I tried to get them to not rob it because that was too much money. Attract too much attention.

It did.

They called all their men in from Washington and all over the United States. They picked out fifty of their best men. "That's your job. Stay on it until you get it solved."

That's the kind of deal when you get too big and too notorious. If we had got forty or fifty thousand dollars, they would never have done nothin' like that and we. . . . One of our men got excited and shot one of my brothers accidentally. That's how come we got caught. Course we would have got caught anyway because it was too big a deal.

We all went to Leavenworth. My big-talkin' brother, everybody just listened to his stories. They all liked him very much and he only got one year. Me, three year, because I was twenty-three years old. My other two brothers, twelve year each because they had been in trouble before.

That was in 1924. I had lived well, traveling all over the country. Drove a good car. Wore good clothes. Stayed at the best hotels. Ate at the best cafés. It was exciting all right, but I don't know anybody who liked it. You were after the money. It was strictly business.

Getting away was the main thing. Anyone can get the money but to get away with it. . . . The reason we got away with it was that we drove a Model T when we left a bank. We drove away at only about twenty-five to thirty miles an hour!

That's right. The sheriff would ask, "Did you see a high-powered car go by here driving fast?"

"No, seen an old Model T go along out there."

There isn't anybody going to pay no attention to that.

We wanted a car that looked like what everybody else had. With a Model T Ford you could go through the country the next day and nobody would pay any attention. They didn't know whether you were Dan Jones from down on the next farm or what.

If we robbed a bank in the corn season, it would look suspicious, three or four men in a car. So after the robbery at night, one man would drop us off near a cornfield. We'd hit a railroad track, walk on the railroad track so they couldn't see our tracks, then find a whole section of just solid corn, higher than your head. Take somethin' to eat along and a little water. Everybody would lay down and go to sleep except for one man and he had to stay up and he had to walk all the time. He couldn't sit down because if he sat down, he would go to sleep from being up all night. If he was walkin', he wouldn't go to sleep. In two or three hours someone else would get up and let him go to sleep.

That would keep somebody from walkin' up on you accidentally. If somebody walks up on you accidentally, you got to catch him and keep him till night. Then the whole town, the whole country is out lookin' for him. His wife would say "He just went down to the field." So if I were up, I would hear him comin' and I could wake everybody else up and we could move on over out of his way so that he didn't find us.

We'd stay in those cornfields all day. The next night we would be picked up again.

Robbing banks was damned difficult, but I went with experienced men that knew how to do it.

For a long time I was just the outside man that looked to see that nobody come around. We were blowin' safes in them days. You put the nitroglycerine in and "boom."

You know, it's a funny thing. Sometimes you would go to town. You would catch the night marshal. Every little town had a night marshal in them days, got about thirty dollars a month. Anyway you had to catch him first and keep him with you. Tie his hands in front of him and keep him around with you.

Then we would cut the telephone wires so that they couldn't call the next town.

Then we got into the bank and put a charge of nitroglycerine in the vault. It would make a sound that they could hear from here to Crystal City. All those banks had plate-glass windows and doors. Them big plate-glass windows would go to fallin' and hit the concrete sidewalk and that made more racket than the damned shots.

We put in five, six, seven shots and sometimes, after those shots and all that glass hittin' concrete, everybody was up shooting at ya. But we had several times that we didn't wake anybody up.

We usually worked from twelve o'clock to one or three o'clock in the morning. They had electric lights in these towns. It wasn't all dark. It didn't make any difference whether the moon was shinin' or not.

It's a lot safer and it's damned sure just as exciting.

We knew what kind of banks we could blow open and how we could get the money. We went in the summertime and looked around over the country. We would find a bank we liked, one we thought we could get the money out of. Then we would come back and see where the telephone was, if we could cut the wires, and all like that. The main essentials in the summertime. Then the next winter we would come back and rob it.

We waited until winter because everybody stayed in the house in the wintertime. In the summertime they were out walkin' up and down the street at twelve or one o'clock at night.

That's what I say. We knew our business. It was strictly business with us. In the summertime we would scatter out and somebody would be in this state and somebody in another state. We would be lookin' around and if we seen anything that looked good, we would tell about it. Although we robbed about eighty banks.

My brothers were all older. I guess I looked up to all of them. You get to doin' somethin', all your brothers together. It's damned hard to quit and come back and do something else. If I had it to do over again, I sure as hell wouldn't rob banks. I would stay with that bronc-riding.

BARNEY HUBBS:
RANGE WARS,
SNIPE HUNTS,
AND BADGER FIGHTS
Pecos, TX
Born 1896

Barney Hubbs was named for one of his father's early saddle buddies, a Pecos gunfighter named Barney Riggs, about whom it was said that "he never killed anybody that didn't need killing." Gunplay figured strongly in Barney Hubbs's history in Texas, too, because his father got caught up in a range war between cattlemen and sheepmen along the North Concho River near San Angelo. Barney's father was on a cattle drive to Kansas about 1895, when a sheepman sneaked about ten thousand sheep onto the Hubbs winter pasture, only to be discovered by neighboring cattlemen who ran off the critters, killing several thousand plus some herders. Though all the cattlemen, including Barney's father, were indicted, none would talk. Even after they had migrated west in search of more open range and free grass, that murder indictment hung over those ranchers.

In the trans-Pecos country where the land was so dry that you needed a hundred sections just to make a go of it, Barney Hubbs wisely decided to forgo the pleasures of cattle ranching because he "had seen too many people go broke." Instead he built up a media empire of small-town newspapers and then rural radio stations. When he began, printing presses had changed little from Benjamin Franklin's day and the local editor might have to defend his views with his fists. When I talked with Barney Hubbs in his award-decorated office at *The Pecos Enterprise,* he described a Texas far different from today's media center, where the latest in electronic communications can link everyone through space satellites to everyone else.

In 1907, when I was eleven years old, we homesteaded and estab-lished a ranch out north of Pecos and I drove a chuck wagon out from Sterling County. We were sixteen days bringing our cattle across. My mother was driving a team of broncs and they would run away from her every morning. But she was a pretty strong person even though she was heavy with child. She broke that team of broncs to suit herself so that she would have a good buggy team. Back in those days before automobiles, people got around by horseback, buggy, or wagon and it behooved you to have a good team. Being from Kentucky, she was used to having good horses, so she broke this buggy team on the way—in addition to cooking for six cowboys.

My mother was raised on a ranch. That was her life. She could ride a horse as good as a man could. All women out in this country, most of them did that. I had four sisters that was as good a cowboy as the men were. There is nuthin' unusual about that in those days. Of course, it would be unusual today, but back there it was just a way of life. It was pretty rough but we didn't know it was rough. She did the cooking for the cowboys on an open fire, sixteen days she prepared three meals on a campfire and thought nothing of it.

We got to Pecos on our way up to the ranch with the cattle. My dad left Mom here with a friend of ours that we had known back yonder. Seven days later, my kid sister was born. Four or five days after that my dad came to town, took her out to the ranch, and there was a baby sister. Mom's brag was that she had ten kids and hadn't missed a washday. Figure that one out!

Barney Hubbs "enjoyed starting things," meaning creating new newspapers and then radio stations. "I was a maverick in the news-paper business and then in radio, too," he says. "I guess the old-timers didn't think we needed radio." In 1935 he and his partner put in the Pecos radio station, KIUN, and had to make their antenna out of old oilfield tower equipment. How to get the two-hundred-foot-tall contraption up? Barney puzzled over it and eventually he "raised that radio pole with a winch truck, two gin poles, and a long cable." The thing stood there until 1962, when it was replaced by a manufactured pole.

Mr. and Mrs. Hubbs.

The same type of curiosity led Barney in 1921 to research his father's murder indictment at the courthouse in Tom Green County. That turned out to be quite a snipe hunt!

IN ABOUT 1921 I GOT curious about that murder that the cattlemen had been loaded down with after the sheepman was killed. With San Angelo being sheep country, everyone had been very upset over that. Some of the people was very vicious because that incident started a war between the sheepmen and the cattlemen in 1895. They went gunning for each other. It got pretty rough. The cattleman felt like he was there first and he was entitled to this free grass. The sheepman felt like, naturally, that it was public domain and he had as much right to it as the cattleman. His sheep wanted grass, too.

If you go back to the early days of the laws of Texas, you will find that there is a law that if you are caught on a horse with a pair of wire cutters on your saddle, you was committing a felony for cutting fences. People started building barbed-wire fences and that was against the law, you might say, of the land at that time. People didn't want fences. So we had what we called the fencecutters. It was pretty rough living back in those days, because you had to fight your way through.

By 1921 times had changed and the smell of sheep had been dispelled by the high price of lamb and wool. A lot of cattlemen had gone into the sheep business and old enemies had gotten friendly with each other. But I was curious to know what had happened concerning that murder indictment on my father. So I went to the records of Tom Green County in San Angelo. Come to find out it was a kangaroo-court deal. The indictment had never been entered.

The average cowman in those days did not know how to read or write. He just worked cattle. He didn't have any type of education. So when you went to pulling a written record on them they didn't know what you was doing. So my father and his neighbors never realized that it was a kangaroo-court process.

I don't know if you know what a kangaroo court is. You are a tenderfoot and to our way of thinkin' you are very stupid. To your way of thinkin', you know we are stupid. It depends on where you are and what your environment is. Back in the early days of West Texas, we would sometimes have a little fun with a tenderfoot at what we called a kangaroo court.

People generally came in by train. There was saloons all over town. Some of them tenderfeet, the first place they would go would be the saloon to get a little refreshment. We knew they were tenderfeet when they came in by the style of their dress. They had a derby hat on and they didn't dress like we did. We knew they were strangers, so in order to have a little fun with them they would be arrested. Some guy would have a star and he would arrest them. They would be violating the law because they didn't have on a pair of boots or they had a derby hat on. They had violated the law. They would have a trial right there and we called it kangaroo court. They would get a bunch of cowboys together, jurymen, and appoint some old long-whiskered guy as judge. You have heard of Judge Roy Bean, I'm sure. All that was just a kangaroo-court deal that he was pullin'.

We would have kangaroo courts and we would try these people

for violating the laws of West Texas because of their dress. Generally their sentence would be a round of drinks for the bunch.

Judge Roy Bean was an expert at it. They found a dead man in the Pecos River down there one time at Langtry. Judge Bean had to rule what happened. They found out he had a six-shooter on and sixteen dollars in his pocket. So he being a dead man, he couldn't defend himself. So Judge Bean fined him sixteen dollars and drinks for the crowd for carryin' a six-shooter.

I found out in investigating my father's murder indictment that it was nothing in the world but a kangaroo-court proceeding. But it had caused lots of people to leave Tom Green County and come out to West Texas and establish ranches out here.

But that murder indictment wasn't any more serious than a badger fight.

What's a badger fight?

Your education has been neglected. Of course this happened in saloon days, when men would gather together in a group to have fun. They had to create this fun for themselves. Like I said, a tenderfoot is a man that is not acquainted with our ways out here. He would be a recent visitor that has just come to town. He is trying to get acquainted with everybody and trying to be a good Joe. So they take advantage of his ignorance and they go to talkin' about a coming event, a badger fight. A very vicious badger that could whup any dog in the country.

The boys would build that up and finally invite the tenderfoot to attend the badger fight out in a vacant lot somewheres. They would have this badger in a box and they would have a very vicious dog to make everything look realistic.

The highest honor was to pull the badger out of the box to begin the fight. Well, bein' a newcomer, they would let him—the stranger—pull the badger out of the box.

Everybody was there, the dog was ready, and at a given moment they would say "Pull the badger out."

Well, this tenderfoot would jerk the badger out of the box and what kind of a badger was it?

Back in the early days in every room of a hotel, you had a water bowl. The toilets were out in the back yard. If Nature called and you needed to go to the outhouse, you had to go down the stairs, out the back door, out to the outhouse. O.K., most of these hotels had what they called "thunder mugs." A big bowl that you could use instead of going out to the outhouse. It always had a handle on it. When the tenderfoot would jerk that badger out, it turned out to be a thunder mug full of water, crackers, and different things to make it appear like what it wasn't. I'm being pretty rough with this story, but I have to tell it like it is!

So when this tenderfoot pulled that thunder mug out, the laugh would be on him. Then he would have to buy drinks for the group.

That's what they called getting acquainted. A tenderfoot learning the ways of the West.

Snipe hunting was along the same route. They would build it up to the tenderfooter about these snipes. They didn't describe whether it was a bird or an animal or what. They had a range out there several miles from town where there was a good population of snipes. Snipe hunting was always at night. They would rig up a sack for this tenderfoot to go out and hold in a gully or something and the rest of the bunch would drive the snipes in to him where he could catch them in this sack.

He had to set there and hold that sack to catch the snipes until his new friends could drive them to him.

Instead of driving the snipes in, they would go home and go to bed and leave him holdin' that sack out there the rest of the night.

That was snipe hunting!

LARRY L. KING:
TEXAS PLAYWRIGHT
Washington, D.C.
Born 1929

Novelist and playwright Larry L. King is best known for his Broadway musical *The Best Little Whorehouse in Texas.* No other Texas hit has ever achieved such fame and fortune. I believe that long after its creator has gone to Boot Hill *Whorehouse*'s sheriff, madam, and Marvin Zindler will be entertaining audiences from Anchorage to Atlantic City.

That degree of popular success is surprising for someone who is a self-described "outside agitator." There is a bite and a sting to Larry King's work that can slip up on you and strike with the speed of a diamondback. It is a venom brewed out of the loneliness and frustration of dead towns, hopeless times, and empty vistas. But this Texan-away-from-Texas is not bitter, but upbeat. He whipped his alcoholism. He became the writer he wanted to be— and then some. He tells his Texas tales with humor and he colors his characters' talk with the rich accents of home.

Larry King's formative experience was to grow up as the last of the horse culture faded away and modern Texas came in with its sudden wealth, explosive growth, and nomadic shifts of population. His world is the West Texas of oilfields, twisters, drought-ridden ranches, hard labor, and booms gone bust. In 1988 in Washington, D.C., I had the pleasure of seeing this playwright take the role of Gus the bartender in his new play *The Night Hank Williams Died.* I got the feeling that that nation's capital audience was full of West Texans who understood Gus's lament, "I imagine God figgered he'd give us so many sand dunes and jackrabbits and Meskins we didn't need nothin' else."

Like many another self-exiled Texan, Larry King likes to visit but not to stay. A returnee in *The Night Hank Williams Died* says:

I forget how ugly this country is when I'm gone. Then I come back and it hits me fresh how flat and brown and bald it looks. . . . Like some old man that won't take enough baths. And lonesome? My Lord! Nothing to do but listen to the wind howl, or drive around dodging tumbleweeds and orphan dogs.

WHO WAS MY MENTOR? WELL, there was a West Texas fella who was a great influence on me by the name of Aubra Nooncaster.* When I was about fifteen years old in Midland High School, he came there as a football coach from just out of the Army. It was during World War II. And he had been a coach at Brownfield in Terry County. And I'd never heard of him. Hell, when you're fifteen, you haven't heard of anybody. But I later learned that he had quite a reputation as a coach when he came there out of the Army.

So we football players learned that he was giving a course in literature. I was a sort of secret poet. I read a lot and I wrote a lot but I didn't want my teammates to know about that "sissy stuff."

So anyway we football players all rushed over to sign up for his literature course because we assumed, as had been our experience with other football coaches, that if you enrolled in their courses, you got good grades and you stayed eligible to play football. Well, we rushed over there and here was this damn fella Aubra Nooncaster, a big six-foot-five, two-hundred-and-fifty-pound guy. I thought he was an old man then. I've since figured out he was thirty-two.

And he was just tough as hell on us. I suddenly realized that this man cared as much about Shakespeare and Shelley as he did about beating San Angelo and Odessa and this came as a hell of a shock to the football players.

---

*In 1988 Coach Nooncaster reminisced about Lawrence King. "I did not know at that time that he had any interests in literature. He seemed much like the other students in class, just sitting there letting my words bounce off their empty noggins. But we never know, do we, when we are influencing someone. If I did encourage Larry, it was my deep love for literature and my modest skills as a teacher that did the trick. Sometimes we teachers get lucky and have someone like Larry in class."

I remember one day he played a recording of himself reading a Kipling poem. "Tommy this and Tommy that and Tommy fall behind." About no one caring about soldiers except in time of war. And another one called "Boots." So we football boys were all sitting there kinda snickering. And he was sitting with his eyes shut listening. He finally cut the recording off when it was finished and he said, "All right, what does that mean to you, Boone?"

"Hell, Coach, it don't mean nothing to me."

"How about you, Drake?"

"Hell, Coach, it seemed kind of silly to me."

And he went around the room and he came to me. "King?"

And I said, "Me neither, Coach."

And he looked at me a minute and he looked at the class and he said, "I hope after the end of this school year that you never darken the door of another schoolhouse again. Class dismissed."

And we all jumped up and started to run out, happy. Then he said, "Not you, King. Come back here."

I thought, "What have I done?"

He grabbed me by the shirt like this, and in effect he said to me, "Scharbauer," and he named a bunch of other guys, "their fathers are oilmen and businessmen and it may not be very important that they learn anything about literature, but your father's like mine. He hasn't got a pot to piss in. And the only way you're ever going to amount to anything is to do that which you can do. And you are very bright and you can write very well. And you like this kind of stuff. And you hide it."

And he really got all over me. He said, "I'm gonna make you do A work in here. And if you don't, I'm going to take it out of your ass on the football field."

Actually I was scared of him, but I was pleased at the implied flattery. I'd been singled out among all the heathens as someone at least half-assed interested in cultural matters. But mainly he kept my attention engaged about writing in a time when nobody else did. In fact, he and I would get off together a lot of the time, away from the football players, and talk about books and poetry. He'd recommend books and writers to me. He himself was a poet and a pretty good one.

He learned that my father and I were having a lot of problems so he became sort of a surrogate father. My father and I had had a fight with shovels and Dad had said I couldn't live in his home unless I did things his way. So I moved into a little room in the high school gym. Took a shower in the gym and cadged meals at a few friends' houses until their parents discovered that I was sort of a runaway. Then I became persona non grata at the homes of my buddies.

Coach Noon figured this out. He spent several days talking to me about my responsibility to my father and what all my father had been through. He got it so that he made an uneasy peace where I went back home. My father and I still didn't have anything to say to each other. We avoided each other but Nooncaster did all he could.

Actually, my father was the person who first got me interested in language. Clyde Clayton King. Born February 18, 1888, in Texas. He only had a third-grade education, but he was a man who had a great sense of narrative. He could really tell stories.

He used so many colorful expressions! He was very good at metaphors, and so forth. And so I became very conscious of language.

My mother wanted me of all things to be a Methodist preacher, and I missed that by a great deal. She taught me to read very early, assumedly so I could get a jump on all these other young saints who were gonna devote their lives to Jesus. She read a lot of the Bible to me. So I got into the biblical roll of language of the Old Testament, which is ever so much better written than the New Testament in terms of literature.

My father was raised on a farm. His father was a farmer before him.

Dad was also a blacksmith. When I was born January first, twenty-nine, Dad was doing very well. He'd just built a new house in Putnam. Putnam had a little shallow-field oil boom going on. He had a blacksmith shop and was making very good money. Just bought a new car. New house. And then, November of that year came the Crash. The oil boom faded out almost immediately. And I heard him talk all the rest of his life about how he was owed about twelve thousand dollars in hard-money dollars by different oil companies around there. In that time much oilfield work was still done with wagons, horses, and mules, and they needed a black-smith.

So he was doing well and the Crash came. The oil companies all left town. They were fly-by-nighters and they didn't have any money to pay him.

So he hung on there in town a little while because my mother, who was a fearful person about the world, didn't want me to ride the school bus to school, to first grade. Dad was trying to farm a leased farm by commuting to it—which was tough to do since he didn't have a car. About eight miles a day each way. Fifteen miles by horseback to farm. Then finally that just didn't work and we moved on back to the farm on which he had grown up.

So he went back to his old home place but, God almighty, I learned to hate rural life and the farm there because of the hard work. What I saw my parents go through and what I went through. Constant work—around the clock. No end to it. And after the crops were laid by and the debts were settled you'd go back to the bank with your hat in your hand the next spring or late winter to borrow money for seed crops so you could work your ass off another year without having anything to show for it.

My parents didn't know that I was awake, but I remember lying in bed in an adjoining room to theirs when I was a small child and hearing them worry about whether or not they would be able to raise money enough to buy me a pair of shoes to go to school. And very early, I thought, "My God, what sort of a life is it that you work this hard and you have this little?" And it just keeps repeating itself.

That was one of the things that my father and I disagreed about. He starved off the farm. The Japanese did us a hell of a favor economically in bombing Pearl Harbor because all the young men went to war and my dad, who was then a middle-aged man, I was not quite thirteen, he could suddenly get a paying job in the oil-fields. So that's why we moved to the Midland–Odessa area. He went to work in the oilfields and within a year I did, too, summers and some after school.

He died in Midland, Texas, in 1970 at age almost eighty-three. Six weeks before he died he had talked to me about trying to go back to the farm. Of course, it was a pipe dream with no realism in it at all. But it represented what he wanted to do. I never understood why the man wanted to spend his life in that drudgery.

Of course, a lot of new-rich Texans immediately buy a ranch. My dad called such people toy farmers and toy ranchers. Some of them buy ranches for romantic ideals and others because for years it was a hell of a tax dodge. But Dad simply loved all the things about rural life. Tilling the soil. He even loved the solitude of it, which I despised as a kid.

I remember years later, after I came to work in Congress, when I was in my twenties, talking to Speaker Sam Rayburn. He was by then a pretty old man. And he was talking about how lonely he had been on the farm when he was a kid and how he was glad now that people had cars, and television, and radio to bring in the outside world. He remembered he used to walk from his house near Flag Springs up an old country lane on Sunday afternoons and set on a fence, just hoping that somewhere on this old country road somebody would come by. Walking. Horseback. However. Just so he could see another human and maybe get to talk to 'em a little bit.

I felt much that way. And when Mr. Rayburn told me that, I really had a sense of identification with him because I had literally done the exact same thing on that farm in Eastland County. Gone up to the old country road and hoped somebody would come by in a Model T Ford or whatever. I'd meet the mailman every day that I could just to receive his wave and his "Howdy, boy."

I was raised almost as an only child because my siblings were fourteen, fifteen, and sixteen years older than I was. Since I've grown up I've often thought that maybe that enforced isolation and the time to think about things had a lot to do with my becoming introspective and becoming a writer.

There was so little opportunity out there to interact with other people that I became a big reader at an early age. The summer between first and second grade, I had whooping cough. My mother bought me the first book that I had ever owned. It was *The Adventures of Tom Sawyer*. She read it to me and then I fought my way through it many times.

Mark Twain was the first writer that I became aware of as a name. And I remember asking her after that, "Has this man written any more books? I'd like to have one."

So the following Christmas, it must have been December of thirty-seven, she gave me *The Prince and the Pauper.* From then on I was hooked on Mark Twain. And he still remains my all-time favorite writer.

He was the most American of writers. I believe that he got America down better than anyone else writing at their respective times.

And also, he was the funniest man. I learned a lot from him about humor. It's the juxtaposition of unusual words that brings unexpected laughter. And unexpected laughter is the best sort. It generally gets you belly laughs. I just used to read that stuff and howl. Still do. I have every book Twain's ever written. And I wish the man had lived to have written much more. God knows how many books about him I have.

My biggest success, *The Best Little Whorehouse in Texas,* was a total accident. Certainly the Broadway show was. It's still the luckiest fluke I ever saw. I didn't know anything about musical comedy. And Pete Masterson was an actor/director, but he'd never written a show. And although Carol Hall had written and recorded a lot of songs, she'd never written a show. It was kind of amateur night in a certain sense. It just worked. I saw the story as funny because that little town down there was so goddamn aroused. Families were splitting. Brothers weren't speaking. The fight wasn't about whether or not they ought to have a whorehouse but over whether or not it ought to be publicized. I mean there were a certain number of moralists who said they had always been ashamed of the Chicken Ranch, but the body of the townfolks mainly resented the publicity. Me and the other reporters coming in and Marvin Zindler with his TV stuff. It was "You're meddling in our local affairs; get out of here." Which is typically Texan and Southern! During the civil rights troubles of the fifties and sixties everything was always "outside agitators." Anybody who came from more than twelve miles away was an outside agitator.

Well, I was an outside agitator and that's what the town was mad at. And seeing them and seeing the old sheriff being so mad and cussing, it just struck me as funny. Sort of a black comedy. And I wrote it like that. Marvin Zindler coming out to close this little eight- or nine-girl whorehouse and making this big stink about the whole thing when he could have walked out of his Houston TV studio and got his ass tickled with a feather for three dollars by streetwalkers and call girls. It just hit me as very incongruous and funny. It probably felt like a tragedy to some of 'em but to my eyes it was a damn comedy.

Most people in our old West Texas world were not sophisticates. They'd never traveled or been anywhere. My mother made one trip in her life outside Texas, except for a brief time we lived in New Mexico, and that was to Washington, D.C., in 1955 at my insistence. I got my mom and dad to come up here when my second child was born. I pretended that I needed Mother to be up here to help my then wife just so I could get them to make a trip. They wouldn't fly. They came on the damned train. Sitting in the day coach all the way up here. Two nights and three days. And then went back the same way.

They didn't like it and wanted to go home the minute they got here. They were supposed to stay two weeks but only stayed one week.

I suppose my mother was forty-five years old before she was ever over a hundred miles from home. And that was true of a lot of those people.

They came up in a brush-arbor culture with hellfire-and-brimstone preachers.

Brush arbor. I used to go to brush-arbor churches in the summertime. They'd cut down little ole small trees and build an A-frame deal, stacking the bushes or leafy parts of the trees on the frame for shade.

People believed all that fundamentalist religion stuff. Screaming and crying at the mourners' bench and rolling in the aisles and talking in tongues. It was a circus of superstition, but a person growing up in that and not having anything to contrast it with would take it very seriously.

My mother had a fifth-grade education. Her father thought that sixth grade, tops, was all that women needed. He was a pretty big landholder for his time and place in Texas. He had nine daughters and two sons. The daughters he took out of school after the sixth grade maximum and had them work in the fields to raise money to send his two sons to college. One to become a physician and one went to Texas A & M to major in ranching and farm management. And so the boys became very successful but the girls didn't get shit out of it and didn't learn anything and didn't get to leave home. And they resented it all their lives. Naturally. I don't blame 'em.

Being isolated, being uneducated, and knowing nothing but that which was forced on them led those people to. . . . And maybe the desolation and barrenness of their lives. That'll drive you about half nuts. I think those fundamentalist religious people are just really goddamn walking crazies. So there you are! [Laughter]

My father and I were a lot alike in certain ways. Both headstrong. And he was determined to rule. And when you've got two guys like that in the same house, you're gonna have some problems.

Also, there was quite a generation gap because my dad was forty-two when I was born. And by the time I got to be a teenager and wanted to set my own agenda in terms of what was popular in the culture and among my peer group, he had absolutely no appreciation for that at all. He was a man who believed in working and working and working and working some more. That was his recreation and his hobby and his religion and everything else. And I did not take to that kind of work. I did a lot of it. But I knew goddamn early that it wasn't the way I wanted my life to go.

We clashed over that a lot.

He was always giving morality lectures tied to labor. Every night he would talk about how much earth he had moved that day. Or whatever it was he was doing. How many milk cartons or crates he had lifted when he worked at the creamery. And how many trucks he had cleaned out. Then he'd get into a song and dance about how the younger guys wouldn't work and didn't seem to want to work and nothing seemed of value to 'em. Life seemed like a joke to 'em.

I'd get in and debate him about who gave a damn about how much you could do on a job like that because in the end it didn't amount to a hell of a lot anyway since the corporations and the companies you worked for didn't give a shit about ya and wouldn't care about your death except as it might hinder commerce.

I said to him once, "Nobody knows or gives a shit how much you lifted today, yesterday, or tomorrow."

And he said, "By God, I do!" It was a matter of pride to him, being a hard worker. He would always say when I would bitch about that, "Well, you hired out to work, didn't ya?"

So we had those kind of conflicts. As he put it, he always felt that I was "too damn fool dreamy." I always had big plans to get away and to write and to become my own man. And yes, fame and fortune. That whole bit. I mean, I was driven by that.

And he'd say to me, "Son, you're just gonna get your heart broke. Life ain't like that."

I'd say, "Life ain't like this either for me and it's not gonna stay this way." We had a lot of problems about this as I grew up. We later became very, very close once I quit rebelling and got out from under the family thumb. I got married young—unfortunately—and had children of my own, and suddenly I was faced with making a living for a family and being a father. I think when that happens, you have a hell of a bigger appreciation for more senior fathers than you ever had before. Because now the shoe's on the other foot. Suddenly you're responsible for somebody and got to take care of 'em and guide 'em and you will inevitably try to superimpose your values on those children just as your own father tried to superimpose his on you.

So that gave us much more in common.

From the time I was fifteen years old and we had a fight with shovels to when I was about nineteen years old we went without having virtually anything to say to each other except to fight and fuss. Then I went off in the Army and when I got out I began to work for various newspapers in New Mexico and West Texas and I got married young and I moved away for a while and I didn't see much of him.

So by the time I finally grew up and he'd gotten old enough to mellow a little bit, then we suddenly found that we had much more in common than we ever had before. We went through a rather awkward peacemaking period I guess of a year or two, and then suddenly that old trouble just wasn't there anymore. Then we wound up being very, very close.

Dad was always interested in reading. The way he worked, though, he just had damn little time to do it. When I was a kid, before he'd go to bed to get ready for the next day's hard labor, he always had something in his hand to read. The Bible. *Farm and Ranch Magazine.* The local weekly newspaper.

Eventually he became very proud that I was a writer. And he read everything that I wrote. He took a great deal of interest and pride in it. Much more so than my mother.

That was a shock to me, because as I came up she was the one that urged books on me and urged me to get an education to "make something of myself." Dad never said anything like that. "Why don't you work harder?" was his only attitude. "And why don't you think more of your work?" He meant laboring jobs, grunt work.

But Mother became disappointed because she had always lived a sheltered and I think a dreamy life and she had this damn fantasy somehow of producing a son for a preacher. She was very much of a constant churchgoer. Hymns. Memorizing the Bible by rote. And spouting Scripture and all that crap, which I detested. I obviously reacted very strongly against it because she was so into it. She got me reading early and encouraged me to write when I was a kid. So I had thought that because she had kept urging me to become educated that she'd be the one that cared about my work later on when I became a writer. Instead she was very disappointed in it.

I sent her my first book, a novel called *The One-eyed Man,* and I got back a letter from her with the economical comment that she found it "interesting." And I knew her well enough to know that that was a sign of disapproval.

When I saw her the next time I visited, I said, "Mom, all right, what was it you didn't like about my book?"

And she said, "Well, Lawrence, just every time I read one of those old ugly words I just wanted to take an eraser and scratch it out."

And I laughed and I said, "Well, go ahead, Momma. You can do whatever you want to with it. It's your book."

And she said seriously, "Oh, Lawrence, but there are all those *other* copies."

And that's the true soul of a censor. They'll constantly want expanded territory. And my mother got so upset by some stuff I wrote that she told me once, "I'm just tired of apologizing to my friends for that stuff."

And I said, "Well, don't apologize."

Once in her later years, she finally said to me in tears, "I wish I'd kept ya on that farm and ya'd never learned to read and write."

MARVIN ZINDLER:

HOUSTON TELEVISION

CRUSADER

Houston, TX

Born 1921

What can you say about a man who wears his toupee to his facelift operation? Or how do you react to a celebrity television muckraker who champions the poor while receiving a million-dollar salary for what he admits is "entertainment"?

A 1976 book, *The Many Faces of Marvin Zindler,* chronicled the Houston television personality's years-long escape from the family clothing business to careers in (1) news reporting (including pioneer roving camera work in 1949) and (2) law enforcement (including the vice squad). As a police department consumer-fraud scourge he chastened and antagonized the used car industry—until a newly elected sheriff fired him in 1972. That was not to be his last run-in with a hostile sheriff.

What interested me most about meeting Houston's airwaves showman was not so much his famous peruke, rebuilt chin, nine cosmetic surgeries, or flashy duds. Mostly I was amazed (1) that a sixty-five-year-old man, wig or no, could hang onto a prime-time TV news job and (2) that everyone I met had such strong opinions about him. A competing station once received the following analysis of the Zindler audience from its pollsters:

Marvin Zindler is more than a personality—he is a phenomenon. Viewers despise him and adore him, scoff at him and respect him. They are irritated by him and entertained by him. But whatever the case, they are fascinated by him. As one viewer put it, "You can react to him." And react they do—sometimes very positively, sometimes very negatively, but most often with a great deal of each.

And what was *my* opinion? Publicity-conscious Marvin is such a blend of vanity and sincerity that I could not help but be charmed by the unexpectedness of some of his stories. Some of the most poignant concerned race relations in a Houston which he had seen grow from a small town of one hundred fifty thousand to what he says is now a small town of three million. He told me about his old black nurse Eva (who was with him until he got married):

When I was a kid and I had to go downtown I'd have to sit in the back of the bus with her. If we went into a picture show, we had to go upstairs where the blacks sat. When I'd go to Catholic church with her, we'd have to sit in the rear of the church. When we traveled with my father, they wouldn't let her come into a restaurant. And I saw all this. And that made me very sensitive about the way black folks were treated.

They still treat them that way. It's a little better down here, but I go to these big dinners and I look around and there's no black folks in there. I don't care where it is. There's no black folks. In fact, my friends are the biggest bigots in the world.

One of the reasons I always ask about people's heroes and mentors is because the answer acts like a radar beam to outline hidden facets of character. I was pleased when Marvin Zindler told me that one of his heroes had been newsman George Karmak, who "believed in exposing the wrongdoings of politicians." That, says the serious side of entertainer Zindler, "is what television is all about."

As this TV showman says of his own crusading zeal, "It doesn't take much to get me pissed off." Here are two examples of classic Marvin Zindler stories. The first concerns his response to a poor black family's housing crisis. The second is his description of his most famous crusade, the closing of what became known as "The Best Little Whorehouse in Texas." (The place reportedly offered an eight-dollar "Aggie Special" to A & M students. Aggie "Four Get" service meant, "Get it up. Get on. Get off. Get out.")

In 1972 Marvin had just exchanged his sheriff's office consumer-action job for a TV spot focusing on the same issues. A former law enforcement colleague then in the state attorney general's office asked him to spotlight the goings-on at two politically sensitive brothels. The resulting closure of those landmarks brought down the wrath of innumerable good old boys on Marvin Zindler's well-coifed head.

To appreciate these two stories fully, you should try to imagine the bejeweled, white-suited crusader signing off with his famous bulldog closing: "Maarvin Zindlerr, Eyewitness Noos."

MOST OF MY STORIES ARE not based on the money that I get back for people that have been cheated. There's usually some lesson involved, like teaching kids the value of a dollar.

To give you an example, I'm doing a story next week because I got a letter from a very poor black family in Eagle Lake, about seventy-five miles from here, asking me if I could help another even more destitute black family. They have seven children. The father is seventy-seven; the mother is forty-six. They live on Social Security. They live in a leaky house and they cook on a hotplate. And they have no toilets or water inside.

So I called the sheriff of Colorado County where this little town is and I asked him to go by there and to see if it's as bad as the letter said.

The sheriff calls me back on the phone later and says, "Mr. Zindler, it's worse than you described."

So I went down to Eagle Lake and I met the sheriff and I asked if they had a black preacher there that was kind of the pillar of the community and who knew who the politicians were who would be most likely to help the black community. So I met this preacher and I showed him the letter.

We went over there. It was the most horrible sight that I have ever seen. No human being should ever have to live in that house.

There are five boys and two girls, four, five, eight years old, and it is just absolutely horrible.

They have one light bulb in the whole house. Electric wires hanging out. If the place ever caught on fire, there would be nothing left of those children. There is no way they could get them out.

They had grandchildren laying on the bed there sleeping when we walked in. The beds were absolutely the most horrible. . . . The preacher said he had never seen anything like this in his whole life. There were rats running around there just like a bunch of ants.

I asked the preacher if he could find a place for these people and he said, sure, he thought he knew of two or three places. And the sheriff said he could help. And I said that I would make sure that they got new furniture—beds for all the kids and whatever they needed.

And I want to tell you something. While I was there, what do you think that some of the white folks that came over told me? Of course, it was a big deal for me to go into Eagle Lake and they all came over to see what was going on. Guess what the conversation was? The white folks told me, "Why, wherever they would go the house would look the same as this."

Do you know why they say this? Because they have a complex

that I have pointed out something in their community that was so bad. They cannot understand that these people have a right to live in a decent place like they have.

When I point out that this family has been living like this for nine months, it embarrasses 'em. So they have to make an excuse that this family would live like this wherever they went.

So I'm going to see to it that the city condemns the house. If they don't condemn the house, they're going to end up with a new mayor and city council because these black folks over there are going to see to it. Cause they control the vote in that city and that county.

That family has been paying eighty dollars a month for that house. They are renting it from a person who could care less about the house. All he is interested in was the eighty dollars. Nobody really cares or ever goes by there. Like I always say, out of sight, out of mind.

You Don't Change a Leopard's Spots

If a girl wants to. . . . I don't care about prostitution. It has gone on forever but I don't believe that local politicians have a right [to make money through protecting whorehouses illegally]. If the people want it in their county, let 'em vote it in.

In 1972 the organized crime unit kicked it around and finally this assistant attorney general proposed that maybe he could get me to do some investigative work on TV and expose these two whorehouses and what was going on. That I could probably get 'em closed down by the new governor, Briscoe, who had just been elected.

These whorehouses were well-known all over the state. And I would say that many who went to A & M and the University of Texas had been in them. It had been going on for about a hundred and some years. Oh, it was nothing new. In fact, some of the most powerful men in Texas had been in that whorehouse. Senators and congressmen and probably a president of the United States.

The local sheriff finally learned that the intelligence division of the Department of Public Safety [Texas Rangers] was investigating it. He went out there and found two agents sitting outside counting the cars going in and out. One of his deputies threw a shotgun down on the two intelligence men and the sheriff told them to get their butt out of town, that he didn't need 'em there. And he got ahold of the Rangers and they were called off of the investigation.

Local sheriffs used to do things like that. They don't any more. Not since that particular little incident. But that sheriff had had the political power and the right connections.

So I pointed all of this out during my television reports. I interviewed the sheriff over there and he kinda cried and said, "Marvin, you know you're gonna close these places up if you do this story."

I said, "Well, Sheriff, that's why I'm up here."

So I put him on the hot spot and his every other word was a cussword. We had to bleep them all out of the interview.

Finally after I did this for about a week I went to the governor. And within four days we had both the whorehouse in La Grange and in Sealy closed down. And they never opened again.

Of course, I never dreamed in a million years. . . . At first, when the Austin media found out what I was doing they thought I was some kind of goof. But there was one young reporter with the Austin *Statesman* that happened to be sitting outside the governor's office shooting the breeze with me. I told him what I was doing and he ran the story. When it came out on the wire services, Houston reporters began to run little stories. And first thing you know Johnny Carson made a big joke out of it on his show.

Then the newspapers started running story after story.

Then in '74 Larry King of Midland writes an article about "The Best Little Whorehouse in Texas" and he pans me and says that I think a pimp is four black guys that beat some gal with a coathanger. Then two Houston boys who are pretty good at writing musicals went to Larry about making a musical out of it.

If you'd asked me to put up money for a musical called *The Best Little Whorehouse in Texas,* I'd have said "You've got to be crazy." But it was a success and it made a lot of money. They gave the sheriff and the madam each twenty-five thousand dollars.

Our station didn't do it for ratings like everybody said. We did it because I was asked to by the attorney general's office. And I felt that if you have local politicians involved in allowing these things to run. . . . And you know they don't let 'em run because of their health. They let 'em run because there's money involved. Then when they move out of local politics to state and national politics, eventually, if they ever stole when they were in local politics, they're gonna steal when they're in Washington.

You don't change a leopard's spots.

PERCY FOREMAN:

SHOOTING FROM THE HIP

Houston, TX

Born 1902

Houston's well-known trial lawyer Percy Foreman began his career as a public speaker on the old Chautauqua circuit. In pre-electrical times Chautauqua was often rural America's main cultural entertainment. "In those days," said Percy, "people were hungry for any sort of drama."

Those hour-and-a-half lectures were good practice in public speaking for the man who would later become a notorious and eloquent defender of the allegedly guilty. Especially those guilty of murder!

As fellow Houston celebrity, former lawman Marvin Zindler, puts it:

He always tried the dead husband and the poor sumbitch couldn't come back and testify for himself. By the time the jury was ready to decide guilty or innocent he had already found the husband guilty. And the husband couldn't defend himself.

Texas does not necessarily always lead the nation in murder or even in the use of its famous Saturday-night specials, cheap handguns easily bought at a moment's notice. That is merely a superstition comparable to the preseason hope that the Cowboys will win the Super Bowl.

Yet I for one continue to hope that Texas's gunslingers will be the biggest and baddest and that their lawyers, such as Racehorse Haynes, will be the most eloquent and flamboyant. Dapper Mr. Foreman was no stranger to best-dressed lists, but in his youth he almost went too far for Texas sensibilities. Originally he was on the verge of styling himself by his first initial instead of plain old Percy! Fortunately, governor Pat Neff convinced him that Texas jury good old boys would not cotton to that.

Many lawyers would argue that Houston, Texas, has the strongest criminal bar in the United States. Percy Foreman was a leader in developing that strength for more than three decades, but this did not always endear him to the general public. "Most people don't think beyond the end of their nose," he said. "And they don't remember that when Jesus was on earth he paid more attention to sinners than to the better people."

There were moments in talking with Percy Foreman when I realized that he was not always on the side of the "better people." And that made him very interesting.

He had gone to work at the age of eight shining shoes and at fifteen he had left home for the bright lights of World-War-I Houston. His flair for talk and language had been apparent as early as the fourth grade, when he had published a "newspaper" on an old Oliver typewriter. "Two girls wrote the paper," he says, "and we'd sell it for three or four cents each at the Happy Hour Theater every Friday night." During his precollege year at Stanton Military Academy, he was editor of the *Cablegram* newspaper. By age twenty-one he was already lecturing on how to get the most out of life.

Chautauqua developed young Foreman's habit of taking a popular book such as Sinclair Lewis's *Main Street* or a popular song such as "That Old Gang of Mine" and converting it into a lecture and a published article. For each of these lectures he used to amass as much as eight hours of material. "But we only lectured for an hour and a half," he said. "In those days if you didn't talk an hour and a half, they figured they'd been cheated. Now if you talk an hour and a half, you'll lose your audience in less than thirty minutes."

And now, ladies and gentlemen, wanting neither to lose you nor cheat you, here, as if on a modern Chautauqua stage, are some short nuggets of the wisdom of Percy Foreman.

Family

I COME FROM A LAW enforcement family. My father was sheriff in Lufkin, Texas, where *his* father had been sheriff. My brother was county attorney. Another brother was chief of the highway patrol.

My father did not inspire me much. My mother was every inspiration there was in our family.

I went to work for myself at the age of eight shining shoes. The fact that my father was sheriff and that his office was across the street from my shoeshine stand meant that I was in the courthouse at every trial. That perhaps influenced me from the age of eight to fifteen. That probably had something to do with my being a lawyer and the type of lawyer I am.

Chautauqua

I went to work at the age of eight. All the time I was in school I had jobs working with people. I had a managerial job most of the time, even when I was eight to fifteen. I had a half-dozen other boys working for me on salary. I'd get the jobs and supervise them. I had people working for me all my life.

In Chautauqua I would have a hundred to one hundred fifty people under my directions. If you are intelligent and trying to learn, you can't work with people without learning about human nature. I *have* studied people.

Chautauqua gets its name from Lake Chautauqua in New York. It was started by Bishop Vincent in 1870. At first it was a resort for Sunday School teachers. Later it lost its religious significance and people would go there for cultural meetings. Various public people would come there to lecture. The circuit Chautauqua that I eventually worked on had no connection with Lake Chautauqua; it was just the name. It was a summer diversion before radio, television, and talking pictures. Rural communities and small cities had very few cultural events.

I was only eighteen when I started in Chautauqua but I looked to be thirty-seven.

I was "last day lecturer" and circuit manager. As circuit manager I'd address groups of people, trying to sell them on signing up for the next year.

At first, from 1920 to 1925, I was with W. L. Radcliffe in Washington, D.C. In 1925 I switched to United Chautauquas, owned by and operated by Roy D. Newton of Des Moines, Iowa. I worked for him until 1933, which was when Chautauquas ceased operating.

I enjoyed Chautauqua. It was getting to know people and seeing the country.

Under Radcliffe out of Washington we had lectures on every program, afternoon and evening. In the afternoon we'd talk inspirational subjects, usually of interest to women. One of my lectures was "The High Mission of Woman in the Twentieth Century." Another was a father-and-son lecture, "That Old Gang of Mine," a subject taken from the most popular song in the United States at that time.

I also lectured on how to get the most out of life. I was about twenty-one then.

One of my lectures at eighteen was Main Street versus Broadway. About the advantages of living in a small town. I know the psychology of the small town. I learned that the personality of each individual holding a job—the depot agent (we don't have them now), the Ford dealer, the postmaster—they'd be almost identical individuals wherever they were. They were affected by their work. I learned a great deal then which helped me later in selecting juries. I'm primarily a trial lawyer and the things I learned in Chautauqua helped.

I saved a great deal of money, over one hundred twenty thousand dollars, that I brought here to Houston when I came to practice law in 1927. But I continued going out for five more summers.

The Depression, good roads, radio, and talking pictures were the death knell of Chautauquas. These new things brought to the small cities and towns the same advantages in the way of entertainment. But Chautauqua had carried me to forty-four states and to practically every county seat.

The Baptist Church

I have always taught Sunday School classes and I've organized several Baptist churches here in Houston which are still functioning. I don't go to church now at all because the average layman in my Sunday School classes cannot understand how I can defend people charged with crime. Most people don't think beyond the end of their nose. They don't remember that when Jesus was on earth he paid more attention to sinners than to the better people.

I don't think there's any church in America today, Baptist or otherwise, even a Catholic church, in which Jesus would be happy.

I have occupied the pulpit of every church that permits a layman to do so because in that Chautauqua work every Sunday some church would ask you to talk. I didn't preach in the sense of being a minister but I would talk on a subject fit for Sunday and for the pulpit.

I'm an ordained Baptist deacon but I don't function as such and I never was a patented. . . . I started drinking at the age of four. I used to drain the Old Forester drops which my country cousins'd leave when they came to town on Saturday. I drank bourbon until the First World War, when you couldn't get it. The kind of whiskey you could get was dangerous to your health and not at all palatable. I couldn't stand bootleg whiskey.

I never let my church tell me what to do. That's the reason I don't function in a church now.

Any educated man knows the Bible. A little boy came home one Sunday. He was six years old. He said, "Momma, my Sunday School teacher said Jesus was a Jew."

His mother said, "Yes, dear, Jesus was a Jew." He said, "Well, I knew God was a Baptist but I didn't know Jesus was a Jew."

The Legal Profession

When I entered the legal profession, a criminal lawyer had about as much social standing at an annual bar association meeting as a

Gentile in New York City. But the reason that there are better trial lawyers in Texas than in any other state is because we have a tradition here of trying cases, not of settling them out of court. But now the world is so much with us late and soon, as the poet said, that they don't want to take the time to try a case. They want to rush it through. Or settle it out of court. And that doesn't help young lawyers' ability to try cases.

I've never had any trouble with judges. Oh, I've had a few that didn't like me to take the time I take to try a case. They wanted to get on with it.

I'm not bashful about charging fees if a client has it because eighty per cent of my work is for nothing. "I never charged a client more than he had." Well, I said that to try to be funny. I try to help anybody that comes in this office—whether I take the case or not. I turn down at least nineteen out of every twenty cases that are offered to me. But I try to help them get a lawyer.

I saw the legal profession at quite a different time, when we had a different concept of the law and of our responsibility.

Anybody who has a case in court makes a big mistake not having the best lawyer. The ordinary person does not know that. And therein lies the tragedy of the legal profession. Most people think that what one lawyer knows, everybody knows, and that it doesn't matter which lawyer they get. But what you get at the courthouse depends on the lawyer you have and what your lawyer, I'll say gladiator, can take away from the other person according to the rules. Law is a bunch of rules to fight by. If you don't have the best fighter, you're likely to lose.

Most people go to the penitentiary on account of the lawyer they hire than on account of what they're accused of doing.

Courage is more important than brains in a trial lawyer. It takes guts. And your adversary is not the other lawyer. It's the judge. He's trying to keep you from getting reversible error where if you lose the case, you can come back again and get a new trial.

Frontier Justice

In 1943 Barry Hardie wrote a series of articles for the *Daily Mirror* of London. The series was called "Murder Town, USA." And it was about Houston because an article in *Time* magazine in

1943 told how I represented thirteen women for killing either their boyfriend or their husband. All were acquitted except one and she received a suspended sentence and didn't have to go to prison.

Texas people are not more hotheaded than others. But there was a time when all Texans were a law unto themselves. We didn't have many courthouses. People carried their Colt .45 on their hip. That was Texas tradition in the 1870s and eighties.

Law is just an enunciation of the mores of the people.

I know half a dozen judges in Texas who collect pistols from the murder cases they try. Well, I probably have four or five hundred pistols that were used in my cases.

The Saturday-night special is not a typical Texas gun. It's for some hoodlum kid. A cheap gun. Harrington and Richards. H & R.

You can buy any gun immediately in Texas, but I think the crooks and the thieves and the hijackers would run the country if we didn't have guns.

I have a .44 double-action Smith and Wesson that I keep by my bed. I'm in favor of people having the right to bear arms, as the Constitution specifically says.

I don't think the average home would be safe without a pistol.

TAMMY SUE DAVIS:

URBAN COWGIRL

Texarkana and Houston, TX

Born 1945

Texas is one of the dancingest of states. Its men and women are not shy about kicking up their heels to Western ballads, Mexican mariachis, Polish polkas, or cowboy square dances. By 1980, Houston's dance craze had been dramatized in the movie *Urban Cowboy.*

Tammy Sue Davis of Houston became addicted to two-stepping everywhere from tiny honky-tonks to Pasadena's Gilly's. She had been high on dance euphoria since college where, with a seventeen-year background of classical ballet and a pretty face and good figure, she never lacked for partners.

What she did lack during her failed marriage was a man who could understand her feelings and give them a high priority. Of course that is a common complaint throughout contemporary America, but this chapter is about how such loneliness is felt in urban-cowboy Texas.

Tammy Sue Davis has a love/hate relationship with her dashing Texas pardners.

"Most of the women love it," says Tammy Sue. "This dominant figure in their lives telling them what to do and what not to do. They gripe and fuss, but tradition is a big thing here. I have done a lot of reading and thinking on it and I feel that I have changed. Women will get to the point where they do not accept it any more and they start making the same changes I have.''*

TEXAS MEN ARE FUN-LOVING, EXCITING, a lot of fun to date. Texas men have an overdose of ego and not all of them ever really get in touch with that fact. Maybe that is part of their charm.

There are a lot of things that are appealing and part of that is their independent nature, their roguish attitudes.

I think that if you marry one, you can be prepared for him to be a good family man who likes the home fires burning type of thing.

Texas men are chauvinistic to a pretty good degree. You stay home and cook. You wash, you clean, and you take care of babies. If you can juggle a career and your home life successfully, you probably won't get any problems in the relationship. If you cannot, you are more than likely going to get some flack about not holding up your responsibilities in the home.

I have dated a lot of men who were not born here in Texas. Their attitudes definitely are different about women. I am not saying that they don't have some of the ego problems, but they are more open to showing sensitivity. The Texas man is just on the other side of macho and is unable to allow himself in front of a group, especially of peers, to say something that would be sensitive to his date, his wife, or his lover. He would be more likely to say those things only in private and only after five or six beers.

Some evening a Texas man may come on like gangbusters. I love it that night. But the next day they are back to being their old self. They lose their gangbuster attitude. They get up for the evening and they go for it and the next day it is like a let-down period for them.

All of a sudden you are back to square one again. You thought that you had made a lot of progress in the relationship but it may have been due to the atmosphere of the evening, the dancing, and the socializing. Where you perceived it one way as a female, he

---

*Four years after this interview, Tammy Sue (not her real name) remarried and said that her feelings about Texas men had completely changed thanks to her improved love life.

perceived it as just a fun evening. The evening built up to a crescendo of excitement and he went for it balls out.

I have gotten to where that is old.

I have a passion for dancing and I am liable to let go of a lot of my shoulds when the opportunity to do a lot of dancing is involved. I let go of my feelings for that reason, too, and end up going for it like they do.

In a relationship that I am working on, I am not willing to accept that any more.

I have lived in Texarkana, Lufton, Dallas, Denton—all parts of Houston and West Texas. I think that is a pretty good span of area to be able to say that basically Texas men are all the same. In reality I haven't found much difference in them from place to place over a period of twenty years.

I am working very hard on me. I feel that if I can get happy with me and comfortable with the way I am and the goals that I have set and work on just this person, then possibly I might have a chance. If I run across somebody that is doing the same thing, we may both have a chance.

I'm not saying that I don't enjoy going out with Texas men or that I don't have a lot of fun with them, because that is not true. They are absolutely wonderful, but at the same time I am saying that I would be very cautious about a permanent relationship with one unless he was someone who could hear what I am saying.

Don't think that I am trying to be some sort of a negative bitch about Texas people, because that is not true. They are wonderful. I'm just not sure where I stand with them. They are warm, friendly, loving, and caring to friendships. You make dozens of friends and you are drawn back to them wherever you go because of their openness and acceptance of you as you are. So it is real difficult for me to say anything negative about them. I don't want to live anywhere else now. I am real happy here.

But these men have to have this feeling of being in control and having the power in a relationship. Definitely being the dominant one.

It is real difficult to deal with that unless you are a submissive person.

And then here comes this jealous business. If you speak with, walk with, or visit with another man, they don't like it. They don't understand women's friendships. They just understand "You are mine."

If you are willing to be in that kind of a relationship, it is definitely going to come up. Texas men just have to be the boss. That means of all their property, and wives are definitely a possession.

Texas is such a big state that women are alone out in the boondocks on these ranches a lot while their husbands travel in the cities. Wives are home with children and managing their homes. They are left alone and severely neglected. Not because the husband doesn't love the wife but because the most important thing that he can do is make this wonderful living. Because the better the living he makes for his wife and his home, the better he feels about himself and the better the community thinks of him. If you can't "provide" this wonderful income for your wife and family, you don't measure up.

So husbands go out and do more and more work. They may work from sunup to sundown on the ranch. When they come in they are dog-tired and they drop dead on the bed. There is no nourishment for that wife, because he is involved totally in making a living. So she is very neglected.

I'll bet you that for seventy-five percent of the women in this city and surrounding communities that that is the number-one problem in their marriages. It is not that they don't love one another, but they just don't take enough time. She doesn't demand the time and isn't able to convince him that it is important. Eventually they lose touch with one another and divorce. So a little less money is better if your relationship is better.

You go to the dance hall and there are girls there from eighteen to sixty. Every one of them are after the same thing, that real high that you get off these guys. When they come in the door to have a good time, they plan on doing it. There are no holds barred. It's wonderful. It's intoxicating. It's exciting.

Women will put up with any kind of behavior to get that wonderful excitement from the men, though that is not what they are after in the long run. But once they get caught up in the whirl. . . . You may wake up one morning and the cowboy on the right is not the one that you went to bed with, so to speak, and you may decide to change things.

At twenty I was at North Texas State University and I had danced my way through the entire school. Every day between every class I was in the Student Union dancing.

Dancing was a big thing at North Texas and there was a specific kind of dance that we did every day, all day long between classes at the Student Union. The North Texas cush is a wonderful dance that only people at that university do. It's very difficult and requires a lot of practice and timing with your partner. It involves a lot of intricate turns and is exciting and beautiful to watch. Being involved in a lot of ballet training, I loved to dance and I realized that the North Texas cush was really a beautiful movement and rhythm which took a lot of practice and natural ability. I was very good at it! When I look back on my college days, that was probably the happiest time in my life. It was so carefree and I loved every minute of it!

I was doing something that I loved all the time and I had ample partners. From that feeling, I evolved to this dancing syndrome that I have. I do it for enjoyment, pleasure and I do it without a lot of expectations.

Basically I was doing that in college, but I thought some wonderful dashing person would dance me off the dance floor into his life and on and on.

I had a Cinderella syndrome then but now I don't. I feel a little bit better and more secure about what I am doing and now I don't set myself up for disappointment.

What led me to this way of thinking was the urban cowboy movement—the Gilly's dance hall routine which I was caught up in because we lived close to Pasadena. My husband and I went there frequently before the movie was made. I saw the changes happening.

Being a dancer, I was involved closely with the attitudes there at the dance hall and other similar places.

Today's urban cowboys have the old attitudes and feelings about being a macho, heroic, cowboy figure but they are working in the Houston Ship Channel or all around in various labor jobs. The urban cowboy is trying to live that heroic persona, no matter that he is in the middle of the city. His attitude toward women is "I'm the boss." It's pretty primitive.

I saw it happening, but I wasn't really aware until after the movie came out that although the drugstore cowboy has no manure on his boots, no hay in the back of his pick-up, he *does* have a pick-up and boots. He *does* have this heroic macho feeling that he must get across.

A lot of it has to do with dominance over the feminine—his partner, mate, wife or whomever. Of being stud. In the movie, of being able to ride the bull. It was real important for him to ride the bull and he busted up with his girlfriend when she decided to do it, too. He thought that girls don't do that. "I'm the one that has got to be. . . ."

Texas men are wonderful. So part of me is hooked. My passion for dancing has become my method of communication.

It is true that the girls get prettier at closing time. But it is also true that the boys get prettier at closing time. It is just as much the women accepting less than they might if they were not on that intoxicating high.

The big fever in this whole state is "dance hall fever." That's where the relationships are born and that's where the attitudes are formed. It's how suave can you be tonight and we don't worry about tomorrow because tonight is so great. We will handle tomorrow, tomorrow. We will just wait till the next wonderful evening and just live from evening to evening.

Lots of the kids do. They go for a good time and then finally some smooth-talkin' devil will flip them away and they will be caught up in how debonair and dashing he is in front of everyone while he dances.

It is definitely a promenade, a strutting promenade of who is the coolest.

But you always have to wake up the next morning. You wake up by yourself or you wake up with this wonderful person who's not so wonderful the next day. Who is back to business. Who is back on the ranch and running the show. Who is off to work or whatever and all the stardust is gone.

He is not so sensitive to your needs that next day and thereafter until he is ready for another good time. Then there you go again with the charm.

It is a depressing cycle but sometimes the goin' up is worth the comin' down. It just is. It is difficult for me to tell you how really exciting it is! I can go to a dance and if there is someone there that is really good, I can dance with that someone all night long and drink Cokes and be higher than anybody who had a zillion beers.

Dancing is absolutely the most wonderful high that I can ever obtain. As long as I go into it with the awareness that I don't have a bunch of expectations for the next day or for the relationship thereafter. Knowing that this cowboy is probably going to fizzle out by the time he gets back out to the stockyard or back out to the ranch. Knowing that it will be just a real fun evening and not trying to make anything else out of it. I can have a hell of a good time and just love it. It is the young girls that have expectations of the relationship being as wonderful off the dance floor as on.

In Texas the dance floor is a common place to create that wonderful, superstud image of. . . . They cock those black hats and you are gone. You get sucked up into it and it is wonderful!

SPIRIT:

"SCOOTER TRASH"—

"ALL WE WANT

TO DO IS PARTY!"

Arlington, TX

Born 1938

The park ranger raised his eyebrows when I told him the name of the campground where I wished to spend the night. He listed the good points of other areas along his lake. But I thought I knew what I wanted. The rascal never said anything at all about the thirty or forty people who were to be my new neighbors. And just as well, too, or I would never have met Spirit, Nomad, and Pit Bull.

Swastikas, chains, studs, leather, and bikes—big bikes. I soon found myself in the midst of Arlington, Texas's Over the Hill Gang. Asking about fishing was my entree. A tall biker with a winged tattoo NOMAD on his arm was preparing a trotline. Unlike many of the other men, his swastika belt buckle did not sit atop a beer belly. He was muscular, clean-cut, and enthusiastic.

His motorcycle gang was a group of workingmen from the grim environs between Dallas and Fort Worth. Despite their pleasure in shocking the public, these "scooter trash" liked to portray themselves as a family group, not only because of the loyalty between the men but also because of the many "old ladies" and kids who participated in their long rides and campouts.

A few burly characters resented my presence, but I kept talking with Nomad and some other men whose paranoia about strangers was at least under control.

Bearded Spirit was the oldest member of these over-thirty riders. A sixties hippie in spirit, he was a short, likable fellow from upstate New York who looked out of place among the big, leather-clad desperadoes. Though the oldest man in the club at forty-eight, he was to stay up the latest partying with beer and golden oldies.

Stocky Pit Bull was one of only two native Texans in the group. He was walking around with a little puppy for which he had big plans.

Before my arrival the gang's tents had been flattened by a sudden squall. I helped Nomad and a heavily tattooed woman pour water out of a soggy dome. Although women stayed in the background, talking among themselves, attending children, or fetching beer for their men, my intuition in watching them was that they were not as subservient as the men liked to think.

The sky darkened, Harley engines roared and died, and corn, beans, and fajitas emerged onto paper plates. It was not a church picnic, but I had fun with the "scooter trash." As Spirit, the most eloquent of them, said, "There's a lot of stereotyping. Marlon Brando movies and all that shit. I *know* we're not as fuckin' bad as the movies make us look."

"It all boils down to one thing—being free," Pit Bull added.

NOMAD: We're from all over the place. Florida. New York. Virginia. Vermont. But we're one family.

SPIRIT: We got together and we've stayed together. I came down in January of '80 and we've all been together since then. We have something in common. We like to ride bikes. And we take care of each other. We met in a biker bar, Cactus Jack's in Arlington. That bar was a classic. I think it should be made a national fuckin' shrine.

NOMAD: A do-you-anything bar. And it looked like a do-anything bar. You had to be open-minded to come in that bar because there were a lot of motorcycles sitting out front. As long as you didn't invade on anybody else's privacy or space, you could do whatever the hell you wanted.

Hang your dick out in your hand—go ahead! Nobody cared. It was all up to you. If you had your old lady with you and she wanted to suck your dick, that's all right, too. Nobody would pay any attention.

SPIRIT: We owned it. That's why they wouldn't let us reopen it without a legal license. We tried to rent the place and open it as a private club. So they condemned the building on us. They just didn't want us there.

NOMAD: We're family-oriented. The other guys've got families and kids and house payments and rents. We're definitely not a band of gypsies. We like each other's company. I get off on his energy and he gets off on mine and vice versa. All of us do.

PIT BULL: We have an oath like in any club as far as helping your brothers. Like if I wasn't in this club, I might need help. Fifty percent of the good friends of mine might help me and fifty percent might not. But I do know that one hundred percent of the people I'm with right now would back me up whether I'm right, wrong, drunk, sick. They will do whatever they can because I'll do the same for them.

We haven't heard the women's point of view yet.

WOMEN: You're not going to.

PIT BULL: That's another thing. The women don't have say-so about shit.

SPIRIT: It's definitely a chauvinistic society, man. They don't speak unless they're spoken to. That's good. I like that in a woman.

BYSTANDER: It's not their club. It's our club.

SPIRIT: If you run around with somebody who rides an American-made V-twin and wears a black T-shirt, you'll find an old lady who keeps her mouth shut.

PIT BULL: There isn't a man alive that likes a woman to interrupt him and jump in front of him and take care of business or conversation. And that's one thing you will find about scooter trash's old ladies is that they will shut their mouth, listen, let you do the talkin'.

Respect. And if they don't, they suffer the consequences.

SPIRIT: We're scooter trash and we ride Harleys. There's only
one motorcycle made. That's a Harley-Davidson. The
rest of that shit's minibikes. Jap bullshit.

How far are you likely to ride on weekends?

SPIRIT: This one's pretty short, but we've gone to Tennessee,
Missouri, New Mexico. Hell, wherever the wind blows
ya. That's independence. And wherever we go we're
always asked back. We clean up our trash. They respect
us and we respect them. But the public expects us to
be like in the movies, raping and pillaging.

NOMAD: Hollywood blows us all out of proportion. We're supposed to be bad-ass. Kick, rape your chickens, your
cats, and your dogs. We ain't that way.

PIT BULL: It's just like dogfighting. I fight dogs. Some people look
at people that fight dogs as very cruel, real inhumane,
no respect for animals. Only sorry people'll do stuff
like that. But it's real funny that when I go to dogfights,
sheriffs, mayors, lawyers, and doctors are sittin' there
fightin' dogs. [Laughter] It's like that.

They build it up to look so bad. But once you see it,
it ain't so bad. It ain't no dog getting his legs torn off.
It isn't no damn dog dying in the pit and they throw it
outside after it lost and shoot it. It ain't none o' that
shit. That's all hearsay bullshit—just like it is about
scooter people.

They think we're up here to steal from 'em. Rape
them, their children. Mess with 'em. Cause trouble.
There are people that do that but that's the people that
are geeks. They're independents. People that ride with
no [club membership] patch. They're just out ridin'
around thinkin' they're bad asses, tryin' to build up this
big-biker Harley-Davidson image. They have to fuck
with people to make an impression on 'em. We're all
past that shit. We know better 'cause that's nuthin' but
trouble. Of course, if the geeks get in a fight across the

lake, the cops are gonna come down here on us because we have a patch on our back. But we're over here doin' nuthin' and they're over there causing trouble. But I can guarantee you the cops will come to us. As soon as we pull out of here they will pull us over and if you've got loud pipes, they'll take you to jail. Instead of writing you a ten-dollar, fifteen-dollar ticket, they're gonna take you to jail and it's gonna cost you a hundred on up. Impound your scooter. Big fine. It's ridiculous. They just can't accept what we are.

SPIRIT: All we want to do is party, man! We don't want to bother anybody else. But we don't want somebody to come in here and try to crash our party. But, you know, there's always somebody that's got to try it.

PIT BULL: We have a patch on our rags. Me and Spirit made it up. Everyone wears it proudly and it sums up our feelings about brotherhood. It's quoted out of the Bible but we changed the words a little bit. It says, "Yea, though I walk through the valley of the shadow, I fear no evil because I have my brother with me."

PIT BULL: That sums it up. Whether we're right or wrong or die we ain't worried about it.

SPIRIT: We don't recruit. We don't go lookin' for members. If people want to come and party with us a while and get to know us and hang out and if they decide they want to try to earn a patch, then they can probate for it. It's not something that's given lightly. We do not recruit members, man! Somebody would have to be introduced into the club by somebody who was pretty well known. And then he would have to hang out for quite a while while people got to know him.

PIT BULL: We'd have to be one hundred percent sure he is not an asshole. He's not comin' in this club to use our patch for a crutch, like if he's got a debt or if someone's after him.

NOMAD: We're a dying breed.

SPIRIT: Yeah, really. After this generation of bikers there won't be any more.

PIT BULL: In the 1800s you had your cowboys, driving cattle into town and raising hell. And they didn't give a shit what anyone said. They were there to have a good time. We're the same but a hundred years later.

People look down on us because of what we look like. They don't know that most of us are working people just like them. But we don't let the fucked-up life we're in get to us like they do them.

They are envious. We do a lot of shit they wish they could. Like get on the bike and go. Get on it Friday and where you end up is where you are.

DOROTHY OWENS:
ON THE ROAD AGAIN
Markham, TX
Born 1926

Nomad and his biker "brothers" are not the only footloose Texans in this book. To further represent the burr-under-the-saddle aspect of Texas culture I want you to meet Dorothy Owens. Hers is not the rootlessness of wagon trains, cattle drives, oil field booms, migrant work, Dust Bowls, rural flight, or 1990s homelessness. Instead, Dorothy Watkins Owens and her husband live on the road by choice. Modern technology has given them the option of taking their Texas with them wherever they want to go. In driving my Volkswagen camper, Hodge, through Texas's many regions, I soon realized that I was not the only nomad out there on the FM[1] roads. One spring day at a campground at Guadalupe National Park, I met this refugee from Markham who said that she was a "one hundred percent Texan", meaning that she was born and raised in Matagorda County and that her great-great-grandfather Emelius Savage, had fought in the Texas Revolution. I wondered if Emelius had had as much wanderlust as Dorothy Owens. She and her husband Adrin had been posted to Libya and Indonesia by his oil company and had done so much traveling that it had become an addiction. "It's really a carefree lifestyle," said Adrin. "You leave your worries behind. We just got tired of maintaining and paying for a typical suburban home."

When I met them, Dorothy and her husband had already been living on the road for more than a year entirely in Texas. Now five years later they are still following the center line, sometimes as far

---

[1]Farm to Market roads.

afield as the Pacific Northwest. Dorothy is not ready to give it up. She says, "We still enjoy sunrises, sunsets, birds and animals, and watching water rush by in mountain streams. But this definitely is not for everyone. If you enjoy your mate, it is a great way to spend many happy hours and miles seeing this great land of ours. Adrin and I have a running list of places to go. Our dream is to keep taking one off the front of the list and adding two to the back."

THIS TRAILER IS A VERY adequate place to live. The upkeep is minimal and you have all the conveniences of a home. We carry a satellite dish and when we are where we have electricity, we have any type of TV we want. We carry a solar panel so we do have at least lights and we can use our water and everything inside. When you go to a washateria to wash, you can wash and dry in an hour and be finished instead of taking all day one washer at a time.

We have found that a lot of the husbands, when the people retire, the men help the women. At home they would never do this. They help with the washing. If the wife cooks, they wash dishes and vice versa.

I was a secretary and went to work for the oil well service company Adrin worked for. After three months we were married and the moving and seeing what was around the next corner and over the next hill was our lifestyle even then.

It is just a lot easier style of living. When you are in a community, you have certain commitments. Life is just easier without those commitments.

We have run into a number of people that are full timers, some twelve or thirteen years. One couple had been at it full-time for thirteen years. They told us that they were fixin' to quit and go into an apartment because of health and their age. Yet they were each blaming the other for them doin' this. Because they really enjoy this style of living.

We met a couple in their mid-seventies that migrate from Washington to Florida, following the sun, and they hate to go home, back to their problems. We still cross paths with this couple each winter.

We meet a lot of interesting people. A really lovely group of people to be around.

You can travel at your own pace. You can stop whenever you desire. We like to just see the countryside, do trails, watch birds.

We had a house in Kerrville northwest of San Antonio but we don't miss being settled. No, not at all. I have always said that I am part gypsy and part crazy to live this kind of life but I enjoy it very much. Through the years my father rodeoed and I barrel raced along the Texas coast. And my son rodeoed throughout Texas. Rodeoing keeps you on the road even if you don't do it full-time for a living.

I am always searching for the best weather, the good places to bird, and the good places to camp.

If you live in town, you've got to be there to keep your yard and house up. With taxes rising every year, a lot of people find that it is really cutting into their budget to stay. Couples who camped for years finally say, "We don't need this big house like we did when we had children. We don't need to keep this stuff anymore. Let's just hit the road."

ROGER ALLEN:
PRAYING FOR A LONGNECK
San Angelo, TX
Born 1943

Roger Allen is one of those good souls who remembers his high school days with fondness. Not because, as is the case with so many Texas men, he is fantasizing about down-home high school football but because he remembers the adolescent passion of scurrying after that sinful drink, beer.

Roger Allen is a cultural fixture of West Texas, having converted some old poultry buildings in San Angelo into an artists' mecca known far and wide as the Old Chicken Farm Art Center.

WHEN AT THE RIPE AGE of fourteen I first entertained the thought of drinking beer, the closest you could get it was Hobbs, New Mexico. I mean the closest beer was one hundred twenty miles away!

Or you went to the bootlegger. And in Lubbock it was just a thriving business. Somebody would hand you a card and you could have beer delivered to your house. Bootleggers were well-known. They had souped-up, jacked-up cars. I worked in a TV shop where we used to fix the two-way radios they used running the back roads bringing in carloads of beer and whiskey to sell in town.

At Texas Tech, driving sixty miles to Post was just the start of a date if you wanted to drink anything. And a lotta times you got a carload to sell on the side to everybody else, too. Bootleggin' was a real way of life in Lubbock for years and years.

When you had to drive way out of town to get it, that was a hell of a lot more fun than just going to Lubbock's Strip like they do today.

As a young person in high school I grew up either driving those

long miles or buying bootleg beer in rough parts of Lubbock. Then driving around town and getting caught.

One night when I was fourteen years old I got stopped by a policeman. He shined his light on the three cases of beer I had in the back seat. He shined his light on my face, looked at my age, and he said, "Son, you're a little young to be driving around in this part of town." He said, "There were two guys killed on this corner last weekend in a knife fight. If I was you, I'd get the hell out of here."

He didn't take my beer away. He didn't give me a ticket.

I drove back down to the Hide-E-O parking lot and drank two cases of beer that night and had a *good* time. Went home and got in trouble.

'Cause I grew up a preacher's son.

RICK HAMBY:
THIRSTY IN A
BAPTIST DESERT
Big Spring, TX
Born 1947

The day I first arrived in West Texas's Big Spring, they were having a local election on whether or not to permit the sale of liquor by the drink. To most Americans the prohibition of this or that liquor practice seems as quaint as running boards and spats. However, in many parts of Bible Belt Texas booze is still seen as a burning social issue—as in "burning in hell."

Liquor by the drink became legal as a local option after the legislature amended the state constitution in 1970 and passed enabling legislation. This reflected the state's transformation from a largely rural population to a primarily urban one. As things now stand, the voters of each county precinct can now decide for themselves on this issue. Of course, the crazy-quilt pattern of cheek-by-jowl dry and wet precincts continues to create opportunities for bootleggers to make a mockery of the efforts of good citizens to control this menace.

As of August 31, 1989, fifty-nine counties were totally dry, including Martin County but not Howard and Glasscock counties. Big Spring's Rick Hamby is the district attorney for all three counties, and I asked him to relate to me his experiences with the area's liquor laws.

I WENT TO HIGH SCHOOL in Plainview. You talk about a seedbed of Baptist and Church of Christ philosophy, that's Plainview.

Plainview is in the Panhandle thirty-eight miles north of Lubbock, between Lubbock and Amarillo.

If you wanted beer, there was a place north of Plainview called Nazareth. Like in Jesus of. [Laughter] Ironically.

Of course, Plainview has private clubs now, but the only way you could get a drink when I was going to high school was to go over to Negro-town, to be euphemistic from what it was called in those days. To go over across the tracks and honk your horn for some fella to come out and sell beer in quarts. A dollar a quart—like a big old Coke bottle. Real obscure beer like Burhoff and Blatz. Old Greasy Dick. Louisiana beer. It was a dollar a quart except Coors, which was a dollar and a quarter.

I remember that the sickest I've ever been is when we all loaded up, my buddies and I, and we went over across the tracks, honked the horn, and they brought out these Coors quarts that we'd bought.

Nothing but the best! We were juniors in high school!

Then we went out to the irrigation ditch and we parked there and we started drinking.

And getting out and doing what you must do whenever you drink a lot of beer.

And somebody as they were doing that opened the door and the dome light came on just as I was about to pry the top off a bottle of Coors beer.

And it had a Hamm's cap on it!

Which made you wonder if they didn't perhaps refill the bottle in a way that we would have found disgusting. [Laughter]

It got me kinda sick.

Later I was going to school at Tech and had a job as a bartender. Twenty years ago in Lubbock they had what they called the locker system in private clubs. That's all they had was private clubs. And you'd come in as a member of a private club and you'd sit down and I as a bartender would go up to you and say, "Hi, my name is Rick. There'll be no charge for the liquor but there'll be a charge for the service."

And so you'd get around the liquor laws thataway since you'd be drinking from *my* locker. Theoretically I had this locker full of liquor. And these people were my guests, but I'd charge 'em a dollar fifty to pour them free liquor.

Some members of the club would have their own locker because of their preferences in booze. In other words, the bar booze—the stuff in my locker—didn't suit them. They might want Tanqueray gin where we used something made by Phillips 66. So they would bring their own booze and have their name on it. And they'd say "Pour me a drink from my locker."

Well, being faithful to the rules, even though it was their booze, we'd have to charge them the same price, a dollar fifty, because it was for the service.

And I remember, oh, not too many years ago right after I'd gotten in, elected district attorney. . . . My brother was the newspaper editor in Weatherford, Texas, and the sheriff there had a name, Booger, that's kind of common here in West Texas. His real name was Royce and so he preferred to be called Booger. Booger Pruitt. Fabulous fellow. And my brother had noted that this private Weatherford club that he was a member of didn't have Jack Daniel's. So he had to bring his own.

He got to noticing when he asked for one drink from a new bottle of Jack Daniel's from his locker that the next day half of his bottle was gone. Of course, he had his name on there. Rendell.

And so he decided that somebody was stealing his liquor. So he stopped putting Rendell on the bottle. He started putting Booger on his bottle instead.

No doubt people came in to steal some liquor and picked up that bottle and said "Oh shit, that's Booger's bottle." [Laughter]

He never missed any more booze.

JAYNE BECK:

IN PRAISE OF TEXAS MEN

San Angelo, TX

Born 1942

Texas is justly famous for its beauty queens and pageant sweethearts but is not generally known for the seductiveness of its men. Certainly the enduring image I have of the breed is of a leathery, sunburnt hombre in a Stetson and old boots.

Jayne Beck* is a housewife and mother and aspiring artist from San Angelo and a woman whose perspective I value—even though she thinks that I, as a non-West Texas man, am somehow submarginal.

SOUTHERN MEN I DO LIKE. But not compared to a Texas man.

I have met men from all over and I definitely prefer Texas men.

Until I grew up a little bit, I used to think that all others seemed feminine in some way. I think a lot of it was a very Yankee accent that was not attractive.

But I have gotten over that.

I still think that Texas men are more chivalrous. And most of them are not threatened by the women's movement as much. (I'm not a woman's libber but I will say that it has its merits.)

In an elevator in New York, an elderly man asked me if I would mind if he took his hat off. I said, "Of course not."

He said, "I really hate to ask a lady now because sometimes it makes them mad."

---

*Her great-grandfather was instrumental in founding Deaf Smith County. Her grandfather started the Episcopal Church in Amarillo.

A Texan *wouldn't hesitate* to take his hat off or to open the door. I like that.

Even Houston is too far east for me.

I prefer West Texas men. Our area is known for its warmth and friendliness. I believe this may be reflected in my feelings for Texas men. Most of the ones I know have a depth of stability and strength. Coupled to that is a gentleness and tenderness that they are not afraid to show. I like that. To me that's real masculinity!

HOWARD TAYLOR:

IN PRAISE OF

TEXAS WOMEN

San Angelo, TX

Born 1943

When I met him in 1986 Howard Taylor was an apprentice Texan, having just moved from Philadelphia. The assimilation of this Buffalo, New York, native was being spurred along by such experts as cowboy sculptor Garland Weeks. The irrepressible Garland told me that he was just helping greenhorn Howard out with a little advice to keep him from going off the road into the bar ditch. "If you really want to meet you a good gal that will do anything you want," said Garland, "start goin' to the singles classes at the church. Whatever church you go to, just join the singles class and you will meet a lady that will. . . . She may go to church on Sunday morning but she likes to get down and get dirty on Saturday night. There's no sense wasting goin' to church."

Howard's new buddy also said:

Go to any mall in Dallas, Texas. A week later they will have to pull you out of there with your tongue hanging out. You can't really describe it until you have set in those malls and watched the women go by.

And:

If you date in Texas, you drive. That's all there is to it. I got fixed up with a blind date here about three years ago with a girl whose family has a ranch several miles north of here. I knew what it was close to but I had never been on the place. So I was talking to her that afternoon on the phone, getting arrangements lined up, and she said, "I can either come into San Angelo or you can come by here," 'cause we were going to go to Big Spring to the rodeo.

Big Spring is eighty-five miles up the road. That's no big deal. I said, "I'd like to see your place, so I'll come out there and pick you up."

So she gave me a map over the telephone and it was way the hell out in the boondocks. A big dogleg out of the way. And from her place there was no way to cut across country to go to Big Spring. I had to go all the way to Colorado City and then get on Interstate 20 and come back to Big Spring.

So we went to the rodeo and we drank gin and tonic and we danced and we had us a large time. Then I had to bring her back to her ranch.

The point is that had I gone straight to Big Spring and back, I would have been on the road for one hundred seventy miles. But when I got back I had driven three hundred twenty some-odd miles that night. But, damn we had a good time!

I've driven farther for less!

And:

You tell the age of a horse by lookin' at their teeth. We were at a party here not long ago and one of my drinkin' buddies was playin' guitar and singin'. Howard, you had a date out there and we got to tryin' to guess how old she was. So we decided to gear her down and toot her.

We didn't get that done because she was raised on a ranch and she was very conscious of the manner of our speech. We were talking about twisting her ear. When cowboys used to have to ride colts that were not broken, they had to get somebody to twist their ear. That took the colt's mind off of the fact that somebody was getting on their back. If you cause a lot of pain on the front end, he don't know that someone is getting on his back.

She knew that we were teasin'. There might have been two or three city people in the crowd that went "AAAAAAAH, what are they fixin' to do to her?" But she knew that we were just bullshittin' with her so she just started bullshittin' back.

That is the nice thing about Texas women. I have lived a lot of other places, and the attitudes are not the same. I don't know that I could describe what that difference is.

I'll give you an example. There was this rude behavior by two intoxicated men. She just kind of blew it off. She just looked at my guitar buddy and said "What are you jawin' at?"

I thought she was goin' to flatten him. He didn't really affect her at all. If this had been one of those uptight Yankee women, she would have. . . .

She began to come back word for word, phrase for phrase. She was ready to play the game. One minute she was a gracious lady. The next she was like a wildcat, but absolutely in control.

MY FIRST EXPOSURE TO TEXAS ever was 1970. I came here for a museum convention in Fort Worth. I will never forget what the hotel manager said when the hotel ran out of liquor. He said, "We have sold more liquor at this museum convention than any convention we have ever had except for the Southern Baptist Convention."

Can you believe that? He was absolutely serious about it.

There are a lot of datable women in San Angelo that are good-looking. I can guarantee you that the best-looking women are in Texas. That's not a brag. That is pure fact. I just went and spent two weeks in Missouri and Oklahoma. I did not see one good-looking female the entire time I was gone. Texas is the world champion as far as producing gorgeous women.

Texas women, I don't know where they learn it but even women from the smallest towns wear a lot of makeup and do it well. They tend to dress up a lot. I had a friend from the Northeast who came down here to teach. Everybody up there wears jeans and sandals and that sort of thing. Here they really dress up just to go to class every day.

If you are a young lady from a proper family in Texas, you have two choices, SMU or TCU, so I'm told. If you want to see good-looking country girls, go sit down at those campuses for one hour between classes and watch the women parade by. They are all rosy-cheeked, blond-headed, beautiful ladies, by the thousands.

Another phenomena that I noticed here. It may just be West

Texas, but I'm not sure. There are a lot of available women but I have never seen so many women that married so young! That just amazes me. It really does. A common Northeastern phenomena, especially if a woman has been to college, is that she is very rarely married before her late twenties or early thirties.

Texas women are real. They are exuberant, unrestrained and enthusiastic. They usually let you know where you stand.

They are not as uptight as. . . . Recently I was back in Philadelphia. Most of the women that I met there were pretty well-educated. All in their mid- to late twenties, early thirties, and very uptight. Yuppie-type women from New York. Well, like I went out with this one woman and after a while I just said that I was looking forward to getting back to Texas and Texas women. She wanted me to explain why. I did the best that I could. I explained to her that I thought the Northeast's educated women were all uptight and neurotic.

I'll tell you the truth. Texas women complain about Texas men a lot. They really do. From my viewpoint, Texas men guard them like they would a good horse. About the same attitude. Which Texas women understand. That's why they appreciate men from other places. We tend to look upon them as human beings.

In one sense Texas women are not very liberated, but in another sense they really run Texas. This is a true matriarchy down here. True, the men go hunting and fishing a lot. They don't generally go in much for the visual arts. They are a little old-fashioned. They expect dinner to be on the table and they don't really like their wives to be working. That hasn't caught on down here. They consider extra income an oil well that they weren't expecting or something like that.

[An attractive woman approaches who is obviously a close friend of Howard's.]

HERE COMES A TEXAS WOMAN now. See what I mean: they come around a lot and they smile a lot. They look out for you and usually ask you if you want a drink or something to eat.

God help you if you hold the door open for a woman up in Philadelphia. I mean literally you can get physically assaulted for doing that. Around here they expect it. One of the funny things that happened after I started dating here, I got out of the car and she just sat there. I thought, "What is her problem?" Then I realized she was waiting for me to come and open the door. I hadn't experienced that in years.

The Texas woman is very excitable and laughs. . . . It's the way Europeans used to talk about the "ugly American." Makes a lot of noise and that sort of thing. Sometimes Texans traveling have that kind of reputation. I understand in New Mexico they can spot a Texan fifty miles away because of their loudness, brashness.

Texans are just unrestrained and enthusiastic! You go out with a bunch of Texans somewhere, they talk, they laugh, and they are very loud and very, very uptight.

I like Austin best of all the cities in Texas. Texas wasn't cut out to be a state of cities. To me Philadelphia is a city because people are actually walking on the streets and living in neighborhoods.

West Texas, to me, is a little paradise. You have fresh air, the most wonderful weather I have ever experienced in my life—if you overlook the occasional tornado.

People exaggerate West Texas's weather, the dust storms, hailstorms, sandstorms. My hometown is Buffalo, New York. All they have is weather. They make weather. They ship it out. I swear, I have been here almost four years. The weather just never changes, relatively speaking. It rained today, and that is quite an event around here. In fact, a common expression here is "Pray for rain." You get your change in the store and you say "Thank you" and they say "Pray for rain." Invoices from suppliers here in San Angelo are printed "Pray for rain."

Their problem here is not the weather. It is the lack of weather. The air is fresh, there is never a cloud, pleasant all year round. Christmas is often sixty degrees. It is beautiful.

And the women here are like that, too.

There's a lot of almost nationalistic pride here in Texas that I never encountered anywhere else I lived. I remember a couple of occasions where I tried to exploit that but it backfired on me.

For example, not too long after I moved here I thought "I can't wait till I take a trip somewhere and somebody asks me where I'm from and I can tell em *'Well, I'm from Texas!'* " And soon I just happened to be in Colorado. In fact, I was in a bar. And I was just getting ready to tell the bartender that I lived in Texas when Nature called and I had to go into the men's room. It's a good thing I did because, I swear, written on the wall in what looked like blood in letters four feet high was something that said KILL TEX-ANS. So I went back to the bar and I paid my bill and told the bartender I was from New York and driving a rented car and left.

That time I learned the relationship between Texans and people from Colorado.

Then another time, again I was in a bar, I thought, "Well, the women here are just like the men in being very proud of being Texans." So I had been talking to this attractive young lady and I said to her, "You know, I've never kissed a Texas woman."

She looked at me and she said, "Darlin', when you finally do, y'all are in for a real treat!"

J. W. JINES:
WAGON TRAIN
INTO THE FUTURE
Perryton, TX
Born 1910

The Ochiltree county seat of Perryton is about as far as you can get into Oklahoma and still be in Texas. But if you are fool enough to say Perryton is not really Texan, J. W. Jines will set you straight!

In 1986 I met J. W. and his friend Fred Shivers at San Elizario, Texas, where the Sesquicentennial Wagon Train had halted for a fiesta at the old Spanish mission. J. W. with his patriarchal white beard looked like he had stepped out of the pages of a history book onto a movie set where mariachis, dancers, drivers, cowboys, and mules strolled, two-stepped, and grazed beside the thick adobe walls of the ancient church. This was a long way from the northern Panhandle's Anglo settlements, but somehow it was all Texas!

J. W. Jines's Illinois father had become a Texan in 1896 thanks to a wagon and team and a sturdy butt. J. W. had grown up in an era when Indians still made pilgrimages across the Jines's spring-rich spread to their ancestral homes at Adobe Walls. Before he was school age, J. W. had broken a team of mule colts by dropping onto their backs from a hackberry tree at their watering hole. "No tellin' how many times they threw me," says J. W., "but I stuck with it and on the first day of school, I hooked them to a wagon and drove to school behind that team of mules." By age ten J. W. was breaking horses for hire. Then he worked himself into dozens of other "honest ways to make a living" such as cattle drives, butcher shops, grocery stores, service stations, bulldozing, and cement mixing.

Decades later, in 1976, J. W. had driven a Bicentennial wagon from Houston eastward to Valley Forge, Pennsylvania, and in 1986 he spent six months and ten days driving his matched mules Joe and Agie from one end of Texas to another in honor of one hundred fifty years of statehood and in memory of his father's westward-ho spirit.

Fred Shivers and J.W. Jines with J.W.'s
mules Joe and Aggie.

I felt that the Sesquicentennial Wagon Train was an exercise in Texan-ness that was genuinely touching. I and thousands of others were heartened by as many as a hundred fifty wagons and by our chance to meet folks who were carving out their piece of the American dream.

I suppose that to some people wagon trains will seem like sentimental folly at a time of homelessness, illiteracy, and bank failures. But I liked these wagoneers for their cooperative spirit and resourcefulness. Though looking toward the past, they were symbolic to me of Texas's gusto for stepping into the future.

"Wagons Ho!"

MY DADDY NEVER WENT TO school a day in his life, but he was the third richest man in Ochiltree County when he died. He could figure faster in his head than ninety-eight percent of the people could with a pencil.

My daddy run horses, mules, and cattle. We used to ride all day long in the buggy with a team of high-stepping horses, my daddy and I. Cross water six or eight times and camp about seven miles from home. The next day we would hook up the same team, circle on to the south and west, and come in the next night and never get out of our pasture.

My daddy died in a flu epidemic before I was ten years old, but I remember a lot of things that he told my older brothers. And I have tried to live a life like his, helping people.

We had quite a large family. Eleven children and Pa and Ma made thirteen, and three or four extry. If a family drove in and sat down at the table, no sweat, we just scooted up closer and put more plates on the table. Who can say how much thirteen or fourteen people are goin' to eat? Another four or five, you just clean up the platters a little cleaner is all.

In this wagon train we are a family like that. We are happy fools. Doing this, we gain a direct appreciation for the individuals like my daddy who came West this way with all their goats, cows, kids, furniture. I used to wonder why they *walked* so much behind those wagons. Now I know why they walked. Those wagons were too rough to ride.

FRED: Common practical sense is the reason they did everything the way they did it. You are reminded of that out here. Why they traveled so many days, then rested. In what season they left. We are out here now because on a typical year this would be the best time to be in this part of the country as far as rain, snows, high winds, and the heat. You wouldn't want to be out here in July and August in a wagon train.

J. W.: Back in the old days, they didn't have any feed to haul with 'em. Eight to ten miles would be a good day's run. They had to let their horses and animals graze. They had to forage their own groceries. People had this all planned, what animals they would kill. They sure weren't vegetarians, I'll guarantee that, but they could find roots and herbs to eat. Some fruit from the trees like Indian bread. It is very delicious if you get it while it is young in spring. It is sweet and white.

Do I prefer the good old days? Let me ask you a question. Is it easier to do your washing with a rub board or throw it in an electric machine and let it wash for you?

Of course, back then you had time to visit, go see your neighbors. Nowadays you are too busy.

FRED: That is part of what attracts me to the wagon train. I see my neighbors every morning, sometimes at ten o'clock water break, noon, when I get in and unharness. Anytime I want to step over and visit with them. We see each other ten or fifteen times a day and we holler at each other every time.

J. W. and I got a little joke between us. I call him "Grampa" and he calls me "Papa Fred." There is another guy on the train that every time he goes by I holler, "Bless you, my son." When you are drivin' down the road, you are a little bit isolated in your wagon unless you have a visitor. The camp life, just knowin' that Albert and Alice Nicely are parked right next door to you, you can lay down and go to sleep better at night. Knowin' that if somethin' happens, you have friends that you can depend on right there, just one holler away. You are probably willin' to tackle some things and take some risks that you wouldn't do if you were out at the house.

J. W.: If you need any help, all you got to do is just say so. Just like right now if you step out there, "Hey, you guys, I need some help." I'll bet that at least ten men would be there immediately.

FRED: They wouldn't ask you what before they come. It don't matter. That's the thing here. If you need help, you are going to get it.

That's part of the attraction of this thing. There is no cost to it either. You couldn't pay them. You go to town, "Hey, anybody need any ice? I'm goin' to town." Shucks, maybe he will bring back fifteen bags of ice. They just make a list and bring it back.

Every one of us out here is independent and yet we are some of the first people to go help other people, even in our communities. Yet we are probably the last ones to ask for help for ourselves. Out here that is one thing you kind of do. Most times you have to kind of watch people because the majority of the time we try to do it ourselves. You kind of got to watch and go help somebody when you *think* they need help. We are independent and we would rather help people than be helped. We are kind of like the teams we are drivin'; we are just a little bit ornery. Otherwise you are going to be home away from the dust and the flies, watching TV, swimming in your pool, and living the easy life.

This is the good life, but it is not always easy.

FRED: Right now this wagon train is averaging close to twenty miles a day. That's an easy day. At thirty or more miles, the days get pretty long. On the Bicentennial, didn't we make a forty-two-mile day that one time we didn't get in till dark? We left an hour early; we had four breaks that day.

J. W.: I think the longest day I can remember is that first day you drove the wagon. You had the sorriest pair of mules that I have ever saw in my life!

FRED: That was a day—a new wife, a new team, a new wagon, and new way of life. A lot of new friends!

I met J. W. in 1976 on the southern route of the Bicentennial Wagon Train. I didn't know anything very much about driving a wagon at all. Very green. He was one of the people that helped teach me the correct horsemanship, what to look for, and how to fit harness. How to take care of the horses and make a good camp. J. W. taught it through soft words and example rather than comin' over and bossin' people around. I don't take bossin' too good, but I sure do like to watch people that know what they are doin' and learn from that.

J. W.: The first time I saw Fred was the day he got married, in Henrietta, Oklahoma. I won't forget his first day because I started out with an accident. People had climbed up on my wagon that night and broken the tongue out and I didn't know it until the wagonmaster hollered "Wagons Ho!" and I just about fell off my seat when the mules jerked me with the line. A young fella jumped off his horse and grabbed my mules and held them. At ten o'clock they got my wagon fixed and I took out after the wagon train. This happened to be a thirty-seven-mile one that day. I caught up with them after five hours and forty-five minutes.

Fred was last in line and he was driving a team of black mules and I could tell when I pulled up behind him that he didn't know straight up about driving a team. He would pull on the left-hand line and the mules would go out to the center. He would pull on the right-hand line and they would go to the edge of the pavement. He must have drove at least forty-three mile that day while the rest of them were driving thirty-seven.

One time down the road, his wife asked me, "Do you suppose I can live with Fred after this wagon train's over?"

I told her, "Girl, if you can put up with him in a wagon the rest of the way to Valley Forge, Pennsylvania, you can live with him the rest of your life in a house."

FRED: We were going to get married anyway. We heard about the Bicentennial coming through and one thing led to another. It was really Debbie's idea. She said, "Let's move the date up and go with the Bicentennial Wagon Train." I laughed a while and she kept on until I said "O.K., it suits me."

J. W.: Honeymoon wagon, that's what it was called. Every night when we would get to camp for a long time, you took everything out of that wagon, put it on the ground, and started insulating your wagon because it was cold. After you finally got it fixed, though, you made wonderful progress with the wagon train because you forgot your fast pace of living. We only averaged twenty miles a day and we had all day to do it in. So you just relaxed both physically and mentally. I don't know, we are kind of like a person on dope. We get hooked on it, take our time, relax. Politicians will only bother us just long enough for the parade and speeches, and then we are through with them and we are left with the good people. I'll guarantee that if you can ride in a wagon three days, you will be hooked bad!

DR. WILLIAM HALL:

OUT FOR A SPIN

Wichita Falls, TX

Born 1926

Texas weather, like hot peppers, has a way of taking its revenge on the unwary. One fine spring day I was driving east of Lubbock near the town of Crosby. I heard on the radio that a storm was rolling my way, but when I saw the black, evil-looking front I was not ready to believe that it could hit *me*. It was, after all, far away and I was moving north as fast as my old van Hodge could go.

After about forty-five minutes the cars approaching me were glistening wet and their headlights were burning yellowishly in the sunny afternoon.

I was now close enough to the horizon-length storm to see lightning zapping Crosby up ahead. Then, as the first drops darkened the pavement, I heard a hailstone ping off my windshield.

In a moment the largest hailstones I had ever seen were carpeting the two-laner and bar ditches like shotgun pellets. I drove on, thinking that I would quickly outdistance this little disturbance.

But the hail and rain fell with such tropical intensity that the road and the flat fields were soon as white as an old-fashioned Christmas. I was so blind that I pulled off at the first opportunity and waited for the hailstorm to pass.

By the time I learned that a tornado had hit not far away, the sun was shining and the white landscape melting into spring again.

Wichita Falls, Texas, has a reputation for violent weather, and when I met a tooth-twister named Dr. Hall there, I asked him about the cyclone that had extracted his house and office in 1979.

It was really comical that my wife had been cooking some steaks for supper and had just taken them out of the oven and set them on the stove. The tornado removed the roof of the house and everything else but it didn't touch those steaks.

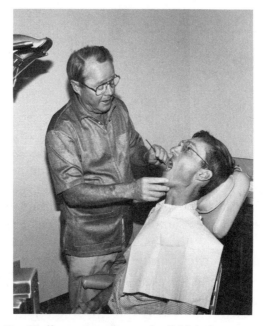

Somehow Dr. Hall managed to rebuild his house and office and eventually as co-chairman of his church's rebuilding committee got that back together again, too. But about three years after the 1979 tornado a major flood hit Wichita Falls. "I had thirty inches of water in my house," he said. "A flood is slower than a tornado but it is more damaging. I prefer a tornado to a flood!"

WICHITA FALLS HAD BEEN HIT by tornadoes a couple of times before, but the others had been out around Sheppard Air Force Base on the northern side of town. I stood out behind my office one day in the 1960s and watched a twister strike the base out there. My side of the town, the sun was shining and it was beautiful. On the north side of town, it completely wreaked havoc.

April 10, 1979, had been cloudy, rainy, and a cold front had passed through. Dr. Bill Coulson who is in the office here with me now, a friend of mine, he was practicing downtown and had just recently had major surgery. So I had started to go down there and I thought, "The weather is so bad I'll go home first and then I'll go down there later on tonight to the hospital to visit with him."

I got home approximately around five o'clock or so. Wife was fixin' dinner. Daughter was home. Allison was eighteen at the time, very apprehensive about storms anyway. She was watchin' out the front door and my wife, like I say, was cookin' dinner for us.

My daughter had always been apprehensive about storms and now it was lightning and wind was blowing some, raining and so forth.

So we were watchin' TV and I was reading the paper. I thought, "There's nothing to worry about."

I watched the news and long about quarter to six, something like that, Allison said, "It sure is black out here."

Then the TV announced that there was a tornado out by the football stadium, which is five or six miles from where I live. I thought, "Oh, there is no problem; it will be back up in the air." Tornadoes generally hit the ground and then bounce back up for maybe a mile or so. I wasn't concerned.

But Allison kept watchin' out the front and soon the TV went off.

When the TV went off, I got up and walked to the front door and looked outside. About two blocks away there was a huge black mass. I could see things up in the air. Chunks and boards. Maybe roofs flying!

I didn't stand there and try to verify what they were. I knew that it was a tornado. I didn't have to ask twice.

So I grabbed my wife and daughter and we ran into the back bath off of our bedroom. There was a walk-in closet there and we got into it. We took some pillows. We just grabbed them because we only had two or three minutes to get in there.

My daughter had grabbed her cat but the cat got away when the phone rang. It was my son from Houston calling to talk to us. My daughter says, "We can't talk, we're having a tornado!"

So we all went and got in the closet and closed the door.

Well, it hit in probably two minutes. You could just feel the vibration when it hit. Just like a train hitting. A tremendous roar and a musty smell from the dust, dirt, and ground. It didn't last over probably two to three minutes maybe.

All that time I was in that dark closet thinking that I might have a heart attack any instant.

It was totally dark in there. In fact, my daughter panicked because the roar was so loud that she couldn't. . . . I was on one side of the closet and my daughter and wife were on the other side of the closet laying on the floor down low, to keep things that might fly through from hitting us.

Anyway, the tornado took the top off the house, flattened the house out completely, and blowed the walls down. I don't know where the roof went to. The fireplace was laying in the middle of the living-room floor. Four cars in the back driveway and they were demolished.

Everything was demolished except this little bathroom area that we were in. That closet and bathroom stood up. Sort of a gable that came out from the back where the bathroom was.

We weren't in that closet over three or four minutes. When the noise stopped, we got out and there was just like a nice gentle breeze blowing.

I was in World War II and when we came out of the closet, what we saw reminded me of a battlefield. Like I say, the roof and walls were gone.

One of the window curtains was blowing back and forth in a gentle breeze. It was all quiet and peaceful but my daughter was hysterical. And I figured there were probably hundreds dead around us. The whole area looked like a war zone.

My mother lived about half a mile from us and the tornado had went right in her direction. As people began to come out of closets and wherever they had hid, I recognized a patient of mine and she loaned me her car to go over and see if I could find what had happened to my mother. I couldn't get over there because of the conditions that the storm had left.

So I came back home and we walked across the golf course over to some friends' house and then I walked up to where my mother lived. Her house was gone, too. One of her neighbors told me that they had taken her to the hospital but she was all right.

My office was just about a block or two from there; it was gone, too. I had lost everything in the tornado. Things were busy and I was so concerned about my mother that I didn't worry then about losing my cars, house, and office.

After they told me Mom was all right, we went back to our friend's house. Their daughter had been in some apartments that were struck and she had a laceration of her scalp and she went down and got it sewed up. There were quite a few of us that spent the night there sleeping on the floor.

The National Guard came out, but not that first night. That's when the looters came. In fact, my neighbor that lives behind me, Dr. Gary Brown, only his roof was damaged, and he set out in the back yard with a gun all night to keep away looters.

My looters were really comical! My fireplace had fallen down into the living room onto a couple of couches and chairs. The looters moved this tremendous weight of bricks and pieces of chimney to take away a couple of chairs and a couch that I didn't want anyways.

I really had no time to stop and think about being depressed about what had happened during the two weeks we stayed with friends. I needed to find another place for an office. My mother's house was destroyed, so I had to find a place for her and for my wife and daughter. So with all these different things. . . .

And no cars. In fact, I had a friend that had a dealership here and he loaned me a new Chrysler. Afterwards I stopped to keep from running through a lot of water and an elderly fella ran into the back of me and just crated it. My friend the dealer was real nice about it!

I eventually rebuilt my house and my office but we have never forgotten how it felt to be huddled in that dark closet with the roar of that wind destroying everything around us. It has really left an emotional scar on my daughter. She came home from Arlington a couple of weeks ago and called twice on the way home to check on the weather here. The weather was threatening in Wichita Falls and she wanted to know what she was driving into. She was very apprehensive.

No, moving is not in my plans. I don't see anything wrong with Wichita Falls. A safer area? A lot of things can happen in any area.

There have been a lot of tornadoes in Florida and back East. That volcano erupted in 1980 and caused more problems than this tornado did.

At the time of the tornado I was treasurer of our First Baptist Church. The building would have been totally paid for by that November. On April 10 it was destroyed.

Out of the rubble we were brought together in a way which probably would not have been possible otherwise. The tornado built a bond among our congregation—which had been going down, down, down for years. Before the tornado we usually had seventy in attendance on Sunday morning. After the tornado it doubled to a hundred and fifty.

That makes some sense. The Lord works in strange ways.

LILLIAN STIELER:

RATTLERS AND DOG TROTS

Utopia, TX

Born 1894

Before the advent of rural electrification, farm wives carried an incredible burden of work. Even seemingly simple chores like filling a tub with water were labor-intensive since water had to be fetched, not turned on. For instance, when newlywed Lillian Stieler wanted to wash her family's clothes, her soap just didn't appear off a store shelf. She had to make it, sweating beside a wood fire and stirring a large pot of tallow, lye, and water. The wood fuel had to be cut by hand from local trees. The water had to be hauled by hand from not-so-nearby creeks and springs.

When the young Stielers' finally managed to pipe in water from a spring, it was "a lovely, lovely experience" to have all the water they wanted.

Fritz Stieler and his wife began married life living with his brother and sister-in-law in a traditional dogtrot house. At first the problems of snakes, wolves, droughts, and plain hard labor might have seemed overwhelming. That does not come through in Mrs. Stieler's account, though I felt her relief when she finally got indoor water and plumbing and when the other couple moved to the "upper ranch."

Mrs. Stieler, unlike her youngest daughter, never hunted and cannot even fire a gun. But when she had to, she could kill a rattlesnake with a hoe. "I'd be at home by myself and it would just be up to me to kill them," she said.

One time in the yard, a big rattlesnake kept coming toward me weaving back and forth. I wanted it to coil so I could hit in front

of it with a hoe but it got so mad that it started toward me. I closed
my eyes [Laughter] because I was so frightened. I closed my eyes
and all I thought of was to stop that snake. I lifted the hoe up and
came down with all my might. And when I opened my eyes, I had
chopped off its head! It was still weaving back and forth even
without its head.

The Wilke/Stieler story is a parable of the German Hill country.
Mrs. Stieler's complex family relationships with a whole county of
cousins, aunts, and uncles was too obscure for me to follow. But
I was fascinated to learn that although her suitor Fritz Stieler
[1890–1958] was also German, no German was spoken on the
dates described in these stories. "Everybody spoke English during
the war because there was prejudice against German," she told me.
In fact, German was not even taught in school during and immediately after World War I.

I WAS BORN CLOSE TO New Braunfels in 1894. We learned to speak
English as very young children and we could speak and understand
English when we started school at the age of seven. But it was
mostly German that we spoke in the home or with neighbors. We
just had nine grades and we spoke mostly German on the school
grounds. It was a German community with very few English-only
speakers.

I first started playing basketball while I was in the seventh grade,
but baseball was the biggest sport of all.

On Sunday we dressed up in our Sunday shoes and Sunday
dresses. In the morning we'd go to Sunday School, all in German,
and Sunday afternoon in summer we went to the baseball game.

My parents were born here but my grandparents came from
Alsace-Lorraine in 1845. They landed in Indianola in 1845 on the
coast. It isn't there any more because they had a terrible hurricane
which wiped out the whole community.

My grandparents traveled by ox cart to New Braunfels. The men
walked and the women could ride in the wagon.

My grandfather was a schoolteacher in New Braunfels for a
number of years. Then he bought a small ranch about twenty miles

out of New Braunfels where they lived the rest of their lives. And, of course, it was still Indian Territory.

My mother inspired me very much. She was very energetic. And she wanted a better life for her children than she had had.

We always had good books in the home. And in the evening we would talk about what we had read. More so than people do now. We didn't have the opportunity to go out every night. We would just be at home and read. We were always a very close-knit family.

I really don't like the life some kids have now. The freedom they have. I remember that I lived in a town where there were so many saloons. And my mother would say, "Now you have to pass the saloons when you go to school. Just walk by. Hold up your head. Never even look if someone should call to you. Never look in the saloon. Just keep on walking."

And we'd hold up our heads and we'd walk by.

My mother sewed all of our clothes and even our coats. We wore much heavier clothes in those days. And always long black stockings and high-topped shoes. We didn't want to be sunburned. We thought that was terrible.

When I graduated from high school, I wanted to go to college— my brothers did—but I went to work to support my parents. My father wasn't well so I didn't go to college.

Let me tell you about how I met my husband. I had a friend from the university visiting us over the holidays. It was leap year and on New Year's Eve we went to a dance in Comfort. Walked all the way to town to the dance. A little over a mile. I didn't dance, but during the evening this nice-looking young man came up to me and said, "You are Miss Wilke, I believe." I said yes and he introduced himself. We talked a little while and then he asked me to go to dinner with him the following day, New Year's.

I was twenty years old at the time so I told him that my mother didn't know him and I didn't think she would let me go by myself. We'd have to have a chaperone.

I said that I had a friend visiting me and that I would like for her to go, too. And he said that he'd find a date for her. And he did. A cousin. But when that cousin learned that we'd have to take a chaperone he said, "Let's call the whole thing off. I don't like that."

But my future husband seemed to be interested and he said that he knew a good chaperone.

He asked his aunt to go with us. She was a very happy person. She was full of fun. And we had a lovely time.

We drove to a neighboring community called Turtle Creek about thirty miles away from where I was living in Comfort, Texas. We pulled down the window flaps and we fastened them on the doors so that we could see. We had a lovely turkey dinner at the home of another of his aunts and then went to the dance. This was in 1914, when I was twenty. He was twenty-three but he already owned a nice ranch. He'd owned a Dodge car for about a year! Before that he used to ride to dances on horseback.

I was very impressed with him. He was everything I had always thought I would like to meet. He was very handsome. He had a good education. He owned a beautiful ranch and was known as a very eligible bachelor. It was just love at first sight!

But I didn't even see him again for six months because I was also dating someone else in another town—Burney—where I was working in my family's drugstore. Fritz had stopped by once or twice on his way home from San Antonio but I had been out driving with another man.

Driving was all there was to do in the evenings. Several boys and girls would go out riding. That was a new thing then, especially since there wasn't much money around for cars. We just enjoyed being out and we didn't do all the things kids do nowadays. [Laughter]

I hadn't seen Fritz for six months when finally I met his sister in town and I talked to her. We had met before. And she went home and told her brother "Guess who I saw today?"

So that night he called me and asked if I'd like to go to a barbecue his sister was having in Fredericksburg. So, of course, I was delighted to go. And that was the beginning of the actual romance. [Laughter]

And we were married in 1917 and I moved out to his ranch. Fritz's brother had married eight months before we did and so we two couples lived in the same house. They lived on one side of the dogtrot and we on the other. And we called the dogtrot no-man's land. [Laughter]

The dogtrot, the breezeway between the two sides of our house, was a hall thirty-two feet long and fourteen feet wide. While my husband was growing up, everybody ate in that dogtrot at a big, long table, winter and summer, and they didn't seem to be cold. They wore their coats. But my father-in-law enclosed it because his four children's teachers complained about being cold eating out there.

Several times after I moved there we found rattlesnakes in the house because they could come in through the dogtrot. Oh, I had terrible experiences with rattlesnakes.

When I moved there there was no electricity. No running water. We had to get all of our water from a spring about a quarter of a mile from the house. We walked and carried big buckets in our hands. Oh, it was hard work.

During the drouth we had several springs in the creek bottom. We would just have to follow the springs wherever they came up. And my husband would get someone to dig a larger hole and we'd dip the water out.

We had big tanks to catch the rainwater. That was good soft water for washing. We didn't have washing machines. We had big tubs and washboards. And we boiled all the clothes in big copper pots. Everybody did. That was the custom. We'd get 'em nice and white.

We had to cook our own homemade soap with tallow from the beef that we'd killed. We used so much soap that we would have to buy some of the tallow from the meat market.

We boiled about twelve pounds of tallow, ten gallons of water, and three cans of lye in big cast-iron pots outside. We stirred it constantly to keep it from burning. We'd let the soap stay in the pots overnight to harden. By the next morning it would be ready to be cut into pieces. We'd cut it into triangles because that was easier since it was a round pot.

That beautiful white soap washed very well. But especially during the summer it was hard work to make soap. The weather was hot but you'd have to stand very close to the hot water to stir it.

We'd just been married a short time when my husband said that it was hog-killing time. Well, my sister-in-law and I didn't know anything about making sausage. I had never lived out on a ranch.

I'd always lived in a small town. All I knew was that we went to a meat market and bought our meat and sausage and bacon.

The men didn't seem to know too much about hog-killing time either, because they missed the hog the first time they tried to shoot it and shot through the copper pot and all the hot water spurted out.

They cut up the meat and ground some of it for sausage. The sausage was put into hog-intestine casings.

We bought the casings, but my sister-in-law and I didn't know anything about them. They were supposed to be soaked overnight in warm water and cleaned very well because they had been put up in salt.

Then the men said that they were ready for the casings and that we should bring them down. So we didn't know. We just brought the package of casings down. And my brother-in-law looked at my husband and said, "I don't know. We married some awfully dumb girls, didn't we?" [Laughter] Because they couldn't use those casings that had just been bought.

I remember that my husband just smiled. He didn't agree with him. And I was just very grateful to him for that.

Oh, we had a difficult time getting accustomed to all of that. Of course, in a year's time we both had babies. She had a little boy and I had a girl. And that was a lot of work.

Also, we were not used to having to cook for hired hands. We always had one or two hired hands to cook for.

And another thing, there were so many wolves at the time that would come at night and kill the sheep. So my husband bought ten wolfhounds. Big dogs. He sent to Kentucky for 'em. And he'd go out every evening with the dogs and try to locate the wolves. That was very hard, working during the day and riding after the dogs at night. Sometimes all night. But finally we got a government trapper and he killed all the wolves.

There were years when we had terrible drouths. Once in the middle thirties a drouth lasted seven years. That took all of the money we had saved and we even had to borrow money to buy food.

It was very difficult during a hard drouth, but somehow we got over it. The Depression was very hard for everyone, but by that time we had big gardens and all our own meat.

But there was always a great deal of washing to be done. And you had to manage well. Not only the men but also the wives.

We were always happy and had a good home life. We had two daughters and they had a good education. They graduated from college.

There were always hard times, but altogether it was a very lovely life.

EARL SCHWETTMANN: HILL COUNTRY TAXIDERMIST

Fredericksburg, TX

Born 1943

President George Bush surprised the nation after his 1988 election by returning to Texas for a few days of quail hunting. Never since Theodore Roosevelt had there been a president with such a lust for feather and fin. Predictably animal rights groups were outraged, but hunting and the love of guns is as Texan as, say, chili cookoffs and beauty queens. Earl Schwettmann's story is not about duck-blind camaraderie or about wily quarry but about the bottom line: how Bambi looks up on the wall.

Earl Schwettmann, grandson of a German immigrant, grew up on a dairy, cotton, and corn farm in McGregor, Texas, near Waco. His favorite hunting as a boy was rabbits, squirrels, and ducks. A degree in wildlife science from Texas A & M University continued his sporting interests with a major in "upland game." In his spare time at College Station, Earl worked for a local taxidermist. Joe Palermo recalls that "Earl knew nothing about taxidermy when he began to work for me but he originated good ideas in my shop. He was lots of fun to work with, always joking with us."

In 1971 Earl moved to Fredericksburg to teach sixth-grade science. That taxidermy hobby he had begun at College Station soon became a flourishing business in a region where the population of exotic deer, boar, sheep, and other trophy animals is a major source of income for ranchers.

IT IS NOT NECESSARILY THE hunter that uses the taxidermist. Quite a bit of my business is selling heads to interior decorators for decorating offices, lodges, restaurants, and large homes where the people want this type of atmosphere but do not have the time to go hunt it themselves. I sell a lot of hides for rugs or for chair upholstery.

The forms are now made so anatomically correct that it is hard to make a mistake unless you are really klutzy with your hands. Of course, instead of using a commercial form, I can create a special position by making an original clay model and casting a mold from it.

What goes into the animals is a polyurethane foam inner structure. We have different sizes and different positions for all the animals. We pour the liquid in a mold and make the forms. The animals are measured as they come in and are skinned. We pick a form to the position that the customer wants. Of course, I have glass eyes, and I use clay around the eyes and the nose under the skin to give it detail. The only part we use of the animal is the antler and the skin. Some animals we use the teeth, but now it is really better to use artificial teeth and tongues. Several guys that have been in the dental business making dentures have retired from that and have gone into making these lifelike animal teeth. They cast real teeth from animals and make the false teeth to the same standards that dentures are made.

The basics of animal mounting are always the same, no matter whether it is a black buck antelope or an axis deer. It is a form of art because you can be very creative with it, sculpting, painting around the noses and eyes. It is very satisfying work.

I started from scratch. I used to have just one showcase in a rented three-thousand-square-foot retail store. Bit by bit I kept putting back into the business what I didn't need to live on. Now I own this large store downtown where you can buy a first-class mounted trophy right off the wall.

The animals have been good for me. I receive game from African safaris. Hunters in Spain send me work. But the bulk of it is from the Texas hill country, the white-tailed deer and the exotics.

In the hill country they shoot these exotic animals year round. We do the mounting and ship them all over the United States and the world.

Some of the larger ranches here have more exotic animals on them than do the original countries they came from. For instance, there are more black buck antelope here than there are in India, the original country. Some, like your Pere David's deer, was nearly extinct and now there is getting to be hundreds of them in the hill country.

Big game is a business. Ranchers raise the animals, the hunting pays for the food, and it all supplements their livestock cattle operations. It is just that you raise big game animals instead of livestock or crops.

I mount the white-tailed deer, the turkey, the feral hog, the Russian boar, the fallow deer, axis deer, Sitka deer, all different types of your African plains game. Some ranches even have rhinoceros, zebra, giraffes, just a multitude of thirty or forty different animals.

I was always interested in wildlife as a kid. When I was at A & M University, in between my classes and labs I got three years of taxidermy experience with Joe Palermo in Bryan, Texas. Just got on the ground floor, kind of, and learned the basics and went on from there.

And then my love for the wildlife and outdoors had a lot to do with it. The anatomy of birds, animals and fish, and all that.

Joe Palermo is semiretired and living in Port Isabell, guiding for fishermen and doing a little taxidermy, mainly fish, on the side. His two sons run the shop in Bryan; it's called Palermo & Sons Taxidermy.

Joe is in his fifties. He was a young man when I worked for him. He inspired me to be creative.

W. O. VICTOR, JR.:
IN THE PATH
OF THE KILLER BEES
Concan, TX
Born 1915

Texas's bees are an endangered species—and so is W. O. Victor, Jr. His family has been raising bees in Texas since 1883, almost all of that time in Uvalde, the state's old "honey capital." African bees are about to put an end to that century of tradition, but even if the exotic migrants had never reached the Americas from Africa, Uvalde's bee business would have taken some fatal stings. Insecticides decimated hives; overgrazing and land clearing drastically thinned out the more than twenty local varieties of honey plants; and honey marketing shifted to capital-intensive methods.

It used to be that if a man had five or six hundred hives of bees and he wasn't in a drought season, he would make a good living for his family. Those were the days that I milked a cow, had a garden, had my bees, and sold honey all over the country.

Nowadays Uvalde County's once-thriving honey business has shrunk to just W. O. and his son Bill (who have greatly reduced their operation because of labor and transportation difficulties). The African bee (known as the killer bee because of its aggressiveness) will further crimp the Victors' last efforts to keep the memory of huajillo* honey alive in southwest Texas.

---

*False mesquite or fairy duster (*Calliandra eriophylla*) is a small-leafed shrub with colorful red clusters of pink flowers.

THERE IS NOT A SQUARE inch on my body that has not had a bee sting on it. Right here is one of the worst, right here on the edge of the nose and on the back of the ear. If you think that doesn't hurt. . . . I could turn handsprings. I snort, sniff, and sneeze.

Any bee will sting you. I don't care what kind they are. You disturb a bee and it will sting you. Old beekeepers like me, I can drive out in the bee yard and from the tone of their flight, I know whether they are working good or not. On a good honey flow it is just a roar. If they are ill-tempered and things are not going good, there is a shriller noise like a scream.

I love working with bees! For instance, I can go out here and prepare what we call a nucleus out of a brood of bees, a frame of honey, and a laying queen that I raised myself. And I can try to produce a crop of honey with that nucleus. It is a gamble. To see that little pint of bees increase, you betcha that gives me a thrill!

In northern Uvalde County our first plant in the spring is algerita. The second plant is a shrub called redbud. Your third plant is mountain laurel; then your next plant is persimmon; your next is huajillo. Usually in the hills around here, when the huajillo is over, that is it till fall. In the lower country, fifteen miles south of here, when your huajillo is over, you have a shrub called cat claw (which has a little long bloom on it). And mesquite starts to come in. Mesquite makes a delicious honey but it's an erratic producer. Above Highway 90, mesquite doesn't produce much to speak of.

Our native honey plants include redbud, algerita, sage, mesquite, white brush, soap brush, and honeydew, all trees and brush, plus a flower we call arnica weed.

Your soils, sea levels, humidity, and atmosphere determines how much moisture a plant will secrete. For instance, around Vernon and Sanford, alfalfa honey is water-white. When it hits, it produces, and it just floods.

You go out there to El Paso Valley, there the alfalfa honey is a light amber. I am sure it is the minerals in the soil.

There are very few parts of Texas that don't produce some honey.

Which is the best-tasting? Well, shall I give a Uvalde answer or shall I give a correct answer?

The correct answer is that the best honey is the honey that you were raised on. If you were raised over around Lockhart on a weed like horsemint. . . . When it rains, horsemint is a heavy producer. For people raised on that honey, that is the only honey in the world to eat.

Just like you can go north; I did this myself. We put a bunch of bees up in Kansas a few years ago and we paid our rent for our location in honey. So good ole stupid me, I thought this wonderful Uvalde brush honey would be different and so we paid all our bee-location rent in it. Shoot, two-thirds of the Kansas farmers said "That honey, we didn't really like it. You can have it back. Can I have some alfalfa and corn honey instead?"

So we gave them what they wanted. It's what you are raised on.

Honey is produced here all twelve months of the year. Theoretically speaking, the darker the honey the more minerals and vitamins. That's what they claim; I don't know. There are some types of dark honey that is not fit to eat. That honey goes into bakeries.

In Uvalde County we raise a honey out in the hills from a shrub called kinnikinnick. I had an uncle who was raised on the stuff and he hollered every fall that he wanted me to get him four or five pounds of that stuff. I would get it for him and my aunt would make a plate of hot biscuits and he would daub the cow butter to it and fill his plate up with that ole kinnikinnick honey and just slop her down.

Normally people can't eat kinnikinnick. *I* don't like it.

On the coast they have a yellow tree called Chinese tallow that leaves an aftertaste for days. People over there near Houston like it but people here think it's horrible.

We are the oldest continuing bee family in the state of Texas. My granddad started in 1883 at Wortham, Texas. He had a daughter in ill health. In those days if you were in ill health, they told you to move to a drier climate. So around the turn of the century he shipped lock, stock, and barrel out to Hondo. He stayed in Hondo just a little while and then moved over to Uvalde, where he finally died. My father continued the business and we worked bees as a family in Kansas, all over Texas, New Mexico, South Dakota, North Dakota, Minnesota, and so on. Eventually I worked in every phase of honey that it is possible for a man to work. We hauled the first load of packaged bees across the United States in a four-wheel trailer behind a 1926 model Chevrolet car. The family shipped bees to Colorado, before I started to school. We spent two summers in Colorado, my granddad and dad shipped bees up there towards Lamar.

I had my first hive of bees at about eleven years old. I started nailing frames up and getting bee equipment ready. I bought my first fifty hives of bees on credit at about fourteen years old. Produced the honey and paid the bees off. Run across a defunct outfit of fifty hives and I bought that. That gave me a hundred hives. I just stayed with my dad. We worked together as partners for many, many years, then separated, and now my son has come in with me.

We honeymen are conservationists because we need all the native plants and flowers to make honey with. Ranchers usually don't care about that. It has been customary in ranching country that a man would lease grassland and overstock it so badly that he would clean it out in two or three years. When he would let it go, it was in pretty bad shape. It would take several years to bring it back.

Huajillo is our main honey crop in Uvalde County. Right down the road here somebody put goats on a huajillo hill and wiped out the huajillo. In fact, people here have been working on wiping it all out during all of my life. They haven't got it all yet, no.

The ranchers today, due to their better education, the news media, they are doing a better job of conserving the ranches than they were thirty years ago. I remember when my uncle was one of the worst abusers of the land. . . .

Bees make our national agriculture possible. They pollinate most fruits and some vegetables. I remember that thirty years ago I used to hire out my hives for pollinating but I quit doing it because the farmers, with all due respect to them, they do not realize the capital invested in a hive of bees. They won't pay you enough to go to the expense of puttin' them in there. Then Pete Jones across the road, he will have airplanes out there and he will dust the H— out of the fields and the wind will blow it over and kill the darned bees. So I quit pollinating.

This food you see on the shelves in the stores wouldn't be there if it wasn't for bees. Where would you get alfalfa seed? Where would you get clover seed? Bees pollinate these fruit trees. Orchard men have to have bees. Farmers have to have insect pollination. They used to say that the citrus and cotton are self-pollinating. But they found out that by saturating bees in citrus country they get better citrus. The cotton germinates faster and better with bees, too.

Shoot, there's all kinds of reasons why we need bees!

DANIEL W. LAY:

ROOTERS, REDNECKS,

AND FIRE ANTS

Nacogdoches, TX

Born 1914

"I wouldn't call this type of person a redneck," says Dan Lay. "That is a *Louisiana* term for a thoughtless individual who doesn't consider the consequences of his action for other people."

In 1938 Dan Lay became Texas's first state-employed wildlife biologist, originally in the Game, Fish, and Oyster Commission, now called the Parks and Wildlife Department. During the last fifty years he has seen so many examples of thoughtless behavior toward wildlife that I am surprised he did not lose heart long ago. Yet he retains a measured optimism and the farsightedness of someone used to seeing today's environment as part of a long series of cycles.

I had expected to find ecologist Lay a spokesman for the ghosts of Texas's wolves, bears, buffalo, and other decimated species, but his focus is broader than wildlife conservation. In *Land of Bears and Honey* (1984) he takes the position that the disappearance of the East Texas pioneers is as indicative of ecological change as the fading away of the red-cockaded woodpecker. With Dan Lay the people environment and the animal and plant environment are part of the same whole.

That unity has been under severe assault in Texas throughout the twentieth century as rangeland has been overgrazed, soils eroded, water flows altered, and diverse natural ecosystems converted to monocultures.

Natural systems have lost their original richness with depletion in diversity and numbers. Many habitats and their species are threatened or endangered. Some are gone forever. Chemical contamination is everywhere. The coastal estuary suffers most of all.

Declining quality of life for people is the net result of even subtle imbalances. Dan Lay speaks of the long-term danger to native deer of introducing exotic game species, which may be as much of a biological time bomb as the African killer bees approaching from Mexico.

I asked him to tell me about a less exotic pest, the plain old piney woods rooter.

UNTIL THE 1950S HOGS WERE free-ranging, almost wild, going on everyone's land. If you didn't want hogs, you had to build your own fence to keep the other man's hogs off.

Acorns are their primary food. In the summertime the rooters go around grubbing up big fields looking for insects, grubs, worms, roots, whatever is edible. They can be very destructive.

In about 1900, there was a letter to the editor of the newspaper at Jasper from a Yankee who had just moved there. He said: "You do some strange things down here. You tolerate hogs. You make everybody build his own fence to keep the hogs out of his house and out of his garden. You build a fence to keep the hogs out of the courthouse. You let the hogs run free though they belong to a minority of the population. Their total value is less than twenty-five thousand dollars, I would guess, for this whole county, yet they have free run and everybody has to watch out for them."

That Yankee thought it was ridiculous that a small group of hogowners could exercise that much adverse impact on everybody else.

Some people love to hunt hogs. Russian boars are thought to be a little wilder but the regular old piney woods rooter can be awfully wild and difficult to hunt. They are wary. They feed at night. It's hard to approach them in the daytime.

Of course, until early in this century bears used to hunt the hogs, too. Naturally the hogowners exterminated the bears for eating their hogs.

The hogowners didn't realize that they themselves were endangered because the oaks were going to be thinned out to such an extent by the 1950s that there wouldn't be enough oak mast to fatten up the hogs. Forty years or so after the bears disappeared, the hogs disappeared because of the decline of the East Texas woodlands and because the hogs were a hazard on the highways.

Today the hogmen are as extinct as the bears.

Wild hogs, like zebras, nutrias, or fire ants, are an exotic species. One thing that I can recite almost directly from Dr. Walter B. Taylor is that exotics are a risk from an ecological standpoint. It is a mistake to bring exotics in, turn them lose, and hope that they will accomplish a certain objective without really knowing what you are doing because the exotic can become a pest. Witness the impact of the fire ant, English sparrow, starling, and water hyacinth.

I think it is better to recognize that native species have survived the tests of time. They have been here since the Ice Age. Ten thousand years of evolution has developed a gene pool that's specifically adapted to that local habitat. No smart management is going to improve on it.

You can take West Texas turkeys and move them to East Texas and they fail. It is a different subspecies because of the adaptation of that race out there to their dry climate, to the species of foods that occur out there. Those turkeys can't find cactus fruit here in East Texas to feed on.

From a long-term standpoint we don't know what we are doing

when we fool with introducing the exotics. They might do well for five, ten, or twenty years, but what about the long-term consequences?

From a commercial standpoint, certainly they have some advantages. They are not game animals under our game laws. So for a rancher it is just like having East Texas hogs out there. He can open his gate to a visiting hunter for a fee any time. That doesn't seem like much sport to me, but a lot of hunters go for it.

"Slob hunter" is a suitable name for some of them. I have always felt that I was working for him, the slob hunters, too, because their *grandchildren* may appreciate our wildlife. Certainly there are a lot of hunters who throw beer cans everywhere, shoot anything in sight, and do all kinds of reprehensible things. We have to hope they become more respectful of their resources and quit misusing them.

I was reared in Beaumont and went to the country at every opportunity. Boy Scouts kept me outdoors a good deal during my teens.

Years ago my hero was Ernest Thompson Seton. I have a full collection of his books right here. Another hero was [Luther] Burbank, the plant breeder. At the time of graduation from high school, I wanted to be a plant genetics scientist. I enrolled at the Texas Agricultural and Mechanical College at College Station for the basic first-year courses in agriculture.

This was during the Depression, fall of 1932. I had to work, as did most other students. The poultry department took me in with work and lodging, so I majored in poultry husbandry.

At graduation in 1936 there was a job waiting for me in agricultural advertising with a national company.

But then Dr. Walter B. Taylor arrived at A & M and I helped him to move into the poultry department's building. As I was helping to unload his gear, I started looking at his library and talking to him about it. That was the first I had known that it was possible to be a professional outdoorsman or wildlife specialist.

That was sure preferable to growing chickens!

Dr. Taylor accepted me as his first graduate student in the Cooperative Wildlife Research Unit. He influenced my interest in ecology more than anyone else. He had been trained at Berkeley,

University of California, as a mammalogist and had worked with the old Bureau of Biological Survey and then had come to Texas A & M as a leader of the Cooperative Wildlife Research Unit. He had just published a book on the mammals of Mount Rainier.

When I got my master's degree in 1938 I became the regional biologist for southeast Texas. During the Depression, there were hardly any game animals left in Texas. They had been used by the people that were hunting for food. In those days any farmer who saw a deer track in his pea patch would stop plowing and go get his neighbors. They would all get their hounds and chase the poor old deer until they caught it—wherever it was. When the Federal Aid and Wildlife Program started in 1938, that first survey showed the scarcity of the deer. One of our first development projects was to trap and redistribute deer.

The pioneer's attitude was that everything out there was for his use if it was worth his effort to take it. A bee tree could be cut down to get the honey out of it. If you found the tree first, nobody questioned it, no matter who owned the land.

Now there aren't many bees because there aren't many hollow trees and there are not many of the kind of flowers that the bees used to use.

We have a residuum of the attitude that trees are not worth much and that one can do what he wants out there in the woods. I manage a timberland for private owners. We have timber sales, and it is not uncommon for me to have great difficulty keeping the loggers from throwing their spent oil cans and filters out in the woods. They don't want to carry them back to town. They never have had to. Why should they start now?

One example happened before power saws replaced the cross-cut saw. A crew of two flatheads needed to sharpen their saw, so they topped a large dogwood at a convenient height, cut a notch in the stump to hold the blade, and proceeded to file the saw. They did not care that it was the only dogwood on the entrance road to my home.

Their ancestors always took what they wanted and used it any way they wanted to. There are too many people in the world now to continue acting like that.

It is a matter of education. Lots of people throw cans along the road because they saw their fathers throw cans out. I pick up beer cans off my lawn here most every day.

People still feel that they can do what they please if they can get away with it. They don't have a feeling of personal responsibility to other people.

The people with pioneering skills and background are disappearing rapidly. There are heirs of the early settlers still around, lots of them. But they are more and more sophisticated, and educated, and oriented toward the cities. They are losing their ties to the land.

There is no question that the habitat for pioneers is just as fragile as the habitat for most wildlife species.

But the inclination remains for people in East Texas to do the things that pioneers did even though those opportunities don't remain. When an early pioneer decided he wanted to build a new fence, he could cross boundaries wherever he wanted to to find the tree that would make some good fenceposts. He could search out the trees like mulberry and chinquapin which would resist rot and be good fenceposts and help himself. Now that is not only illegal but also the mulberry and the chinquapin aren't there. Mulberry is very palatable to cattle. It hasn't reproduced because the cattle are holding the seedlings down. The chinquapin was finished off by a blight.

So now if that pioneer were still around, he would have to go buy a treated pine post instead of going to the woods and getting something superior with his own hands. He couldn't operate like his ancestors did.

What can Texans do today? Habitat is the key. Here in East Texas support is building for managing and conserving hardwoods because they are the key to habitat quality for most game and nongame wildlife. There are lots of different ways that people can get involved to work toward the goal of more hardwoods. They can plant hardwoods themselves. They can go to hearings when the Forest Service is considering long-range plans. They can work toward public land acquisition and work for its proper management.

To rebuild the land requires three things—the knowledge, the means, and the will.

We have the knowledge. We know how to take what's left and build a field of corn, a wood, many kinds of birds or none. A herd of deer and a thicket of quail are pages in recorded science.

The means are there. We live in a time when the signing of a name causes countrysides of hardwoods to fall and columned pines to march in. Forests yield in a year to pastures and palaces. We have the means to endless directions.

But where is the will? The desire to bring back the many kinds of trees and birds, the bears, the April sound of turkeys in the woods? Can we find the will to build the land our grandparents knew?

Or can we find the self-discipline to make the most of what remains, to balance the inevitable decline of resources and rising numbers of people?

This success or failure will have a direct impact on all Texans.

How do you get them to think ecologically?

JOHN HENRY FAULK:

PINEY WOODS KINFOLK

Austin, TX

Born 1913

John Henry Faulk was a Texas television personality and racon-teur. During the 1930s he learned the value of collecting folk songs from pioneer collector John A. Lomax and his son Alan Lomax (one of John Henry's best friends). Then he fell under the spell of J. Frank Dobie and, like Dobie, searched with a voice recorder for the essence of the Lone Star mystique.

In the following tale about his early days as a folklore collector John Henry Faulk told one on some of his piney woods kinfolk (whose names were changed to protect his Austin hide).

NOW THIS IS AN EAST Texas piney woods story. A lot of my kinfolk come from down there in the piney woods. And they're the finest people on the face o' the earth. And they'll kill ya damn quick. [Laughter] They'll cut your throat. But they won't steal from ya . . . while yer watchin'!

No, they are good people.

I went to see Aunt Edith when I was a little boy. I used to go down there and we'd run hawgs with dawgs. That was when they didn't have any hog laws, didn't have any fences down there. And everybody'd turn their stock together in the piney woods. All you had to do was earmark your stock.

Uncle Rip would let me ride a mule because a mule was safe to ride. It wouldn't stumble and fall, runnin' through the brush when the dawgs git after hawgs 'n run em.

Well, Aunt Edith, I adored her. She was a huge woman and I hadn't seen her in years. I had gone to the university and had started collecting folklore back in 1940. Them was just stories back then, not folklore. It was just yarns people. . . . Like Brother Patterson's stories or ole Bill Brett's stories. They was just things that happened in the community. [Laughter]

At any rate I went to see Aunt Edith and I said, "Bless you heart, Aunt Edith, it's sure *good* to see *you.* I haven't seen you in so *long!*"

Well, Aunt Edith was always kind of *jealous* of our *family* that lived up there in *Austin.* Because we were the educated end of the family. Daddy sent all us children to the university and Aunt Edith kinda resented it. But she didn't resent it nearly as much as the fact that Momma *named her three daughters* Mary, Martha, and Texana and didn't give em no second names.

She said, "You know, that's just the high-toniest show-offiest thing I ever seen, not give a child two names. That's just same as handicappin' em." [Laughter]

Well, at any rate, her oldest son was named Toots. And he had lived with us. Daddy had sent him to high school up thar. And I hadn't been down to see Aunt Edith in about fifteen years. Now I'm an instructor at the University; I'm a collector of folklore; and I gave myself airs. And I had this recording machine with me.

And Aunt Edith was sittin' there on her porch swing. And I said, "*Aunt Edith,* what's happened to Toots?"

She said, "I know why you askin' that. You Momma asked you to ask that, didn't she? You all always said something bad was gonna happen to Toots. Always said he's gonna turn out bad. Well, he didn't. I'm so *proud* of 'im, I can't see straight!"

And I said, "Well, Honey, no, I just asked because I wanted to know what happened to 'im."

Aunt Edith said, "Ya know, Toots was the *sweetest little ole thang.* He was my first baby. And when he was three years old, well, little old Willy was born. He's the cutest thang and we had more fun out of Toots. We'd say, 'We don't need you no more, Toots; we got another baby now. We'll throw you to the hawgs if you don't behave.' And oh, it'd make him so mad. He'd pout and sometimes he'd turn black in the face and hold his breath and that sort of thing. I'd whup it out of 'im. [Laughter]

"But," Aunt Edith said, "and everybody said, 'Well, he's gonna turn out bad cause he's got that high temper.' Cause Toots was always trying to git at little old Willy to get little Willy mad."

Aunt Edith thinking back: "And one afternoon, Willy's about sixteen months old and he a-layin' there on a pallet, and I was ironing and Toots got at 'im. Got 'im with a pine knot. Like to takin' his left ear off with it. And it's bleeding bad. And I said, 'Well now, Toots, you've gone *too fur.* You're always trying to get at Willy. And ya just done *too much!* I'm gonna tell ya Daddy on ya.'

"And when Rip come home, I told Rip about it. I said, 'He jes like to knock his brains out.'

"And Rip said, 'Toots, we gonna cure ya of it! Ya ain't gonna do that again.' And then he said, 'We got to take you out there and lock you up in that corn crib and let them ole gray rats eat ya tonight.' [Aunt Edith shouting] Oh, it made Toots so mad. He just squalled and screamed.

"But we locked him up out there. [Laughter]

"And way after dark I say, 'Ya know, Rip, we ain't gonna git no sleep tonight. I can hear that child squalling and he's butting his head agin the wall. He's skeered to death of rats and skeered to death of dark.'

"And so Rip went out and give 'im a good rawhiding and then brought him in the house. And, ha, ha, ha, and ya know, Toots showed off after that. He jerked, ya know. Like this [Demonstration]. His eyes was kinda. . . . Jerked like that.

"But he was the cutest little ole thang and everybody said, 'Well, he's going to turn out *bad!'*

"But little old Toots, let me tell ya something. He went to the Magnolia School and the boys didn't have no toilets in them days. The boys went to the bushes and the girls were the only ones that had a toilet at that Magnolia School.

"And little old Toots was a-going at recess time out there and them old big boys, them two oldest Grogan boys and that ole Simpson boy would jump onto 'im and back him up agin the wall and slap his little jaws and his ears would ring.

"And he'd come home at night just squallin'. And we'd say 'Whatsamatter Sugar?'

"And he'd say them big ole boys had jumped on 'im and slapped his jaws so his ear rung.

"And so Rip got out his 'Dallas Special.' I don't know whether ya ever seen a Dallas Special. It's got a button at the end of it and you throw a blade about that fer. It's about a six-inch blade it'll throw. And Rip always kept it awful sharp so he could skin varmints with it. And so he give it to little old Toots and he said, 'Now Sugar, I want ya to hold it.' [Laughter] He showed him just how to hold it so it wouldn't close on his little fingers, ya know, and cut them. He said, 'Them ole boys jump ya [Shouting], I want ya to cut 'em and cut 'em good and deep—tomorrow!'

"Sure nuf, next day at recess time, Toots started for the bushes. He always had a big-leak bladder. Don't never [Spoken softly] tell 'im that I said this, but, ya know, Toots wet the bed till he was almost twenty-two.

[Shouting] "At any rate he was a-headin' fer the bushes and them two oldest Grogan boys and that ole Jackson boy backed 'im up agin the wall and started slapping his little jaws and his little ears start ringing.

"Toots didn't do a thing in the world but run his little ole hand down those overall pockets and bring out that knife, throw 'at blade, and he started to slice 'em. [Yelling] Oh, he was slicing 'em good. He surprised 'em!

"And he cut that oldest Grogan boy plumb to the holler. If they hadn't laid him on his back, his entrails woulda dropped out just like a hawg at hawg-killin' time. Boy, he got that old . . .

"The funny thing is, he got his own cousin, that ole Jackson boy, a good 'un right across the arm. Right there at the elbow. Like to took it off as a matter of fact.[Laughing]

"That was thirty-seven years ago and you go down to that Sinclair station—he's a-runnin' it—and he ain't closed that left hand yet. The fingers just stand out like that. [Showing hand]

"And everybody said, 'Well, Toots is gonna turn out bad.' But he's the proudest little ole thang. He didn't want me to wash the blood out of them overalls, ya know, he was so proud of it.

"Folks was always telling me that Toots was going to turn out bad. 'He's got that high temper,' they'd say.

"He tore all the pages out of a song book down at the churchhouse. And my sister May called me and said, 'He shouldn't be a-stuffin' them under the churchhouse and settin' fire to it because it looks suspicious.'

"At any rate, Toots turned out good! Oh, I hope ya tell yer momma this, too. He's up there in Arkansas. He's constable. He's the law up thar.

"But that ain't his big claim to fame. Toots has proved everybody wrong. He's a success. He's head of the whole Ku Klux Klan up in that section!

"And he's one of the sweetest people that walk the earth today and I'm very proud of 'im."

WYATT MOORE: POACHER, MOONSHINER, AND THE *TUSH HOG*

Karnak, TX

Born 1901

In 1860 the riverport boomtown of Jefferson was second in Texas only to Galveston in cotton exports, but by the late 1870s steamboat traffic on Caddo Lake had dwindled away and the calls of frogs had replaced the whistles of the palatial steamboats.

Young Wyatt Moore grew up to tales of the glories of the steamboat era. He knew the locations of the old wrecks and knew men who had sailed on the great flat-bottomed, sternwheeled two-hundred-footers. Everyday names still spoke of that colorful time. Whangdoodle Pass. Devil's Elbow. Jeem's Bayou.

The poststeamboat era was much more self-sufficient. Many families fell back on hunting and fishing. Hogs roamed the forests like cattle on an open range. The air teemed with wild fowl. And in the many creeks, bayous, and lakes there was an "inexhaustible" resource of fish.

It was a time when the newfangled fish and game regulations were slow to be accepted by a populace accustomed to exercising its "Indian rights" to unrestricted fishing and hunting. It was a place where county and state borders were abstract labels for vast hinterlands of cypress, alligator, and water moccasin.

It was also home for a hardy brand of Texas individualist. One sunny afternoon we stood by a dappled slough watching an avenue of cypresses recede into the watery distance. Wyatt said, "You can't see no farther than right yonder, can you? Now when I look through there I can see to New Orleans. I can envision all the land from here to Shreveport." He said that until recently Caddo Lake had been the only sho-nuff lake between far East Texas and El Paso because the Dallas, San Angelo, Rayburn, Lake of the Pines, Toledo Bend, and Texhoma lakes had not yet been built.

A visit to Wyatt Moore's outbuildings is sure to turn up a fascinating trove of net-knitting tools, fishhooks, and Caddo Lake souvenirs. "Here's a six-volt sireen I had on the *Tush Hog.* It'll still blow." During a visit to the lake he will draw your attention to the wind in the treetops and tell of the time in 1924 when the boat he was in with his uncle capsized and his uncle drowned. Most of all you will hear about Wyatt's hero, Frank Galbraith, Sr. (1880–1961). "I had great admiration for him," Wyatt says in that serious, unexpected tone he reserves only for memories of copper coils and memorable perch.

Today Wyatt doubts if he could "find enough fish to amount to anything." As I heard the tales, I could only marvel that the destruction of this resource had happened so quickly and so inexorably.

"Well, yes, I destroyed a good many fish," Wyatt says happily. "Back then we never went hungry."

"But nowadays I would because there's two game wardens to one me. [Laughter] There used to be a bunch of us to one game warden."

MISSISSIPPI IS THE OFFICIALLY RECOGNIZED redneck area, but the term *redneck* could apply to any people anywhere who are a little arrogant and hard to regiment and who don't take laws too seriously.

The term *redneck* in Mississippi denotes a person of independent character. The people of Mississippi are not all rednecks but the designation means a man who don't look up to nobody. He sorta feels like he can make it by hisself.

When we were growing up here in East Texas we didn't realize how free we were. But we were living in a sort of a no-man's land right in here, between the Red River and the Sabine River, a distance of forty or fifty miles. We grew up in an environment where we didn't believe in people telling other people what to do or what not to do. A lot of that early unregimented feeling rubbed off and it still kind of sticks to some of us older ones.*

And, unfortunately for the game wardens and revenuers, Caddo Lake lays in two counties in two states and in part of a Louisiana parish. Caddo's so big Texas wouldn't hold it all!

So we always had our outlaw fishing and moonshining camps right around the Louisiana–Texas line. And if it got too hot in one state, you could move over. When the grand jury was meetin' in Harrison County we'd go over and spend a few days with friends of ours in Marion County, where they couldn't subpoena us.

The day was when most farmers would keep themselves a little bateau. Back in the late teens people here on the lake didn't have motors. We pulled a boat with oars. Outboard motors wasn't much in vogue until about 1920. (I had already been fishin' then about four or five years with my uncle.) And we'd pull boats with oars unreasonable distances with big loads in wind.

We fished nets on Big Lake and then later on when the Volstead Act come along these little one-man canoes would haul a pretty good load. And you could maneuver them in among places where

---

*Northeast Texas's border country had been developing a subculture of violence and outlawry well before Texan independence. As early as 1806 the area was known as the Neutral Ground (or Texas Badlands), a home for renegades, outlaws, and runaway slaves. The long tradition of Northeast Texas rebelliousness festered during the Regulator/Moderator wars of the 1840s and in the bloody upheavals of the Civil War and Reconstruction.

a big boat couldn't go. They were very popular to make whiskey with; that's what I done for about a good many years.

The pirogue of Louisiana is usually just open from one end to the other. But our bateau here was fourteen or sixteen foot long and about two foot wide and it had two compartments. It had a minnow well right behind the seat and a four-foot-long live box with a lattice cover over it so the bass wouldn't jump out. Of course, the bateau was used to squirrel-hunt along the bank and to bushwhack ducks and to frog-hunt at night. I builded a lot of 'em and I nearly always kept me one. To the natives of this area that bateau was about like a horse was to a cowboy in West Texas.

Farmers, natives, fishermen, people that lived on the lake would seine minnows at night, keep 'em in this minnow well overnight, and fish the next day with a hook and line. Fish almost all day. Then they kept their catch at their camp or farm in a lattice fish box about four foot big till Friday, when they'd sell 'em and get a little money for groceries and so forth. Of course, the main purpose of catchin' 'em in them days was to sell 'em or eat 'em. No refrigeration back in the heyday of fishin here, and you had to keep your fish alive. If you killed one—say he hooked himself in the gills—you'd dress him and cook him and eat him before he needed refrigeration.

Mrs. Lyndon Johnson's father, old man T. J. Taylor, sold general merchandise and he furnished people supplies to raise cotton and corn and he maintained a gin or two. And charged high prices, but he kept a lotta people from gettin' in worse than they would have been if it hadn't been for him. And if somebody made a good crop, he'd try to get 'em ta spend most of the money with him. And a lot of 'em couldn't pay him and he was really kind of a Socialist but didn't term himself such. But he believed that if people had a good crop year and got kinda paid up, then he'd maybe help carry 'em through lean years. And no tellin' how much he had owed on his books, but overall he acquired about thirty thousand acres of land.

I was eight or ten years older than Lady Bird and at that age eight or ten years means a whole lot. I used to go campin' and all with her older brothers who were the same age as me.

Friday was Fish Day. Her old man, T. J. Taylor, would buy the fish then and you'd get you a few dollars.

From around the mid-teens to '24 or '25, about ten or twelve years, I fished commercially constantly on the lake. That was the best period of my life. Old man T. J. Taylor would order us a five-foot-around-at-the-front and eighteen-foot-long, double-throated hoop net from the Lennon Thread Company in Chicago and we'd catch thousands of pounds.

One time old man Taylor shipped fifty-two hundred pounds of white perch, what they called croppies, in one day. That was an unusual catch, but for years there was several thousand pounds of fish a week come out of this lake. And was shipped to Dallas and points north and west of here.

The bateau was multipurpose. Going to your still out on the lake, you'd appear to be hunting or fishing. Why, if somebody was there waiting for ya (which ain't never happened to me), you would just be a fella that just come along and not the owner of the rig. But if you went out there with sugar and chops and likker-makin' material in your boat, you'd look like the one they were huntin' for.

Back in the teens and twenties and even up into the thirties, there was quite a boatbuilder here from Missouri. Frank Galbraith would order twenty-six-foot-long, twenty-inch-wide red-heart cypress planks from down in Plaqamines, Louisiana. And go in the woods and cut him a stem out of a mulberry tree to build an inboard motorboat out of. And after building the stem he would flare the stem more at the top and give it a little slight twist down to the bottom and would make a most marvelous-looking boat.

He could look ahead and envision what he was going to do. He would never start a boat until he had the measurements of the motor. And he would lay all that out in his mind. He told me that he would lay awake at night in his bed and figure out every inch of that boat before he started it. The *Tush Hog* was one of the inboards that he builded.

Tush hog means bull of the woods. The big shot. The tush hog was a big boar hog that got to where he was boss of all the other hogs in the woods. A man who was a kind of a tough, happy-go-lucky fella and most people were afraid of him, they called him a tush hog. Well, I never did call myself a tush hog. I just called my boat *Tush Hog*.

In 1917 or eighteen when I was down in Louisiana working in the oil fields Frank Galbraith was just beginning to build those boats. His method was to put the boards on the front and lay 'em completely down at the back. And he would put guards on 'em to prevent the stumps in Caddo Lake from bending the propeller.

When I was just a boy he would take a little time and talk to me where other people would ignore me. And when the people out of Shreveport would launch one of his new boats (people with money like the Ford dealer) and they would watch that new boat run all day Sunday, I would think to myself, some day I'm gonna have me one a them boats. And I've finally now had four of 'em and have run 'em a many a mile!

Caddo has had casting and minnow-fishing and worm-fishing. And there was a time when we fished gill nets, hook nets, trammel nets, and wire nets. But fishing on Caddo Lake is not near as good as on a lot of these new lakes. Caddo has been held at a constant level and does not produce fish like a lake that overflows where a river flows through it or where it has access to rivers below it and above it. A landlocked lake'll just kinda play out.

There used to be lots of buffalo, we called 'em here, or carp. They usually run from three to seven or eight pounds. And sometimes you'd get a fifteen- or twenty-pounder. And we'd trammel-net at night and catch up to three or four hundred pounds.

When Mr. Taylor used to order 'em from us to ship to Dallas, there were two passenger trains here—one going north and one going south. And sometimes in the spring he'd have several thousand pounds of fish to ship each week to Dallas, Grangeville, all places north of here. The train would be here in Karnak an hour sometimes, loading fish. They'd pack 'em in ice.

Usually Friday was the big fish day. Sometimes in the spring, if we were catching a lot of white perch with hook nets, we'd also deliver 'em on Tuesday.

This fishing went on from about the turn of the century on up until by about 1925 they had pretty well outlawed the sale of game fish or white perch and bass. But you could still sell catfish, buffalo, carp, spoonbill, grinnel, jackfish, and roughfish.

And there was a lot of illegal bootlegging of white perch. People would still buy 'em. As late as in the thirties I even hauled two or three hundred pounds in a T-model to a Dallas hotel that was gonna have a big party.

What do I like about a wooden boat? Well, I can *build* a wooden boat. I've built all kinds of looks and shapes and forms of wooden boats. I've never built one of them big inboards but I've rebuilded some to a considerable degree.

Well, it don't rattle when you move around in it. You can be quieter while you're dodging the game warden, I guess, if you want to pin me down. You can slink along in it easier. I can row that boat with them oars and you cannot hear a sound. And it's almost impossible to piddle around in a metal boat without. . . .

I guess I spent the best times of my life out in these wooden boats.

I want to find a young fella who will get the *Tush Hog* back into shape and out on the lake again.

There's good wood in 'er yet!

MARTIN "BUSTER" LEHNIS:

"THAT FIREBOX WAS

JUST A-DANCIN'"

Early, TX

Born 1915

A good place to get a dose of railroad nostalgia is Buster Lehnis's front yard. You won't be able to miss it as you pass through what remains of Early, Texas, in Brown County. Just stop at the place with the collection of old-timey rolling stock, a testament to Texas's railroading traditions. The state is still America's leader in railroad-line mileage and was the home, at least on paper, of more than seven hundred railroad companies, including such famous roads as the Houston East & West Texas (Hell Either Way You Take It) and the Atchison, Topeka & Santa Fe (All Tramps Sent Free). The Missouri–Kansas–Texas (the Katy) first arrived in the state in 1872 in a race for the right to build across the Indian Territory. The Katy won and its growth, often along old cattle trails, was accompanied by the Old West drama of immigrant settlement, Indian raids, and armed hold-ups.

Buster took me into his genuine railroad depot (salvaged from Kress, Texas), propped his feet up on the rolltop desk and began to explain how railroading became his "family" after most of his East Texas relatives died in the flu epidemic of 1918. He was "adrift" until an Abilene railroader named Sam Wyatt adopted him.

Buster Lehnis
leaning on the
back railing of
his private
railway car.

IN 1918, 1919, 1920 WE had a big flu epidemic. People were dying in East Texas in those swamps. They were just a-dyin' like flies. There at Romayor, they didn't have no funeral parlor or nuthin'. If somebody died, they laid them out on the dining table on a white sheet and they give them a bath and cleaned them up. Then they rolled them up in a white sheet and put them in a pine box, buried them. That's the way my mother and, I guess, my dad. . . .

Anyway, they were dying down there thick. I had a double cousin and he never did take the flu. He was nine years older than me. His name was Silas Matthew Lehnis, but everybody called him Tie because he used to wear overalls and a necktie.

Well, ole Tie would take one them dugout boats. . . . Did you ever see one of them? Tie took a cypress tree, cut it down, dug it out, and made a canoe out of it. Tie was an expert at manhandling one of them dugouts.

There was a nurse that came up there into them woods and she was going around tending to people and old Tie would take her across that Trinity River when it was running bank-full. That was a treacherous river and he would take her across that river and he would steal her asafetida, steal some of it. Used to everybody wore a string around their neck with a ball of asafetida on the front. When they wasn't talking or something, they would put that ball of asafetida in their mouth. That kept the evil spirits away and deterred the flu bug.

Tie was nine years older than me. He was born in 1906. His mother and my mother was sisters, and our fathers were brothers. His mother died before my mother did. But his father died a long time after my father died. His daddy was farmin' down the river from where the ferryboat was, and in nineteen and thirty I went down the river to where my uncle was, and all that bottom was full of water.* I got down there a little ways and my cousin was comin' to town to meet me. I had wrote them and told them when I would be there. He was coming to meet me by horseback. I had done got across the river over there before I met him. So I got up behind him on the horse and had my suitcase with me. We went back down that road and his old horse was a-wading, water half-knee-deep all the way.

I got down there and the uncle and the kids was gathering corn in a boat. They were poling a boat right down between two rows of corn because that river had been out of bounds and flooded that bottom. That corn, he had a real good crop of corn, but the bottom crop was ruined. But it suckered out and made a top crop. They were gatherin' that top-crop corn to make cornmeal and fatten hogs with. My cousin Tie was a Prohibitionist, a strong teetotaler that didn't drink corn liquor and didn't approve of anybody else drinking it. He used his corn to make cornbread and feed hogs with. If he had a good crop of corn, he had his bread and meat. That was one thing they always counted on, a good crop of corn. He could fatten his hogs on that corn and make cornmeal out of it. If you had cornbread and bacon, you had your own lard out of them hogs.

After my parents died, I left that East Texas life and became a railroader thanks to Sam Wyatt that adopted me and thanks to a roundhouse foreman named Fred Scott. Sam Wyatt took me to Abilene when I was seven years old. He was a bridge-gang foreman for the Abilene & Southern Railroad and lived in a company house right beside the railroad tracks. The roundhouse next door had a great big sign on the door, KEEP OUT, but the roundhouse foreman, Fred Scott, him and his wife didn't have any children, and he was a fine fella. I kept hanging out at the roundhouse until finally the

---

*In May 1990 Trinity River floodwaters rose to record levels.

Abilene & Southern got a brand-new locomotive, Number Eighteen, in 1922, and she was a coal-burner. They put her in the roundhouse in the back shop, where they made the big repairs. I was fascinated by that new engine and I peeped in and asked Mr. Scott what he was going to do with it in the back shop. He said, "Well, it's a coal-burner and we done changed it over to an oil-burner but they are making a tank to go in the tender for the fuel."

It stayed in there about a month until one afternoon when I came back from school I heard an engine down at the roundhouse chuggin'. I made a run down there to see what was going on. They had that new Number Eighteen fired up and running it back and forth, up and down the main line. Boy, I was really proud! The roundhouse foreman was a-runnin' it and the boilermaker was a-firin' the engine; the machinist was doing this, that, and the other; two or three laborers were on there; everybody was on it. They stopped right on Eighth Street. Eighth Street was the street that crossed the railroad tracks right in front of our house. Just as soon as you crossed the railroad you turned into our driveway. Anyhow, they run it up to Eighth Street and stopped. I run out there on Eighth Street and I said, "Mr. Scott, can I get on it?" He said, "Yeah, come on up here, Buster." I said, "Can I blow the whistle?" We were backin' down towards a street crossing. Fred Scott said, "Yep, go ahead and blow it."

Man, I had to jump up beside of him to get ahold of that whistle, but I blowed a long lonesome whistle. I think I blowed Number Eighteen's whistle the first time that it was ever blowed on the Abilene & Southern!

When I was twelve, I was always in and out of that roundhouse. I was a very privileged character!

About five or six blocks up the street from our house, I was in Miss Berry's homeroom at Locust School. The sweetest woman I ever seen. The principal was Miss Christopher. Miss Christopher was a mean ole woman. She wore those pinched glasses down on her nose and boy, when she looked at you, you just kind of dehydrated.

All the time them teachers are tryin' to get me to play football. I ain't got time to play football, because when school is out I haul my little behind right down the street to my house and go out the back door to the roundhouse to help the night watchman work on the engines.

We called him the night watchman, but actually what he was was the hostler, the man that gets the engines out and gets them ready to go. When an engine comes in off the road, they bring it in and park it. From then on the hostler handles it. He takes it to the fuel rack, to the coal bin, to the sand bin, turns it around, or puts it in the house. Abilene & Southern's hostler and night watchman was a combined job, a fella by the name of Jack Miller. Jack was a real good buddy of mine. His wife's name was Elsie. She was a Baack. They were German people and they came over before World War I. They were our neighbors. We loved them people. They was gooooood people.

Jack cussed; he had been in the Navy in World War I on a minesweeper. And he was a muscle-bound fella. When he used to close his hand into a fist, there was a muscle right in here that popped up just like that. He had more grip in his hand than anybody I ever seen. Jack Miller was so muscle-bound that he could pick up a two-by-twelve. . . . I seen him do it one night when we had an engine derailed up there, he picked up a dadgummed two-by-twelve and whacked it across the rail and broke it in two when they were cribbin' up on that engine to get it back on the rail. That will shake the hell out of your hands but he picked up that two-by-twelve, whacked her across that rail, and stuck her in under that wheel. I thought, "Well, old Jack's got more than I'll ever have."

Anyhow, I loved to go down there and help Jack Miller. Those pins, he had to put that pin to open them side rods on the bearings on the wheels. You got to screw that thing out and put a piece of pinned oak. Pinned oak was round, I guess a three-quarter-inch diameter, and you cut it off in about a two-inch piece. You put it in that hole and then you screw that plug down there on it and push that in. Then you screw the plug back out and put another piece in and screw that down. You got to do that about four or five times on each bearing.

Jack Miller was a brother to the roundhouse foreman's wife, Fred Stock's wife. Everything on the Abilene & Southern was kin-folks. If you wasn't kin to somebody, you didn't get the work.

Unless you wanted to dig. If you were a section hand or something like that, you didn't have to be kin. If you got to be a foreman or anything else, you had to be kin to somebody.

Anyway, I loved Jack Miller. He carried me to the circus one time. The circus moved in on the Abilene & Southern. Boy, they unloaded that circus there on Eighth Street and took it out to the fairground. Then they took all them cars and stored them. Then they come back and loaded that circus out about midnight one night. Them elephants left tracks about an inch and a half to two inches deep in the middle of our street!

When I was twelve years old, Jack Miller would let me throw the yard switches for him but he wouldn't let me run the engine. I kept on asking him all the time "Let me run the engine."

He said, "No, you go down and throw the switch for me and we'll fuel her up."

Well, I would go down and I would throw the switch and he would come down through the switch. Then I would line the switch the other way and I would give him a signal to come back on another track. I would hang on the back end and we would back around to put fuel oil in the tender.

Anyhow, one evening we were messin' with Eighteen and we were going to fire up Seventeen. She had been in the shop. I said "Let me fire it up and you breed 'em."

You understand what breeding is? You mate a bull to a cow; that's breeding. Well, you breed a live-steam locomotive to a dead-steam locomotive. She is sitting here and she is cold and you hook a line up from the live engine to the dead engine and that gives you the steam for your blower and your atomizer. Your atomizer is what sprays your fuel and the blower is what gives you a draft on the stack.

Anyhow, we were goin' to fire up the Seventeen and I said "Let me do it."

He said, "Ah, get out of the way. Goddamned, you don't know nuthin' about this."

I said, "Jack, I can fire this engine up."

He said, "O.K., you smart-aleck son-of-a-bitch. If you think you can fire it up, you get right in there and hep yourself."

So he gets back out of the way.

Well, I got me a handful of waste, this stringy, shredded cotton. It's oily. I took a piece of that waste, stuck a match to it, and set it afire.

Jack says, "All right, you little son-of-a-bitch, if you think you can fire it up, you go ahead."

I said, "O.K., Jack, get out of the way."

Old Seventeen, she was a muzzle-loader when she was a coal-burner. The firebox came way back in the cab. In fact, when that engine was on the road and the engineer was settin' on his seat and the fireman was settin' on his seat, they couldn't see each other because the boiler come so far back into the cab. Seventeen had been a Missouri–Pacific engine and then she went to the Katy and then the Abilene & Southern got her. She came there a coal-burner and they converted her to oil on the Abilene & Southern. Anyhow, I was putting my waste down in there and I turned the oil on and got it to dribblin'. Then I turned the atomizer on and got that oil to sprinklin' and scatterin'. I turned the boiler on just a little bit and got a little draft on it and I just kept givin' her more oil, and directly I had that ole hen just sittin' there um um um um.

That firebox was just a-dancin'.

When I got a full head of steam on her, then we disconnected the pipes, we unbred her.

I was just twelve years old.

I worked on the Santa Fe off and on for forty-nine years and Jack Miller, that night watchman, was always my hero.

ARDATH MAYHAR:
PINEY WOODS FEUDS
Chireno, TX
Born 1930

In Ardath Mayhar's science-fiction world of East Texas, remote Chireno becomes the piney woods town of Skillet Bend. A nuclear war has devastated America's cities but has left Skillet Bend unscathed except for a sudden total lack of electricity, gasoline, and supplies. In other words, the Bomb has pushed Ardath Mayhar's woodlots, dirt roads, and Attoyac Bayou bottoms back into the nineteenth century. Back to saddle and ride, hew and carry, grow and can, and aim and shoot.

Of course, author Mayhar has scarcely ever left that world anyway. One evening I shared it with her and her husband and son on the porch of their spaceshiplike house. Night noises seethed from the lush pastures and forests. Stars gleamed overhead and the country's springtime freshness was intoxicating.

Mayhar East Texas, however, is more gothic than bucolic. It is Southern in its feuds and violence. *The World Ends in Hickory Hollow* is a classic good-guys-versus-bad-guys tale. The bad guys are a river-bottom clan of redneck harpies, the Ungers.

That damn Cheri's with 'em, too. Don't ever forget that. She knows our defenses. She knows the way we go about doing things. She was smart, that one, no matter how side-slung her mind was. If she's gone off to them Ungers, she's got some kind of plan for getting back at us. The only reason they ain't wiped us out, before now, is that they didn't have no brains. Now they got one. Don't forget that.

Ardath is no outside critic of the East Texas redneck. Her family has been rooted in the region since before the Texas Revolution, when her maternal great-great-grandfather received a very large Shelby County land grant from the Spanish. She herself worked ten years until the age of twenty-seven as co-manager of her father's dairy farm, doing the work of three or four men. "I had just about pulled my skeleton apart," she says, "when I finally quit to open a bookstore in Nacogdoches."

There she met her husband, a book-lover, jack-of-all-trades, and service station operator. She has since become a prolific writer of poetry, short stories, novels, and science fiction.

The Mayhar house outside Chireno is as crammed with books as the The View from Orbit bookstore in Nacogdoches. Despite its futuristic shape, the house has few modern conveniences. Just books. That reflects the priorities of a young farm girl who passionately wanted to learn but whose circumstances ruled out a college education.

Out on that spaceship porch, with the lightning bugs flickering over the dark fields, cows lowing in the distance, and good conversation flowing like drops from a still, I got the eerie feeling that East Texas fact was stranger than fiction.

For example, consider the matter of fences.

THE OLD GENTLEMAN FROM WHOM we had bought the place drove up while my husband was building fence and pulled a fencepost out of the back of the pick-up and threatened to beat him up with it for presuming to build a fence without paying him something.

Naturally my husband was on our property so he came back to the house and called the sheriff and said, "I'm having problems with my neighbor. He doesn't want me to build my fence. I am about to put the guns in the pick-up and go back down and build my fence." And the sheriff (who had been a friend of ours for years) said, "Just be very careful." And my husband was.

And when our pick-up appeared with our guns in it, no more static arose.

There is a law in Texas that if there is a disputed fence line, both sides must drop back four feet from the fence line. This was not a disputed fence line. The place had been surveyed for our purchase. So we dropped in one foot on our side and built fence all the way around. The neighbors dropped back four feet, thinking that it came under that provision of the law.

So now we have a beautiful double fence with a neat, stickery hedgerow full of rabbits and quails and all sorts of things. And the entire neighborhood has had a nice snicker out of the whole situation.

It was so typical of the rednecks down here who've been reared not realizing that the rest of the world was there at all. These neighbors had been here long enough, having everything their own way, that they just didn't realize that they had to take the law and other people's rights into consideration.

Fence lines and livestock that gets out and into people's gardens are the things that really make for bloodshed.

You have people anywhere who get drunk and fight and shoot or knife each other. But I think that fence-line disputes that go to the ultimate are probably a typically Southern thing. Southern Scotch-Irishmen have a passionate attachment to their land. And you don't take one inch of their land without a fight. [Laughter]

I have been ready a couple of times to kill somebody. Once in defense of my family and once because a man said he was going to come on our property and take something we were sure was not his. I was sitting in the door of the house with a gun in my lap and another one lying inside, waiting to shoot him when he came. Unfortunately I didn't get to! And he was really one of these people who should have been shot pro bono publico.

You have to be willing to shoot somebody in defense of your property and your family. If you're willing to, ordinarily you won't have to. If you're bluffing, you're probably going to get flattened. Because people know a bluff. It's a gut instinct. But if you are earnestly willing and ready. . . .

It was like this big fat character that I was so longing to shoot that time when he was going to come on the place whether we liked it or not. I was sitting on the step. And I think vibrations—"Oh, I would love to shoot you"—were going from me to him. He was a Neo-Nazi scumbag who was as crooked as two barrels of snakes but he didn't set foot on the place till Papa said he could. Not one instant sooner.

It's a willingness. As Shakespeare said, "The willingness is all."

Your general run of East Texas river rat does not respect education. He thinks people who have a lot of education must have something intrinsically wrong with them.

They don't want their children to be well-educated. The school is just to keep the children out of their hair for six hours a day.

But your average redneck makes a wonderful soldier. Very independent and hard-headed. He won't take orders blindly. But you put him in a situation in which the principles are clear-cut, he's one of the bravest people you will ever find. Audie Murphy was a good example of the breed.

In 1942 my father bought a farm which had been worn out with cotton. Cotton severely depletes the nutrients in the soil. Corn had been planted there, but it had never gotten over two or three feet high in years. Or made more than a few little stubby ears to the stalk.

But in 1942 when we moved there, the Soil Conservation Service was giving farmers not only instructions in how to build up their soil but also giving them fertilizer and seed for land-building plants, hairy vetch and singletary peas.

They gave my father the cover crops and the fertilizer. He planted his cover crop and fertilized it well. He let it grow until he had hip-high, beautiful dark-green foliage. He went in there about

January with his team of mules and his breaking plow and he turned all that greenery under and let it rot. Then in the middle of February he planted his corn.

All of the white neighbors had just been laughing at this town fella who thought he was going to grow corn on that piece of ground. My father was from Mississippi. He was from a small town, not from a farm. His grandfather had had a farm where he'd spent the summer and he loved it and he always wanted to be a farmer.

Down here in Chireno, if you're from Nacogdoches, you're a city person. [Laughter] The difference between three hundred and thirty thousand is considerable.

And when that corn came up, it grew and it didn't stop growing until it was about eight feet tall and had three and four big, fat ears to the stalk.

And these old geezers would drive by staring at that corn. Not one of the white farmers asked what he had done. It was their considered opinion that no farmer could learn anything from a man who was raised in town.

But every one of the black farmers asked my father about it and went and did likewise. And most of those black farms are still in the same families. Some of those men are still alive and they have prospered much more than they would have if someone hadn't shown them what could be done with the worn-out land that they were trying to rear their families on.

My father was a traveling salesman, a drummer, who sold Levi Garrett snuff. He had sold snuff in the Kentucky mountains and nearly got shot for a revenuer several times. And the company sent him down here to Nacogdoches in 1923. My mother taught music on the high school campus. And they met and married despite threats by the local young blades that if my mother paid any attention to that traveling salesman, she would be ostracized from decent society. So she married him.

My father was a very well-read man. As a traveling salesman he used as bad English as he could bring himself to, 'cause he was selling Levi Garrett snuff to country storekeepers. And if he had gone in sounding like an educated man, he would have put their backs up and he wouldn't have sold anything. He had to work within their context. And this is true pretty well all over Texas.

A redneck is somebody who is proud of his ignorance. You don't want to call a man a redneck unless you're in the mood for a fistfight.

But it can be deceptive, though. I talked up at the college one day with a lady who had come down to teach there several years before. She said, "I could not believe, listening to some of the professors speak, that they were people who knew anything. They sounded like ignorant rednecks. But these are men with doctorates. I only realized after quite a long time that if you stop sounding like an East Texan, people think you have gone all high-hat and uptown on them and get very angry with you. So you keep sounding like an East Texan no matter what your level of education."

If you are patient and persistent and don't lose your temper easily, you can eventually butt your way through the stone wall.

People here are *very* polite. If you don't want to get your nose broken or your pants shot full of lead, it pays to be polite. I had an editor come down to visit us from New York. She thought everybody here was a hypocrite. And I kept trying to tell her, "No, this is not hypocrisy. This is self-preservation."

You should listen to my discussions with my New York editors about East Texas. For them the fantasy I write is not nearly as fantastic as the absolutely factual things I tell 'em about. Things I have observed personally.

I think they really don't believe in East Texas. Sort of like they don't believe in fairy tales.

"BONES" NOBLES:
WHEN A MONKEY
WILL EAT RED PEPPER

Beaumont, TX

Born 1902

Moving with his family from Jim Crow Alabama at the age of fourteen, Bones Nobles worked as a pine-gum gatherer, as a Jasper, Texas, section hand on the Santa Fe Railroad, and as a sawmill dogger. John is his real name, but everyone calls him Bones because of the two pairs of seven-inch cowbones his fingers click into the most amazing rhythms. When I asked this energetic black man about his unusual music, his ancient cowbones, one dark and the other light-colored, the answer came with an unexpected lesson of racial reconciliation. "I carry a message with these bones," he said, "when I plays for kids at the schools. I show them that black and white can get along so nice if they just unify. If they ever get together, it will make good music."

CONDITIONS WILL MAKE A MONKEY eat red pepper. If there ain't nuthin' there for him to eat, he'll eat that for fillin'.

My daddy was making fifty cents a day from can to can't.

As soon as he could see, he was out there working until he couldn't see. They call that "can to can't."

And he got fifty cents.

That's six days for three dollars. Three big dollars! A wife and three kids.

Could he buy me a musical instrument?

He did whatever kind of work was available. Were those the good old days? Hell, no!

Those are the worst days that I can remember. What was good about 'em? I don't know nuthin' good about 'em. The sun rose and set. It wasn't no good. It was a push and a pull.

It wasn't too long since the Reconstruction time. Well, the blacks didn't have no school. They kept all the books and everything away from them during the slavery time. If they would catch them readin' a book, they would beat the hell out of them.

After Reconstruction, they were goin' to make a sharecropper out of him. "Hey, John. I want you to come and sharecrop with me. I'll tell you what I'm gonna do. My God, I'll give you a third if you'll come up there and raise. . . . I'll give you a third for sharecrop work."

Here comes along another white fellow, a politician, who says, "Hey John, I want you to come and sharecrop for me. I'll give you a vote." You see what I'm sayin'? That's the way the white politicians were toward us. They let us see what they wanted us to see.

I was born in Macon, but I was raised in Opp, Alabama. That was a white man's town and, boy, they put emphasis on that *white*. I'm tellin' you if you was black, hell, you didn't get no frontin' at all. You just had a certain part of the street that you could walk on and all that stuff.

Stores had glass show windows and a black man couldn't walk beside them. You had to walk on the street side of the sidewalk, where the wagons and the horses were. So if they knock you out in the street where the horses and the mules and things are, that's all right. But if you are over here and you get knocked and you break that man's showcase, they goin' to put you on the pea farm for fourteen days to pay for that man's. . . . Because you didn't have no business. . . . "You were on the wrong side of the street, boy. What in the hell were you doin' over there? Mr. So-and-So might have had a drink and he might have knocked you into that window but you didn't have no business over there. You get out there on that pea farm and you pay for that man's window. We ain't a-gonna let you boys take over the town."

Opp, Alabama, was pretty bad. You had these little ole shotgun houses where you can look in the front door and straight out the back door. That was all they would fix for ya'. A farmer, he throw up a cow crib that was a little better than the house he made for his tenants and help. You just had to go along with it if you wanted to survive. Just stay on there and hope for better.

One thing that I will give my dad credit for: givin' us the right start in life. It was easy for me to make friends. All my bosses liked me. Any kind of a way that I could be entitled to a break, I would get it.

You see on the turpentine farm, the Man built a great big commissary. You got to buy all of your food from him. All but what you made in your garden. Every day that you work, you get a coupon. A coupon was five, ten, twenty-five, and fifty cents. The coupon was just good at the store. So you go to the store clerk there and buy your groceries and stuff. He got a little ole clipper and however much you buy in his store, he clips it off your coupon. Your coupon was deducted out of your payday. The payday was once a month. Once a month they would pay off, but your money was reduced by your coupons from what stuff you had bought at the store.

The same boss, he will build a gamblin' house first, honky-tonk next, church last because he knowed the kind of people he had.

My father was a pastor on the turpentine farm. He was the preacher for the camp trying to save they souls.

Let me tell you the turpentine boss was tough. I don't give a damn whether you were a United States marshal, you couldn't come on that premises unless he permitted you. He could hit a gnat's eye with his gun. All them turpentine guys were a hell of six-shooter man and riflemen. Didn't nobody, any colored disturbance come, he was in it.

He was the boss, he was the law, he was everything. If you done too much against him, he would turn you over to the law. But if somebody else come in there and done somethin' or you did somethin' to somebody, it didn't count. They would just go off and bury 'em and that was all. There wasn't a damned thing done about it.

From 1916 to 1919 I gathered pine gum in Jasper County at what they called East Camp (four miles east of Wenasco). After we cut out at East Camp in 1918, we come to Wenasco for one year. Wenasco was named for the Western Naval Stores Company and it was about seven or eight miles west of Jasper on the Santa Fe Railroad. When the turpentine work cut out, so did Wenasco.

We kept chipping each pine for the gum but we always left a lifeline of bark up the trunk of the tree. No tree died from the operation.

A man would come around and chip the tree with a hack, a hickory-handled steel tool. He put a cup under the cut for the gum.

I was raking the pine gum out of the cup with a wooden paddle into my bucket. Then I took the bucket and raked its gum into a barrel. It takes seven buckets to fill that barrel if you got a big bucket. If you got a small bucket, it takes nine per barrel. And then the man come along with four mules and a wagon and rolls the barrel on skids onto the wagon and drives it to the still where they make turpentine and resin.

When we was in Alabama they wasn't payin' but about fifty-five or sixty cents a barrel. When it come to Texas, they was payin' four dollars a barrel. Then they went to payin' seven dollars a barrel. That was durin' World War I, right along 1916, 1917, and 1918. So the prices went up ten times. They was usin' that turpentine for paint and dynamite.

I would go out there and get me six barrels a day. I would get seven dollars a barrel, I'd make thirty some-odd dollars.

But I had that big ole bucket and it would rub against a wart on my leg. So I got my uncle in Philadelphia to take it off. He would say some kind of a ritual. The amount of warts, you tell it to him. He put that many notches in a stick and put it in his pocket. He just carried it around and my wart disappeared in Texas even though he was in Philadelphia.

There have been a lot of changes in East Texas. I was here when it was pretty rough.

I don't suppose you have ever driven a T-Model? You got to have both foots workin', your hands, both eyes. All of you was involved drivin' T-Models. It wasn't nuthin' like no power steerin'. You had to manually pull it over.

My boss man was dabblin' in real estate and runnin' a grocery store. He had a Hudson and I had learned how to shift on T-Models. One day in 1923 he told me, "John, I'll let you drive my Hudson in the country."

Oh man, that was the greatest uplift that I had ever heard tell of, gettin' a chance to drive that Hudson!

I didn't know where we was goin'. I had come to Beaumont from Jasper in 1922 and I thought everybody around here was civilized. I was just glad to go driving.

We got up this road and he said "Turn right." I was a big shot, man, drivin' a shift gear. Went up to a little ole store sittin' aside the road and he said "Stop here." I parked over to the side and he got out and went in the store.

I was sittin' up there, the biggest thing in the world that could happen to me, you know big chauffeur sittin' up behind the wheel. A white boy about eighteen years old came by and he peeked down and he seen me. He ran over there to that car and said "How long you goin' to be here?"

I say, "I'll be here until my boss comes out of that store."

"I sure hope you be here when I get back."

I was sittin' there just as comfortable until after a while I seen them weeds shakin' and the eighteen-year-old comes out of there draggin' a boy about eleven years old. He ran up to the car, out of breath, and he pointed at me. This young boy's eyes were wide-open lookin' at me. The older boy said, "That's one. That's a nigger. Some of them are lighter than him and some are blacker than him, but that's a nigger."

The little boy set there and his eyes were wide-open and he said "Say somethin'."

I said, "What do you want me to say?"

The young boy turned to the older one. "Oh, he talk like we do. I thought you said they jabbered."

I thought "Oh, hell." I started blowin' the horn. My boss came out and I said "Let's go."

He came and got in the car and I took off. I got clear to Benson and he said, "What's the matter back there?"

I said, "Man, don't you know we were in the wrong place?"

He said, "What's the matter?" I said, "A boy come up there, eleven years old, that had never seen a black man. Don't you know good and well that I am in the wrong place? Ain't nobody lives in a place that long and never seen a black man. I know I ain't got no business here."

He said, "Yeah, it is pretty bad around here."

I said, "Why in the hell you didn't tell me that?"

About four or five years after that, they catched a black back there and they gave him all kinds of hell. They made him eat a codfish raw. All of that stuff.

I was standin' right out on the street here in Beaumont in 1926 while the Ku Klux Klan paraded by. The sheriff of Jefferson County led the parade. They passed by me and my partner standing on the corner and they called out "Hey, nigger," trying to scare us. I wasn't scared of them, but I'm tellin' ya' I was on their list to be taken out and tar and feathered because I attended the Good Neighbor organization. Anyone doin' somethin' worthwhile was on their list.

We still got the KKK two miles one way and seven miles the other in two little ole towns here that don't. . . . They meet about every two weeks with all the rituals and everything.

Until recently the main thing was to keep the blacks from acquiring any money. They would give him a dollar and half or two dollars a day. Then he has got to eat and all that. The grocery store would get the majority of it. So he couldn't establish hisself as a number-one citizen. He couldn't have a car, he didn't have nuthin' hardly. If he did get a car, he had to have one that was wore out and full of haywire and stuff that he got to be patchin' and goin on. He couldn't hardly get a chance to do nuthin'.

Well, they put your salary down, they didn't allow ya to join the union, they didn't allow ya to vote. We all had our organization here that was tryin' to get the privilege of votin' but they was stoppin' us from votin' just on account of our color. So when Pappy O'Daniels was running for governor of Texas in 1938, we was glad. We was all keyed up and glad because probably we would get a chance to go to the poll and vote when he got to be governor. But during the campaign, he got up and says, "I don't need the Negro's vote. I just want their prayers. They don't need to vote." I said, "Oh, hell. Here comes some more years of that shit again."

When we did get the privilege to vote in 1944, Beaumont had a polling booth down there at the Century Fire Station. The line would be from here up across the street there and you would be back behind there. You done stood there until your legs got limber.

Finally you would be about the third or fourth from the poll and if a white man was late and he see you in the line, he would just come and shove you out of the line and take your place: "You go on, boy. Go on back to the end of the line. You don't know what to vote for."

What the hell you gonna do? You start a fight there, when they got through beatin' on your head, your head would have been as big as a basketball. You ain't jumpin' no odds, you know. You have sense enough to try to understand the first law of nature is self-preservation.

You just go to the back of the boat. If you don't get to the polls, all right, you haven't been votin' nohow.

Maybe comin' up the next time you will get it.

How did I get started playing the bones? Well, along in 1906, 1907, and 1908 you couldn't meet a black kid that didn't have two little sticks, makin' a noise. It was a fad.

We had a little combo goin' on in Opp. I wasn't preferred; they had another ole boy that was pretty good with the bones. But I went out there in the swamp and found a cow that had been dead a long time and the buzzards had done cleaned his ribs off. I got me a saw and sawed me off some bones and come back playin' them bones. Then they begin to notice and whenever anybody had a little hoedown: "Where's Johnny? Get Johnny with the bones."

Because we could not afford musical instruments, we settled for bones or a Jew's harp which we could get in the music store in town for a nickel, or the French harp which was a dime. Some others would get themselves a jug and fill it maybe half full of water. Another one would have an empty jug. And one had one three-quarters full. They could really produce a rhythm.

Another fellow, he would put a rope in a tub, tie a knot on the end of it, and attach it to a stick and have himself a washtub bass.

We would all get together, some on the bones, some on the other things, and we would have a real hoedown.

Yeah, man. We had a lot of fun like that!

Do you know why they called it a hoedown? Because everybody was choppin' cotton and haulin' corn until they would say "Put the hoe down and let's go to the dance."

So they just kept on telling people to put the hoe down until they just started calling it a hoedown.

That's the origination of it, back there in Alabama.

I like to see people get along together. I would like to see this whole nation, this whole world to come to an agreement that man is man until he proves himself to be somethin' else. I think it should be just like when you go to the store and purchase you a dozen eggs. You have but one request for those twelve eggs, that they all be good ones. Should you find a bad one, you don't give a damn about the color of their hide. The shell can be brown or it can be white.

That's the way you are supposed to be with people, too.

A. J. JUDICE:
TEXAS CAJUN #1
Bridge City, TX
Born 1927

Texas's kaleidoscope of ethnic cultures often surprises the first-time visitor. After all, people throughout the world know what a Texan is supposed to be like. Does a Czech Texan fill that bill? Or a Mexican Texan? Or a Polish Texan? Or a Vietnamese Texan? My feeling is that the state's rich ethnicity more than makes up for any disappointment accorded by the myth of the "real Texan."

What is so noticeable everywhere is the pride members of each group feel in celebrating their own heritages. Cajuns are no exception, and at the risk of plowing too close to the cotton I am nominating A. J. Judice as this book's communal booster. He's a risky choice because he is likely to talk up the Cajuns so forcefully that every other group will be gunning for his coon-ass scalp.

A. J. Judice is not bashful about telling the world what fine people the Cajuns really are. In fact, I spent several days with him once in a whirlwind of crawfish boils, "Jolie Blonde" fiddle dancing, and Cow Bayou boating. I even joined A. J. and his pal Oink Theriot on a Cajun radio program to talk about my experiences as an outsider eating boudain and crawfish for the first time.

When you are with A. J., your motto had better be *les bons temps rouler* (let the good times roll).

My only disappointment was that except for a few phrases like *fais do do* (go to sleep) the French language was nowhere to be heard.

The word *Cajun* comes from Acadian, the name of the French-Canadian exiles who settled in Louisiana after the British conquest of Canada in 1768. Second-class citizens for much of the last two centuries, the Cajuns enjoyed a cultural revival in the 1980s. Strangely enough, music and food are much stronger parts of that revival than language.

And food is the part of his culture that makes A. J. Judice roll his eyes and dance a little two-step in anticipation of roux, gumbo, blackened fish, or a down-home crawfish boil.

Like most things, crawfish ain't what they used to be. Instead of jacklegging crawfish at night in a pirogue, it's commonplace now to buy them at a supermarket.

One day A. J. took me to a backyard crawfish boil—complete with fresh corn and cold longnecks—at the Port Arthur home of Eugene and Lou Boudoin. Gene and Lou are organizers of crawfish dinners and crawfish races for the Golden Triangle Cajun Association. Despite the fact that they have served up jillions of the hapless crustaceans, the crawfish is not in danger of extinction.

Nor is the pig, that other friend of the true Cajun. A. J. kept salivating on and on about a pork sausage called boudain and finally we went to the Boudain Hut restaurant, where I saw huge vats of rice and pork being mixed with Cajun seasonings and extruded into sausage casings. When I finally sat down to eat a boudain breakfast with about a dozen of A. J.'s ubiquitous friends, I was the butt of jokes and merriment. They warned me that once I ate boudain I would be "addicted." Well, that breakfast was a gut-buster! No *cuisine minceur* in the Boudain Hut! I liked the spicy, rich sausage and understood why in the 1980s Cajun restaurants had spread across America like a squall down a bayou. For a while fashion-conscious diners couldn't get enough blackened fish and boudain. I am sorry for them, though, that they missed the best part of the experience, meeting A. J.'s mother.

MY MOTHER AND DADDY HAD to be the most beautiful Cajun couple I have ever seen. My dad was a meatcutter and my mother was a front-end operator checking people out of the store. She had personality!

In those days, everything was cheap. Round steak was twenty-five cents a pound. T-bone might be twenty-nine or thirty cents a pound. In those days small grocers made a profit. My parents made enough in five years to buy a farm on the Bayou Teche, build a brand-new home, buy two mules, a cow, a tractor, and. . . .

It was just an inspiration to see a couple that got along so good, working together. That was my goal. Normally a young man my age wouldn't have liked the grocery business, but I loved it from the very start. From nine years of age, I worked in my parents' store in Port Arthur. I was with them every day and they were a model to me.

The area was seventy-five to eighty percent Cajun except for that little German neighborhood where the store was.

I was born in Port Arthur, Texas, in 1927, the year of the high water. Then we moved to Loreauville, Louisiana, and lived on a sugar-cane farm. After two years my parents got lonesome for Texas, so they came back to Port Arthur and they started a grocery business. I stayed with my grandmother in Louisiana but when I was nine years old I came back, too, and started to work in the store. I loved bagging potatoes and doing everything.

I just loved the business from the very start. We would go to Sabine Pass with a trailer and our 1931 Chevrolet. Man, my daddy's Chevrolet had a tire on the side and little mirrors! What a sporty car! But we would go and pick up a load of watermelon and potatoes with it.

The potatoes I remember well. I put them in ten-pound paper bags and we would sell them, ten pounds for a nickel. Watermelon and cantaloupes, hundreds of them. The cantaloupes might sell for a nickel.

After spending my whole life in the grocery-store business, I am still very particular about Texas vegetables and fruits. For instance, Pecos cantaloupe is considered top of the line because of the Pecos soil, but Sabine Pass has a sandy soil and watermelons grow better and get sweeter there.

[A. J. was expecting his mother to arrive at any minute and he was very excited that she might make some boudain for him.]

MY MOTHER ALWAYS LOVED TO COOK. The things she made! She made hog's-head cheese for the store, right behind the market. She made maybe a hundred pounds of boudain a day. Every day!

All these things make me think about how people would drive far and wide to get a good-quality food.

Cajun food is much different than Chinese or Mexican food, because when you eat it, it sticks to your ribs. It can hold you up for many hours where Chinese food, two hours later you could be kind of on the hungry side. Cajun food is filling.

My mother is gonna be here soon. Boudain! Boudain!

Maybe we'll have fish. This Cow Bayou behind the house connects to Sabine Lake and the Gulf. This water is kind of brackish. Sometimes we have caught fourteen species of fish from our dock. Speckled trout, bass, sheepheads, drum, redfish, white perch, you name it.

Believe it or not, my first name is Albin. Five of my daddy's brothers was A. J. Judice. See, my grandmother was a Cajun and she must have been scared by a broken record because she kept on naming them A. J. Judice. Five boys named A. J. Judice!

They were Albin Joseph, Anthony Joseph, and what have you.

When I was born, initials were popular because some of the Cajun people. . . . Really we didn't have as much schoolin' as others and we couldn't spell as many names, so we made it very simple and we got by with initials.

In 1927 my mother and daddy left Louisiana because there were too many people per farm and there wasn't no work. They bought a little store with five hundred dollars and moved into a section of

Port Arthur that was maybe a hundred German families. No other nationality but German. That was so brave of them to try to invade the Germans. But they conquered them without firing a shot because of the food, the boudain.

Once you brainwash a person with boudain, they got to have it. There is something about it I can't explain. It's a rice dish with meat in it. It is a complete meal in a tube.

Most people on the farm years ago would butcher the hogs and they would use every part of the hog. Nothin' was goin' to waste. They would even use the squeal. They would put that in a little balloon and the kids would play with it.

Of course, seasoning is one of the main things that we have a gimmick on that nobody else does. Cajuns had to raise all these spices.

Corn, now the Indians gave them the secret of raising corn and makin' cush cush. Cush cush is the staff of life for the Cajuns.

And crawfish. Have you been to a crawfish race after the crawfish come out of hibernation? In January we start planning races but the big races are in March. That's when Bridge City has its first big crawfish/crab festival.

Bridge City is the Texas center of crawfish racing. Sometimes we even beat the Louisiana people!

I've even trained crawfish to jump from a little remote-control plane, a little Stearman biplane with two cockpits. Six of them we trained, on their own, to jump with parachutes. It's hard to believe but it happened.

We have lost. . . . After they jumped out the wind would catch them. We had put a lot of money and time into training them and we had to give a prize of a month's supply of boudain to whoever would bring that crawfish back.

One time my plane cracked up and just luckily my crawfish that was in there was well enough trained that it had enough sense to jump before the plane hit the ground.

The secret of it is I have a box of radio controls, nine buttons on this thing to communicate with the plane. The last three tells the crawfish what to do at what time. Once he feels. . . .

You got to train them to do it. They just don't do it on their own. We found that if they are hungry, it helps. Sometimes I rub boudain on the outside of the cockpit. If they are hungry and they sniff it and lean out, then they will fall out, don't you see. Sometimes, this is very unusual, but if they don't jump, I have a little spring rigged up underneath the seat and that's the eighth button. When I push it, it actually springs the crawfish out.

But if anything happens and I can't get him out, I have one more alternative. This is the boogaboo that I can always depend on. That's the ninth button.

My uncle Too Too was the greatest Cajun that we ever had in Loreauville, Louisiana. Everything about him was beautiful, especially his big mustachioed smile. What a smile that man had!

I have Uncle Too Too's picture hidden in the cockpit of the airplane. When I push that ninth button, Uncle Too Too pops up and the crawfish can see that smiling Cajun.

If you are a crawfish and you see a smiling coon-ass looking at you, you are goin' to jump or he will eat you if you don't.

[When A. J.'s mother, a short peppy woman named Lariza arrived, she wasted no time in telling me what she thought about her son's crawfish races.]

A. J. HAS GOT THEM BELIEVING that his crawfish are trained. There are thousands of people that come around that would swear it was the truth. I don't think the crawfish knows what it's doing. But people go far and near to see a crawfish race.

I have a drive in me. I never get tired. I just love to work. I'm still going strong. I tell you if I was younger, I would start the most fabulous restaurant. I am not very educated but I do know Cajun cooking and I knew the culture.

The Cajuns are a very conservative people. Like in preparing food. I have cooked almost sixty years. I have made as much as two thousand pounds of boudain in a week. A ton of boudain!

It is like a German sausage except that it is rice and gravy and pork liver. We cook the rice separate, then we mix it in, and then we stuff it into the casing. It's got a good flavor because it is highly seasoned with onion, bell peppers, celery, salt, red pepper, black pepper, garlic, and paprika.

We sold so much of it! Two thousand pounds a week—which is a lot of boudain.

If I wasn't so old, I would start me a restaurant and get me a big speedboat. Then when I got mad at the neighbors, I would just move on in my speedboat.

CLEM MIKESKA:

MR. TEXAS BARBECUE

Temple, TX

Born 1929

Food is one of the greatest joys of Texas. Some foods are relatively universal from the Rio Grande to the Red River, but a lot of favorites are or were associated with a particular region. For instance, elsewhere in this book A. J. Judice salivates over his boudain sausages and crawfish and Wyatt Moore extols the delights of poached perch.

After serious deliberation I decided that it was only fair in the state of the cowboy and the longhorn to celebrate beef with a chapter of its own. Immediately I thought of fajitas, because everywhere I went in South Texas people were happily chewing into this tasty chuck. Fajitas is actually the flank steak known otherwise as hamburger. Until recently flank steak was decidedly a downscale food but it has been redeemed by fashion and now often commands a high price.

However, I decided to opt for tradition and investigate barbecue. The trouble is that people are so opinionated about barbecue that choosing the best is about as difficult as judging Texas beauty queens. Many areas have their own B-B-Q sage who dispenses wisdom on mesquite versus oak cooking, this or that sauce, and beans versus cole slaw. For instance, at Otto's Barbecue in Houston, Annie and Marcus Sofka claim to have "the best barbecue anywhere." Well, it is sho-nuff good, but over at Marble Falls, Texas, Wilma Hinman and her husband extol *their* homemade sauce. And on and on all across the state.

The Hinmans cook their beef brisket until it is delightfully crusty on the outside and juicily tender on the inside. Wilma stands by oak wood. "Mesquite smokes too much!" she says emphatically. Her husband, F. M. Hinman, was busily poking through a pile of dry beans for debris. He told me that he and his brother had first started barbecuing in Llano in 1964 and had been at it ever since. I especially liked their turkey sausage and I could see why the Hinmans have many repeat customers at their nondescript old house. "We call them friends instead of customers," said Wilma. "But I don't give out our recipe to anyone!"

She did reveal that she is very particular about the beef she buys. And that is certainly one of the keys to the success of Clem Mikeska in Temple, Texas. He and his father and brothers began in the butchering business back on their farm in Taylor, Texas, in the Czech community. His family story reminds us that beef is king in Texas and always will be unless the wimps and Reds subvert our all-American food. Clem encouraged me to eat barbecue breakfast, noon, and night and said that the cholesterol scare is merely a plot by the fish-sellers to turn the public away from Texas beef.

And what about that mesquite/oak wood controversy? I thought I remembered Clem's telling me the night I met him that a mesquite fire's aftertaste was something like turpentine. The next morning over an oak-fired breakfast of barbecue, the old Czech set me straight.

"No," said Clem. "More like diesel."

I USE THE STRAIGHT LIVE-OAK wood. I think it is a slower-burning, hotter-burning fire and it has a lot cleaner-looking smoke. And it does not have that *diesel aftertaste* like mesquite wood does.

I believe that beef is the best thing for you. It has a lot of protein, a lot of vitamins, and it is just good solid food. You eat good beef and you make it through the day without any problems.

I don't think it will hurt you. It hasn't hurt me as long as I've been living. I think it does me *a lot of good!*

The best thing in Texas to eat is beef. Texas beef! As long as you eat it, you will live a long time.

I've seen a lot of this crap on TV that beef is full of cholesterol. But it isn't. What they did was, they was knockin' the beef so that they could promote fish. I'm not goin' to knock fish or anything like that, but I eat a fish that big and thirty minutes later I'm hungry. It's a real light food and the fish industry people, they are like politicians. They will go out here and knock beef. Now the beef people, they got to come out with some kind of a promotion to get back into the saddle.

Here in Bell County we have a strong youth fair and livestock show operation. The kids raise these calves, hogs, or whatever for their projects to show. I have been buying the grand champion steer for the past many years. We go ahead and send him back home with the boy and have the boy feed him for another thirty days to settle him down. These steers are nervous and excited. Then we bring him to the slaughterhouse.

Yes, we do slaughter him! We do barbecue the parts of the steer that we can and the rest we grind up and make our own sausage out of it.

The kid who raised the steer is tickled to death that he won the grand champion ribbon. He feels good about it and he gets quite a bit of money for him, so he is happy. He goes home and puts the money in the bank for future days. Most of them put up enough money to go to college with. I'm proud of them for finishing this steer out. They make a pretty good profit out of it and they are happy. They just turn the steer loose to me and that's the way it is.

I myself raised animals at my father's farm.

My father, John Mikeska, came from Czechoslovakia when he

was nine years old and was a farmer around the Temple, Texas, area for a long time. In 1936 he started a beef club for about thirty or forty Czech families. He was in charge of slaughtering an animal every Saturday morning and dividing it up so that each family in the club could have fresh meat every week. There was no money involved but he kept records of how many pounds of meat each family had received and what animals they had contributed. So if you didn't have refrigeration, at least you would have fresh meat once a week and then whatever was left over you would preserve it the best way you knew how.

All six of us, my father's sons, helped slaughter every Saturday morning. That gave us the experience. We learned right there with him. When I was about ten years old, we were all learning together.

Around 1939 the beef clubs were discontinued because electricity became available and everybody was able to afford it. And then people began to be able to go to town daily and buy fresh meat whenever they wanted it.

After my father married my mother in 1913, he had gotten interested in the meat business because it was hard to make a living farming. My father was quite aggressive about the business and we learned to be that way, too.

What I'm trying to say is, you just got to hustle. You just got to make it work one way or the other. If one thing don't work, try something else to provide for the family. You don't set back and let it happen. You got to make it happen!

Eventually we brothers each owned our own meat markets in different cities and we got the idea "Why not cook some of this meat on a barbecue pit?" It sounded like a good idea to all of us, so we built barbecue pits in the back ends of our meat markets and started cooking beef, chicken, and sausage. We had a dining area for people to come in and eat or to take out.

That went over real good because the food was good and people got used to the idea of not having to cook. We made potato salad, beans, and everything else. Done a complete meal for everybody!

Times change all the time and you have to change with it. Slowly but surely we got out of the fresh meat end of it and just started cooking and selling the barbecue.

I'll tell you, barbecue is good any time of the day: morning, noon, or night. It is better for breakfast than Post Toasties or bacon and eggs, that's for sure. It has a lot of power to it.

Yeah, I eat barbecue every day and enjoy it. When my brothers and I get together, we usually cook steaks on a pit in the back yard at my mother's home in Bastrop and compare notes about our barbecue businesses. We just have a hell of a good time discussing barbecue and everybody pitches in to prepare the picnic. We all have a hand in it, like we are all authorities on it—which we are— and each of us pushes his own opinion on how to barbecue the steaks. But we all agree that when you get out of Texas, you get out of barbecue.

I think Temple is the barbecue capital of Texas and I am glad to be here in Temple. Of course, other cities in the state have good barbecue people, too, and Temple may not be the biggest and it may not be the best. But I'll tell you one thing, whoever *is* the biggest and the best, we got them nervous!

ANTHONY MCGOWEN: "COTTON EVERYWHERE YOU LOOKED"

Goodrich, TX

Born 1911

Anthony McGowen's truck-driving son says that he would not have endured the stoop labor that was his father's lot in life. He would not have picked cotton, pulled corn, and picked peas, but he does not know what he would have done instead during the hard times of East Texas segregation.

In May 1990 Livingston Dam was in the national news because of an epic flood that swept through its spillways. Nothing, however, was said about Swartout, Texas, an 1840s steamboat landing and until 1930 an important Trinity River ferry crossing. The construction of Livingston Dam inundated the town along with part of the farm Anthony McGowen's grandfather had purchased after Emancipation.

Anthony McGowen lives across the road from an old wooden Methodist church still used by local blacks. He told me about old-time church picnics, his family's cotton gin and grist mill, and the times when travelers had to camp overnight after big rains until the floodwaters had receded. Today Swartout (named for a New York politician who helped finance the new Republic of Texas) is at the bottom of Lake Livingston. And the black community's togetherness is much attenuated. What remains are a few old-timers and their church.

The black people used to have their own Methodist conference and the white people had their own set-up. After they united, the white people and the black people could go to the same church, share pastors, worship together, conference together, everything. But we don't have any whites here in our church except just now and then.

MY GRANDFATHER DIED IN 1945. He was a hundred and fifteen years old. He told me he was thirty-five at the time he was freed from slavery. He said his slavemaster was a real good man who would eat with 'em and cared for them more than the other slaveowners, who were kind of cruel.

We have a white man over at Coldspring right across the lake that says that my grandfather was a slave on his grandparents' place. His name is Neil McGowen and he is about my age. At one time the McGowens over there owned lots of property.

My grandfather said that his grandfather was one of the slaves that didn't do very much work because he was used to stay with the slave women and have children. He had thirty-three children that he knowed of.

I heard my grandfather tell often about when he come from across the river, San Jacinto County, where he was born at during slavery time. He come over here after he was freed and bought five hundred and fifty-four acres at seventy-five cents an acre. He had about twelve boys and six girls.

My grandfather was independent because he had a cotton gin and quite a few customers. But when more gins were built, it cut him short because most landowners would send their crop and sharecroppers' crops to their own gins. That forced my grandfather out of the gin business. So my father thought a grist mill would be a good thing to have because so many people was going to other places to grist mills. So Mr. McMurray helped him get one set up here. Mr. McMurray was a white man that owned lots of property and had lots of people workin' for him, both white and black. He thought well of my father from when he and my father had associated together a lot before they were grown. These McMurrays that are living now are his grandchildren.

Farmers would bring their corn to my father's grist mill and get it ground into meal. It was belt-driven by a one-horse motor operated by coal oil. Farmers come with a horse and wagon, riding horses carrying corn, and everything. They paid my father a fourth of whatever they had.

In later years the cotton farmin' got so profitable that the men that owned these large farms, they cut their corn crop and planted cotton. Made corn crops so small that there wasn't much corn to grind, so my father finally sold his grist mill. It was moved to over around Willis, Texas. Pretty soon corn went out over there, too.

Then after World War II cotton went to goin' out. Most people say that pulpwood is taking the place of cotton. Pine trees and oak, too. Oh, yessir, pulpwood is the big thing now!

After my father quit the grist mill, he went into the funeral home business. He didn't do very much with that but he kept his store running until 1938. He became ill in 1938, and he passed in 1940.

Back there in the Depression it was real rough, but it didn't bother me none because I didn't have any money no way. Because I didn't have nothing to begin with, the Depression didn't bother me like it seemed to bother other people. Many East Texas people went to leavin' the rural area goin' to the city. The country just went to nothing!

Looking back, our life doesn't sound so good, but the poor

people was happy because most of them that had the privilege raised just about all their food. Peas, beans, chickens. They milked cows.

Know anything about milkin' cows? When I was growing up, I had three or four cows to milk every morning. Come in from the field in the evening time and I milked. Then you churn that milk and make butter.

Didn't buy no chicken eggs because we had plenty. We raised everything, didn't have to buy nothing like that. Didn't have to buy bacon and pork. Take a notion that you wanted fresh meat, you would go out and kill a hog.

I had plenty to eat and the few clothes I had was decent enough.

For a few years segregation here was kind of rough. Black people were working for the rich white people on their farms raising lots of cotton. Oh, man, there was cotton everywhere you looked! Cotton and corn. Getting out there and gathering a crop by hand was kind of rough but that was the only way we knowed at that time to do it.

People could really get it by hand! Some of them could get three and four hundred pounds of cotton a day. Quite a few would get five and six hundred pounds. I never could get more than three or three-fifty.

To harvest cotton you get down there and pick it by hand and put it in a big sack behind you. You had to bend over quite a bit to pick cotton. It's rough on your back but once you got used to it, it didn't bother you. I could go from one row to the other and never raise up unless my back got a pull and start hurtin'. I could pull eighty-five to ninety pounds of cotton before I raised up, then I'd go on down the next row.

LOUIS RAWALT:

BEACHCOMBER

Padre Island, TX

Born 1899

The Texas coast stretches almost four hundred miles from the Sabine River at Sabine Pass to the Mexican border near Brownsville. Barrier islands separate much of this hurricane-prone territory from the Gulf of Mexico. With their warm weather, abundant wildlife, excellent fishing, and shipwreck booty, the Texas barrier islands are a beachcomber paradise.

Given only six months to live because of wounds suffered in World War I, Kingsville's Louis Rawalt returned to the Texas coast to live out his last days with his hospital sweetheart Viola. Together they built a ten-by-twelve driftwood shack on Padre Island's Big Shell Beach. After recovering his health, Louis managed to eke out a living through fishing and odd jobs, but his true forte was studying the play of sand and surf and the way Nature revealed relics of the Indian, Spanish, and Mexican past. For more than four decades he was Audubon warden of Bird Island, home of the once-endangered white pelican.

WE LEFT KINGSVILLE ON A sunny September morning. Behind me were the years of war, the hospital corridors, the waiting rooms, and the operating tables. I kept the doctor's grim predictions from my mind as much as possible.

Keeping the wheels of the Model T on the parallel planks of the causeway demanded all my attention, but every few moments Viola would cry out over some strange bird flying over Laguna Madre. There were white pelicans by the thousands, snowy egrets, roseate spoonbills, herons, ducks and gulls and terns. Mullet leaped and played in the water, shining like silver in the bright morning sun.

We left the causeway and followed a winding path through the dunes to the Gulf side of Padre. At the beach we turned left and drove along the surf to Corpus Christi Pass, where we set up camp. The pass was open then, and the islands of Padre and Mustang were divided. I don't know what time we reached the pass; we took no clock with us. I didn't want time measured out to me in minutes and hours.

We gathered lumber the rest of that day to build a floor for the tent. Viola did most of the labor, for there was little strength left in my body. When the sun was high in the heavens, we stopped long enough to eat the lunch Mother had packed for us. It had been many months since food had tasted so good, and if the fried chicken was seasoned with a little Padre Island sand, neither of us noticed—or cared.

By nightfall we were snug and secure. We ate a supper of bacon and pork and beans by the glow of our Coleman lantern. Viola had made a table from a small hatch cover the tide had carried in; our chairs were two nail kegs. She stacked some apple boxes, one above the other, to make a cupboard for our supplies. The cots were set up, side by side, at one end of the tent. We turned out the lantern, brushed some of the sand from our bare feet and crawled between the covers. I listened to the pound of the surf a moment before sleep overtook me. From the dunes behind us coyotes howled.

I awoke that first morning feeling refreshed and eager to face the day. I raised the flap of the tent to see the splendor of early morning on the Gulf. Nature was outdoing herself in artistry. The sky, the water, and the clouds along the horizon were all tinted with color—mauve, rose, and copper seeping through the gray. As I watched the sun break through to make a golden path across the water, Viola came softly on bare feet to stand beside me. I had everything. But for a limited time only. That day and the ones following it flowed by; the hours came and went like the waves that broke against the sand, unmeasured and unrecorded. We ate when we were hungry. When we were tired, we rested; and when the time came for sleep, we slept like exhausted children. For the most part, Viola busied herself about the camp, but sometimes she came and

dropped down beside the camp chair where I sat for hours at a time
fishing with my cane pole.

Gradually the sun and the salt air worked their healing magic,
and before many weeks passed I felt the beginnings of strength
returning to my body. The aches and pains lessened. The shadow
of death lingered, but grew fainter.

Our appetites were enormous. In spite of all the fish we ate, our
supplies disappeared rapidly. Neither of us looked forward to the
trip to town after more. Fish were plentiful in those days and would
strike at anything—even a bare hook. I saw schools of redfish a
mile long, their color like a river flowing through the Gulf. There
were many other species of fish, and I think I caught some of them
all. There were the redfish, trout, drum, pompano, pike, mackerel,
golden croaker, whiting, and many less important fishes. The bottom of the lagoon was thick with flounder which we gigged at night
by lantern light.

One cool night in October I caught five hundred pounds of
redfish on my trotlines. Early morning found us chugging across
the causeway with our load. The fish sold for twenty-five dollars;
then we bought supplies and more line and hooks and hurried back
to our island as fast as the Ford would take us. After that, I fished
commercially.

When the first norther' whistled down across the dunes, we
realized that we would have to have a stove to keep the tent warm.
So the next trip to town we bought some stovepipe, a chisel, and
some hinges. I took an oil drum and chiseled out a door on one
side and hinged it on. For the pipe, I cut criss-crosses and flanged
them out to fit snugly. We filled the drum about a fourth of the way
up with sand for insulation on the bottom, ran the pipe up through
a hole in the tent, and there was our stove. Wood was no problem.
The tide took care of that, but cutting it became my chore. Viola
tried it once, but swore off tearfully after a stick of wood flew up
and hit her in the eye.

Winter passed. A short spring merged into a long summer. By
the next October, I realized that I had borrowed six months over
my allotted time to live, and by leave of the Almighty I meant to
borrow as many more as I could. I was strong again and seldom
felt the touch of pain. Fishing was good, and if the proceeds in

those days were not astounding, there was always enough for the things we really needed. Island living agreed with Viola. She was brown and healthy and as active as a ground squirrel.

We moved our camp to the edge of Big Shell the next year, thirty-five miles down the beach. This time we had a shack to live in. A place loaned us by Major Swan, one of the old-timers of the island. I bought a surf net and a used Model A to replace the rust-eaten Model T. We converted the Ford into a pick-up. Viola helped me with the net until I found a fishing partner.

One morning when we were hauling in the net, something kept leaping against it with the force of a huge shark or a porpoise. We couldn't bring it in, so I staked one end of the net into the sand, and hooked onto the other end with the car. Slowly, I pulled in the net until the creature lay in the edge of the surf. Incredible: It was an eighteen-foot sawfish. When some fishermen came by later that day and found me beside the sawfish with a cane pole—no net in sight—they assumed I had caught it on the pole. I didn't enlighten them, and this tall fish story was told about Corpus Christi for years. The sawfish, I regret to say, became food for the packs of coyotes that roamed the wild stretches of Big Shell.

We seldom saw other human beings there, but coyotes prowled close to our shack at night, and in the early mornings and evenings we saw them on the beach searching for fish, which were the mainstay of their diet. I learned by experience just how clever and crafty they were. I have seen them fishing in the surf for mullet and catching them! Many times I saw these lean, hungry animals watching me from over the rim of the dunes. Once I left the beach, they would sneak down and pick up my discards. Sitting on the porch that I had added to our shack one early morning after I had set out my trotlines, I saw two big coyotes slink down to the water's edge and begin dragging one of the lines in to shore. I was too amazed and curious to move. They pulled the line all the way in; then bit the fish off the hooks and trotted with them back to their habitat in the dunes. Many persons doubted the truth of this, but I saw the same thing happen time and again.

One night Viola nudged me awake. "There's something in the kitchen," she whispered.

Listening, I heard the faint rattle of the tin plates we had left on the table. I got up and edged toward the ktichen. The moonlight streamed through the open door and outlined the gaunt, gray form of a coyote. He was on the table licking up the remains of our supper. He sensed my presence and leaped for the door, but slipped on a greasy plate and somersaulted into the center of the room. I gave a swift kick to the astonished animal and sent it rolling down the back steps. Tail down, it trotted up a nearby dune and sat on its haunches barking with venom. As I looked closer, I saw the forms of four or five puppies, joining in the harsh chorus. They continued to bark until I got my shotgun; then they vanished into the night.

During a big run of redfish one night, I caught ninety, averaging in weight from five to fifteen pounds. I kept them on stringers alive in the surf until I was too tired to fish any more; then, nearing midnight, I started to ice them down in the pick-up. There was no ice. I hastily loaded the fish and hauled them back of the dunes, where I put them in a pond. We could net them the next morning easily and hurry them in to market. This catch would bring seventy or eighty dollars which we needed for supplies.

Satisfied with the night's work, I tumbled into bed and slept until dawn. With the first light of morning, I hurried to the pond. I stared in amazement at what I saw: Scattered around the bank of the pond were the headless carcasses of the ninety redfish. The coyotes had outwitted me. Their tracks formed a network around the pond and trailed into the sand hills in every direction. They ate a hearty supper; but what were we going to eat?

I drove in to town that day for a new supply of ice, which was all I could buy. The next night the redfish were still running—so we got our groceries and gasoline after all.

Coyotes weren't the only problem we had to cope with on the beach. In any season, but especially during vernal and autumnal equinoxes, the Gulf might change from peace to violence. We lived in the Devil's Elbow, the bend of the long arm of Padre. It was strewn with the accumulated wreckages of the years, from shrimp boats and freighters to Spanish galleons dating back to the time of Cortez. Salvage from these boats helped us to improve our daily living conditions, and some old coins and jewelry I found at the site of one of the wrecks made interesting additions to our treasure trove of beachcombings.

Some of the castoffs of the waves were unusual and astonishing. One afternoon Viola and I stopped to examine a five-gallon can that had washed up on the beach. I pried the lid off with my fishing knife. The can was filled with clean, white lard. We put it into the pick-up, and before the day was over, we had salvaged more than a hundred cans. There were a lot more damaged cans that we left lying on the beach. The Coast Guard told us later that a Mexican freighter had been torn to pieces by a sudden tumult in the Gulf. She was carrying a cargo of lard; it made a profitable load of salvage for us and a grease bath for the beach. For a long time after that the sand was saturated with lard. The island coyotes grew fat from feasting on it. Even the sand crabs acquired a new look of sleekness.

It was about the same time when the British smuggler *I'm Alone* was shelled and sunk by the Coast Guard cutter in Sigsbee's Deep near the southern tip of Padre. The ship was spotted off New Orleans where she expected to land her contraband cargo of whiskey. The cutter chased her along the coast, finally closing in on her. The captain refused to surrender. He jettisoned the cargo before the Coast Guard cutter blasted the ship full of holes.

I received word by the island grapevine to be on the lookout for the liquor, so I started down the beach in the pick-up, searching the incoming waves and the tideline for bottles of the amber elixir. I didn't see anything that looked like whiskey but noticed a full gunnysack imbedded in the sand. I could check it later, so I drove on, but when I saw several more similar sacks, I stopped to investigate. The sack I opened contained a dozen sealed tin cans. I pried the lid from one of the cans. Inside, was a bottle of "Old Hospitality" Bourbon whiskey. During the day, I salvaged one hundred and ten sacks. I stashed this horde behind the dunes, filled a duffle bag with seventy-two bottles, and headed for Port Isabel. The ferry-boat took me across the channel. The captain's suspicions were aroused by the weight of the duffle bag. I had to explain what I had found and make a gift of a few bottles. It is enough to say that I disposed of the remainder in Port Isabel.

When I returned to the island, a comforting feeling of cash in my pockets and the prospect of more, I met the captain of the ferryboat and one of his crew. They were driving a pick-up with the bed loaded with bulging gunnysacks. I followed their tracks, as they had, from all appearances, followed mine, to my cache in the dunes. Of all my loot, there wasn't even a bottle left!

For weeks the beach was combed by thirsty men all the way from Port Isabel to Port Aransas. At Port Aransas, one boatman got more of the "drink" than he counted on. He spotted a sack and headed his craft toward it. As he reached over the side for the bobbing burlap bag, he tumbled into the water. He was five miles from shore, and his boat was circling away. He kept afloat by using the liquor as a lifebuoy. The boat swung in a circle, finally coming back to him. He grasped the side and struggled aboard. Evidently the thoughts that raced through his brain as he floundered in the water, with drowning almost a certainty, sobered him greatly, for when he got back to town he sold his boat and other possessions and moved inland.

So the days flowed into weeks, and the weeks became months and years. I had grown steadily stronger and seldom gave a thought to the fact that I wasn't even supposed to be alive. I could walk for miles without tiring, and many nights I slept on the sand with only a piece of tarpaulin around me when I was fishing away from the camp. It was one of the times when I had gone alone to a spot thirty-five miles below our shack that the car stalled. No amount of coaxing or tinkering could get a sound out of it. There was nothing to do but start walking. It was seventy miles to Corpus Christi Pass where someone lived who had a car. The tide was exceptionally high, and I had little hope that any fishermen would be venturing down the beach that day.

It was early morning when I started out. A little before sunset I reached our shack. Viola was visiting my people in Kingsville at the time, so the place was still and empty-feeling. I ate, drank coffee, and rested for the few moments before starting again. The tide was rising rapidly. It looked as though a storm might be brewing in the Gulf. If I didn't get the car up out of reach of the water, I wouldn't have a car. This thought kept my bare feet plodding through the sand all night. It was dark as pitch. Sudden squalls blew in, keeping me drenched most of the time. But with the first gray light of morning, I could see by the familiar outlines of the dunes that I was only a few miles from the pass.

Bill White, another fisherman, was cooking breakfast in his tar-paper shack when I knocked at his door. I was too tired to eat, but as I gulped down scalding cups of coffee, I couldn't help crowing over the fact that four years before I had been doomed. In the last twenty-four hours I had walked seventy-five miles!

During the next year I acquired a fishing partner. We called him "Shorty," and if he had any other name, we never knew it. He was a good man on the end of a net. It relieved Viola from some pretty hard work, too. She had found a bale of cotton washed up on the beach and subsequently launched into a quilting project. Shorty set up his tent a little beyond our shack, and until the hurricane of that year [1933], we had a pleasant and profitable partnership.

That was the year the Gulf staged a real shindig. We had several scares that September. Viola kept most of our valued and important possessions packed in boxes against the time we might have to evacuate. The Friday before the storm hit on Monday was one of the most perfect of island days. The water was flat and blue. The skies clear and the southwest wind warm and gentle. Shorty was expecting weekend guests, and Viola, thinking they would perhaps visit us, too, had unpacked the boxes and made the house cozy and neat.

I was fishing early Saturday morning when I noticed that the swells were coming over the beach in an erratic rhythm. Far out over the water, the sky had an ominous look; wildlife had deserted the beach. A squall hit with sudden intensity. I pulled in my line and went into the shack. Viola was still sleeping. I wakened her and told her to get ready to go to town, that I thought there was a storm on the way. Sleepily, she started pulling on her jeans and shirt, mumbling about repacking everything. I walked to the porch and looked out. The tide had risen so fast that it was already hazardous to travel the beach.

"You won't have time for that," I told her. "We'll have to go now, or not at all."

Shorty came in then. He had seen the signs. There was no need of telling him. Another squall hit as we were getting into the pick-up, where we squeezed up together in the seat. The beach was almost impassable where the long sweeps crowded us up into the soft sand and shell. But the Model A came through, and in the late afternoon we reached the house of some friends in Corpus Christi.

I checked with the weather bureau and found that there was, indeed, a storm in the Gulf. It was one of exceptional force and was headed straight toward the Texas coast. They expected the storm to hit Monday. After getting Viola more or less safely settled, Shorty and I began to talk about returning to the island and going down the beach on low tide that night to get some of our equipment. We decided to go, and over Viola's protests we refueled the Ford and drove back over the causeway to Padre.

The island was a place of darkness and fury that night. It rained incessantly and the wind blew in gusts that threatened to blow the pick-up over. We had only gone a mile or two down the beach when we both had to admit that it was hopeless to try to go farther until daylight. So we drove the Ford up into the edge of the dunes and sat there all night trying to sleep, our legs cramping and the water reaching nearer with every heave of the Gulf.

When morning came the rain let up a little. We shoved and shoveled our way through the dunes and to the grasslands in the center of the island. It took all day to reach the shack driving over the rough terrain and through the pools of water left by the night's deluge. It still rained and the wind blew.

We left the truck behind the dunes and walked over to the house. The water was running under it so deep it was over our knees as we waded up to the steps. We estimated that the tide was four or five feet above normal. I knew that unless some miracle happened, the shack was not going to stand much longer. I went inside, and dumping a pillow out of its case, started grabbing some of our valuables and putting them into it. I tossed in a box containing several old coins I had found around the wreckage of an old ship, a rust-encrusted lavaliere I had picked up at the site of the Balli mission-ranch. Then there were the stem-wind gold watches I had found in a wooden box on the beach and my collection of arrowheads and spearpoints.

I was looking around at all the rest of our furnishings and equipment, wondering how much to take, when a giant roller hit the shack with terrifying force. I felt the floor sway and buckle under my feet. The water was running up through the cracks when I went out the back door with a pillow case in one hand. The steps had washed away. As I jumped off the porch into the water that was now over waist-deep, I caught sight of a can of gasoline that I was counting on to use for the return trip to town. I caught the can as it floated by me and waded out of the melee. Shorty, having finished collecting his belongings from the tent, was waiting for me in the truck.

I put the gasoline in and looked back at the house. It had toppled and was being beaten to pieces by the waves. When I started to place the pillow case on the seat, I discovered that I had grabbed the wrong one—I had salvaged only a pillow and a can of gasoline which might not even be enough to get us back to town. Darkness was coming down fast. The storm grew in intensity. We would be lucky if we got out of it with our lives.

Fortune was kind to us that night. By following our recently made tracks back up the center of the island we laboriously made our way to the north end of Padre. There we found the waters of the Laguna Madre lapping over the plank troughs of the causeway. Could we make it? The choice had to be made quickly. We would try. So I nosed the Model A onto the planks, and we inched our way over the water. Wind tore at us and rain poured down in torrents.

It was daylight by then. A liquid, gray daylight in which everything blended and wavered like the scenes in an underwater film. At the ship channel we found that the swing bridge had been torn partly loose. The ends of it were two feet higher than the planks of the causeway. A barge was anchored nearby with several men aboard. They came to our rescue. Climbing from the barge to the causeway, they lifted the Ford and set it on the bridge; then they set it down at the other end. Thus we finally reached the comparative safety of the mainland.

Later we found that during the next hour the causeway was reduced to a total wreck. The planks were torn loose and flung through the air. Some of them were found weeks later in the mesquite forests of the million-acre King ranch, twenty miles away.

That hurricane left devastation everywhere it moved. Much of Corpus Christi was a shambles. Padre Island was cleared of everything for a hundred miles. The contours of the beach were changed and there were thirty channels cut all the way from the Gulf of Mexico to the Laguna Madre.

Within a week after the storm we were back on the island. We got there by loading our car on an improvised raft and poling it across Laguna Madre. Driving the beach was hazardous. It was striped with deep ruts and covered with logs and debris. The passes were filling up with sand, and we were able to drive through them, although we went through water two feet deep at times.

At the site of our former shack there was nothing. Nothing, that is, except an old icebox half sunk in the sand. Shorty's tent had caught around the icebox, and on examination showed its only damage to be a small dent. In searching about the campsite, he found all the things he had left with the exception of a small stew kettle. Viola and I found, as I have said, nothing. Out of all the supplies, the equipment, the bedding, the clothing, and what we regarded as our treasures, there absolutely was not a sign of anything. And Shorty had found everything he owned but a thirty-five-cent kettle!

The ways of the sea are strange. They say that whatever it takes away from you, it brings back. I'm inclined to think that it does. The next few months the tide carried in the lumber and piling for us to build a bigger and stronger house sixty-five miles from the north end of Padre.

Now, many years after the doctors predicted my imminent death, I still roam the wilds of my unsubdued island.

PAUL KALLINGER:

BORDERBLASTER DEEJAY

Del Rio, TX

Born 1922

When Texan Alan Bean literally stood on the moon in 1969 he could be seen and heard live by every Texan in the world who tuned in the spectacle. Yet when many people in this book were born, most Texans, rural people, led what now seem amazingly isolated lives.

Radio was the first of the mass media to break that isolation. By the late 1920s crystal sets were sophisticated enough to pick up nearby stations, especially at night when AM reception was best. By the 1930s vaudeville entertainers such as Jack Benny had made the transition from live stage performances to live radio.

One of the most influential radio pioneers was Texas's own John R. Brinkley, the Dr. Ruth of his day. From his mansion in Del Rio, Texas, J. R. Brinkley broadcasted via telephone lines and his Ciudad Acuña, Mexico, transmitter throughout North America and beyond.

Other states had their Edisons and S. F. B. Morses. Texas had Dr. Brinkley. Like all geniuses Doc Brinkley knew a good thing when he saw it. His enormously powerful XER, unregulated by the federal government, reached most receivers in America with an irresistible blend of patent medicine, down-home religion, and hillbilly music. His goat gland implant operation ($750) was so popular that his hospital and its three hundred employees kept little Del Rio humming throughout the Depression as oldsters flocked in by train to be fleeced. Dr. Brinkley became a multimillionaire in the middle of the Depression.

Stricter Mexican regulations closed Dr. Brinkley's station in

1933 but it reopened, more powerful than ever, in 1934 as XERA after a south-of-the-border political change. Brinkley's new directional transmitter is reported to have put out as much as a million watts of power and was almost certainly the most powerful station in the world. Other borderblaster stations (under nominal Mexican ownership) imitated Dr. Brinkley's formula, but he remained the king of border radio for a decade. His country music, corn-pone characters, and Bible preachers attracted advertisers who hired hillbilly bands to pitch such products as Light Crust flour.

By 1939 an international convention regulating broadcast frequencies and station strengths had been signed between the United States and Mexico, and by 1941 Dr. John R. Brinkley was silenced. Former patients sued and he died bankrupt in 1942.

But borderblasters continued to enliven the Southwest. Doc Brinkley's old powerhouse, renamed XERF, became an important cultural force in the 1950s in helping to determine the course of American musical history. And J. R. Brinkley's inventive mix of warblers, pitchmen, fortune-tellers, and preachers has influenced radio and television ever since.

"People like to have you tell them a little bit about yourself," says radio legend Paul Kallinger. "So I might tell about how I had just gone fishing with my oldest boy."

Paul Kallinger was born in Cedar Rapids, Nebraska, where his father was a shoe repairman and where young Paul grew up mesmerized by early-day radio. So after his World War II Navy service, Paul enrolled in a two-year radio school in California and hit the road looking for work. Paul began as a disk jockey at XERF in 1948 and soon exposure on his country-music show was essential for singers hoping for a big break. Paul did live shows until 1963 and then did taped shows until his involuntary retirement at gunpoint in 1963, when he was run off in a labor dispute.

Dr. Brinkley would have loved it.

I was in the studio announcing. A man came in with a forty-five and pulled the hammer back. I walked out with my hands in the air. He told me to run and I thought, "If I do run, he will shoot at my feet or my back." So when he said "Run!," I walked slower. When he said "Run, run, run!," I walked even slower. When I got out of range, I started running.

IN 1948 I HEARD OF an opening at XERF in Mexico. I sent an application out and an audition disk and they hired me. I had studied all phases of radio, news, interviews, man-on-the-street broadcasts, talk shows, you name it, but I became a pop disk jockey at XERF because most of our audience were rural folks.

Our country music went over real well. I would go off the air and say "Tomorrow night we will have Eddie Arnold, the Tennessee plowboy, on the program. Thank you, Johnny Cash, for being our guest tonight." We kept this up for a number of years, and its popularity kept growing and growing. I laid the pattern for the music. Whatever I would play, the smaller disk jockeys would pick up and this is how we made hits.

Country music mostly told a story. It had to be sad or it had to be a happy song that told a story. What sold a country record was somebody was breakin' up or someone was drinkin' beer in a bar and they cried in their beer and all that. If you could make the people cry or laugh with a country record, it would sell.

Elvis Presley's ballads had a little bit of country flavor at the time he was just easing into the rock field. If he had come up with "You ain't nuthin' but a hound dog" right from the very beginning, people may not have accepted that transition because it was too fast.

In 1955 Elvis called my house in Del Rio after he had just converted to rock and roll. He said that he had just heard Johnny Cash on my show and that he would like to be on the next night. I said, "We don't allow rock-and-roll artists on our program."

He said, "Thank you anyway, Mr. Kallinger."

So he went on to the next radio station to get on.

Everybody was trying to keep rock out. We were trying to keep it country because we were country and western deejays.

Right after his appearance on the Ed Sullivan Show in November 1955 Elvis was guest artist of the week at the Louisiana Hayride in Shreveport and I was the guest disk jockey of the week. I went to his hotel room. The fans, the young girls, were just going wild over him. They were waiting in line to go into his room and have his autograph. We got reunited and shook hands and he said, "Mr. Kallinger, they all did it to me. Don't feel bad about it. All the disk jockeys tried to keep rock out but we were lucky and the good Lord was good to us and we brought it in anyway."

It was up to me to decide what shows to popularize on my show. I'd look for somebody's qualifications and I paid attention to the record label, because if the company didn't have the proper distribution a song could be very good but there would be no way in the world it was going to hit because nobody could buy it and I would see if the song told a story, had a good musical background, and if the artist could pitch the song. I always wanted to know if a song was able to go.

The ones I remember the most are Web Pierce's songs like "There Stands the Glass," "In the Jailhouse Now," "Why Baby, Why?," "I Ain't Never," "Bye Bye Love," and "Wondering."

Web Pierce came out at a time when his style was so unique that everything he touched would automatically turn to gold. He was so hot that even if he took a song that wasn't any good, it would sell like crazy just because he was singing it.

In the early fifties he came down here to Del Rio as an unknown and he said, "Paul, I just got off Four Star (that was a record company out of Pasadena, California) and I just signed with Decca." I knew when he signed with Decca that he was going to get a lot of distribution; that's what it takes to make a hit. He said, "I got this song, I would like to have you audition it, listen to it, and see if it's worth playing on the air."

So I listened to "Wondering" and I said, "Yeah, it sounds real good. I am going to see what I can do with it."

He said, "Anything you can do, I'd appreciate."

Nobody had ever heard of him. Web Pierce was one that I put quite a bit of emphasis on to see what. . . . This was the beginning of helping artists to see how powerful XERF was and what you could do for an artist. So I played "Wondering" and "Wondering" hit. Then there was "There Stands a Glass," "I'll Go on Alone," "That Heart Belongs to Me," "In the Jailhouse Now," and many more.

When I took the job, I started running the late evening show from ten till two in the evening, playing country western music. Way back in those days, they didn't even call it country music. They called it hillbilly music. Five-string mandolin, five-string banjo. They played a lot of bluegrass until we graduated to country music, insisting that it was more of a modern type of western music.

When I started playing country music, artists would come down to Del Rio to be on my show. It just went over remarkably well. I got calls from artists from all over the country, mainly from the Grand Ole Opry and Louisiana Hayride, which is in KWKH in Shreveport. They would come down and I would spend many many hours, maybe days or weeks with them, fishing and entertaining. I would have Johnny Cash one night and I would have Hank Snow the next night, Web Pierce, Eddie Arnold. . . .

I don't think Hank Williams could write a note of music, but he was the greatest song-writer in the country. I was in Fred Rose's office once when Hank walked in. He said, "Fred, I have wrote a song."

"Well, Hank, go on over there in the corner, sit down, pick up your guitar, and I'll turn on the wire recorder."

That's how songs like "Your Cheating Heart," "Cold, Cold Heart," "Lovesick Blues," "Lonesome Whistle," "I Saw the Light," and many others became popular. For instance, when Hank was in his limousine going on a personal appearance at night, he saw the lights of the cars approaching him in the opposite direction and that inspired him to write "I Saw the Light," which had a lot of religious flavor in it.

The big-name singers like him weren't as well known then, but we put on quite a show. *Billboard* magazine called me in 1954 and said, "You are number three in the nation." I was in the top five for eight consecutive years thereafter.

I will tell you this much, XERF had the best announcers, the cream of the crop trying to sell mail-order. The owners offered announcers at other successful stations a handsome salary to come down here and sell mail-order on the air. But most of them couldn't sell any of it. They were very good—but not for our type of rural audience which was, every day, a do-or-die situation. You had to reach the type of people you were talking to. You didn't necessarily have to be one of them but they wanted to be spotlighted; they wanted some recognition. That was the key to it. Talk about them, don't talk about yourself.

If I had been selling beans, listeners would write and tell me, "Yes, we did have beans for supper that night."

You just pull stuff out of the clear blue sky. "Did you get enough rain out there, you folks in Iowa? I understand that Iowa is drought-stricken." Stuff like that.

A truck driver is going along the highway and you say, "Slow down. You know what's goin' to happen if you fall asleep at the wheel. We think a lot of you and we want to keep you around for a long time."

I would get calls: "You saved my life."

You have to visualize what the people are doing.

We introduced a lot of new products. You have heard of D-Con rodent killer? It was introduced on radio station XERF. It wasn't available in stores at the time. The only place you could buy it was from XERF.

I used to say, "The only place you can get this, folks, is right here at XERF. We're having a limited-time offer. If your letter is post-marked by midnight tomorrow, you will get a free gift, something you will value. Folks, if you want to get rid of rats, send your order today to D-Con, XERF, Del Rio, Texas. I gave my father-in-law some and his rats left and went so far for water that they never came back!"

We had the blade man, the diamond man, the toy man, and I have had people from up North come down here and say, "I want to see the diamond man. I want some of those diamonds you have been talking about." They thought all these factories were down here. There weren't any of them down here. They were in New York, Chicago, Minnesota, Wisconsin, and different places like that. We would get so many orders, count them, and then would bill the companies for those orders.

Texas was one of our best mail-order states. When I started in 1948, we were fifty thousand watts clear channel, with all new RCA equipment. Fifty thousand watts back then would reach as far as two hundred and fifty thousand watts today. We had great cover-age of the entire USA.

I think people are pretty hungry for the old type of delivery! Except mail-order. Although I used to pull in thousands of orders a day, even one record-breaking ten-thousand-order day, I don't think mail-order would go over too well now.

Most young disk jockeys are just button-pushers. And if they do start catching on with their audience, it goes right to their head, but listeners want you to talk to *them,* not talk about how great *you* are. Let's talk about them and see what they are doing. That's what they are hungry for. That's not what they are getting and they really want it again.

If we didn't bring in the results, we didn't keep our jobs. It was hard sell all the way through and very difficult unless you were natural at it. Fortunately enough, it was a gift from God that I could speak extemporaneously. If somebody told me to talk about paint for fifteen minutes, I'd do it! If a company sent us a piece of copy which was about a million words long, what to do with it. I had that account on two or three times a night, so I ad-libbed it. Like Dial Finance Company, for example, or More Weight, Pounds Off. I would turn on the microphone and ad-lib the whole show. My commercials ran three to four minutes, sometimes longer. I have had commercials last as long as fifteen minutes. As long as it would sell, I went ahead and delivered it.

Pounds-Off, how to lose weight. Things would come up like a light in my mind. "You couldn't overload the motor in a truck and have that truck perform properly, could you? Of course you couldn't. The human body is the same thing. Your heart was designed by the good Lord up above to pump so much blood from your system. Now if you are overloading your heart, if you overload an engine, what happens? It breaks down. Of course, it does. We are going to talk about getting that weight off so you live longer."

Sometimes we had recessions and I had to come up with something to keep my job. It was a matter of put out or get out. You sold or you didn't last.

I lasted on that radio station for four broadcasting decades, forty years of broadcasting on XERF. Wherever I go people still remember my old station break: "From coast to coast, border to border, wherever you are, whatever you might be doing, when you think of real fine entertainment think of XERF in Ciudad Acuña, Coahuilla, Mexico, alongside the beautiful, silvery Rio Grande River where the sunshine spends the winter. This is Paul Kallinger, your good neighbor along the way, from Del Rio, Texas."

THOMAS QUALIA:
CONSERVE WATER,
DRINK TEXAS WINE
Del Rio, TX
Born 1944

One of Dallas's most influential preachers has reportedly said, "I would rather commit adultery than let a drop of alcohol cross my lips." Of course, scuppernong and imported grapes have been tempting the faithful ever since the arrival of the first Anglos west of the Sabine River. But now in the 1990's, Texas's resurgent wine industry is attempting to outferment California for the shekels of the godless. That will be difficult because though Texans' per capita alcohol consumption ranks seventh nationwide, Texans only quaff about one gallon each of un-macho wine. And, unfortunately for wine producers like Tom Qualia, the dinner-wine business is an iffy proposition in a state where local-option liquor laws make prohibition a scary possibility at every election.

One of my favorite bumper stickers says, CONSERVE WATER, DRINK TEXAS WINE but it does not say where to find a good Texas wine. The place I looked was Del Rio on the Rio Grande River. That was where Thomas Qualia's Italian immigrant grandfather had founded the Val Verde Winery, Texas's first, in 1883, using Lenoir grapes.

DON'T DRINK THAT CALIFORNIA STUFF! Think Texan!

My grandfather produced for his own needs and supplied the local demand. He made wine for love of the vine and for the tradition. My own love of wine and the grapevines was passed from my father to me. A lot of people say, "Golly, you are really tied to this." But growing grapes and making wine is what I enjoy doing.

I call my port Don Luis after my grandfather. It has become very famous across the Southwest. I'm bragging because it wins in every competition it is in and has been compared favorably to some of the better known ports in the world. It is a very complex, dense wine, something that you are going to sip in small quantity.

Our cabernet sauvignon is aged in French oak from central France. Our lenoir of 1984 right now is in American bluegrass Kentucky oak.

No Texas oak yet!

When I went to Texas Tech, I started out in personnel management and ended up with a degree in animal science because I thought I was going into ranching. But instead I inherited the winery; so I am making wine. I have had no formal education in winemaking other than what my father taught me. His method of wine-making was of the old school: "Yours is not to question why; yours is just to do it because it worked before."

Ever since 1978 I have had an oenologist, Dr. Ricky Ferro, who is my consultant in California. I fly him out here anywhere from two to three times a year. We are working anywhere from a day to five days depending on whether there is a crush or not. He has taught me all my lab techniques that are used for following the progress of our wines. My father would be pleased to see the quality of the wines I am producing today.

I enjoy the challenge of making good wine. There are so many variables; every year is different regardless how scientific, how modern your equipment, and everything else. There is always a challenge. It is always a thrill at the end to taste the final product. You can have the most exquisite laboratory in the world, but the ultimate test is the taste test. If it isn't pleasing to the consumer, you are not going to sell the product.

Untold millions have been invested in the Texas wine industry, but we are a fraternity of only about two dozen people and we all help each other. If I need advice or help, I can pick up the phone and call five different wineries that would be happy to help. We all reciprocate. At this point in the game there is not enough supply to meet demand so we are not in competition with each other.

Texans want Texas products and are proud of them. For a while there were some wineries in the state that started bringing in tankloads of wine and juice from California, either fermenting it or buying it and saying bottled by such-and-such winery in Such-and-Such, Texas. Well, Texans were a little naive at first, but after they started learning how to read that label they just left that stuff alone—just like they do the rest of the California wines.

They wanted Texas wine! But it isn't easy to find it yet in the retail stores. You are going to have to look hard to find it. Distribution is still very limited. When you get into the large stores, the chains, you are going to have to supply enough for them to deliver to all their stores or not at all. In our case, we just started selling to a retail market away from the winery in 1985. Prior to that time, we sold all our production right here because, one, it is too delicate to transport and, two, the natives won't let it leave because *they are going to drink it locally.*

DAN WESTBROOK:

TEXAS RANGER

London, TX

Born 1895

The name Texas Ranger looms larger than life in American history. From the early scouts who ranged ahead of the emigrant wagon trains to the frontier guards to today's professional state police, the Texas Rangers have weathered everything from Indian wars to dirty politics. The legend persists.

Texas Ranger Dan Westbrook was the last of the mounted patrolmen. "I was raised on a horse," he said. "I never did much afoot."

Born and raised in Menard County, he ranched goats and sheep both before and after government service. An old Army buddy, Governor James Allred, got him a job as a livestock inspector working out of the governor's office. Dan transferred to the Rangers when Governor Allred left office in 1939. Dan liked the work, whether it was retrieving a cattle thief from Ohio, catching draft evaders, patrolling the border, or setting up roadblocks. And he liked the freedom of wide-open country before the advent of paved roads.

The salary was only one hundred fifty dollars a month, out of which he had to provide his own horse. The nearest telephone might be a sixty-mile ride away, but for this man whose education stopped at the eighth grade learning how to make do came easily "by necessity."

Dan Westbrook's life stretched back to the homesteading days. He said that his uncle and father went to Austin and paid seventeen dollars to preempt a section of six hundred forty acres of state land. Menard County had been organized only two decades before

Dan's birth and it was not until 1905 that H. H. Wheelis built the first net-wire fence there. Menard and neighboring Schleicher County (1901) were livestock country and it was a terrible shock years later when a local ranch family was massacred near Eldorado.

Resolving that case was to be Dan Westbrook's most difficult and controversial challenge as a Texas Ranger.

CALCOTE FAMILY IS WIPED OUT. FORMER EMPLOYEE CHARGED screamed the San Angelo *Standard-Times* on September 7, 1940. "Bullets from a .30-.30 rifle Thursday night snuffed out the lives of the entire Henry Calcote family." Along with grisly photos of the four victims lying in pools of their own blood, the newspaper said that "A posse of citizens and local and state police tonight was combing the vicinity for Emelio 'Shorty' Benavidez, about twenty-nine, former employee of the Calcotes who has been charged by District Attorney O. C. Fisher with first degree murder of Calcote."

Governor "Pappy" O'Daniel posted a reward of two hundred fifty dollars for the man. Eldorado Legionnaires put up one hundred dollars and brothers of the slain man added one thousand dollars.

On September 21 the paper announced the arrest of the Mexican by Sheriff Jim Nance of Sanderson in Terrell County. The "foot-sore and hungry" suspect had given no resistance when captured "about 2 A.M. Friday 60 miles southeast of Sanderson, a short distance from the Rio Grande."

The unarmed suspect told the sheriff that he had caught an automobile ride from Eldorado to Sonora when he learned that he had been indicted by the Eldorado grand jury. "From Sonora, however, he walked toward the Mexican border—150 miles away. When he was almost in sight of the river Friday he was arrested. . . . The suspect denied he committed the slayings. He first refused to identify himself, Sheriff Nance said."

Sheriff Nance told the newspaper that he would claim the thirteen-hundred-fifty-dollar reward.

Despite appeals by the U.S. Department of State and Mexican embassy officials, Emiliano Benavidez was executed in the Huntsville electric chair on August 8, 1941. "Execution of sentence had been previously stayed three times for a total of 120 days to allow full investigation of the case, including a contention Benavides was kidnapped in Mexico and returned to the United States following the death of Calcote."

Benavidez went calmly to his death, stating in English "I die for nothing."

A half-century ago the Calcote murders were a front-page Texas sensation. The mystery of the Mexican half-breed's capture lingered on long after the case had been closed. Many people continued to wonder what had happened down there in Terrell County on the banks of the Rio Grande on the night of September 20, 1940.

Author Ron Strickland interviewing Texas Ranger Dan Westbrook.

As we talked, Dan Westbrook freely admitted that *he* had arranged the kidnapping of Benavidez. "A Ranger is handicapped now and he can't do anything like that," he says wistfully. "We didn't have no damn search warrant."

He adds of himself, "These Irish people, you can't do nothing with 'em. Smile and the world smiles with ya."

Dan Westbrook said that he always had "such good luck in the Texas Rangers" because he wanted to help people, not harm them. Yes, but if I had been a fugitive in 1940, I would not have wanted Dan Westbrook on my trail.

Here then is the story of the capture of Benavidez. As the oldest living Texas Ranger said, "These Rangers tell it like it is. They don't put no bull or nuthin' in."

WE ENFORCED LAWS ALL OVER Texas and were assigned to companies. I worked out of Company E and Company D from El Paso to Brownsville, eleven hundred miles down that Rio Grande River. Company E was El Paso to Del Rio, six or eight men, but not all of them worked on the border. Just Spanish-speaking men. Me and one or two others. We didn't have the amount of crime or the new types of crime then so two or three men could handle it O.K.

Nearly all of us in West Texas spoke Spanish. I could read and write it. I was raised with 'em on my father's ranch herding goats and sheep. They herded goats and sheep on foot. They herded 'em and I was the *bassiero,* wrangler, the man who looked after the whole operation on horseback. The herders'd lose 'em and I'd find 'em and bring 'em back in. I hauled water to 'em long before we ever had any net wire and turned sheep loose.

In the Rangers all my principal work was on the Mexican border. There wasn't any Big Bend National Park then. That was wide-open country, owned by the state and by big ranches. We operated in that country ahorseback. We didn't have but very few cars when I started to work. You could just get so far in with a horse trailer. Then you'd camp there overnight and go up the river one way on horseback and then down the river the other way looking for smugglers smuggling horses, sheep, and cattle.

They'd smuggle both ways. Them thieves from Mexico would come over and sell cattle and horses and then when they were going back they'd steal animals.

I lost a horse to them myself. It's hard to explain to a man that's never been there, but they could cross anywhere on foot. One day I had my pack horse staked out at my camp when I was gone all day and part of the night. When I came back the horse was gone. Somebody had swum that river or ridden across and stolen him.

A Ranger couldn't go over in Old Mexico, but once I got back a murderer who had killed four people—the Calcote family, big ranchers in Schleicher County next to my Menard County. Captain Ernest Best in Del Rio had asked me to work on it to see what I could do. After I investigated, I found out that it couldn't be done legally but would have to be done otherwise.

I wasn't on the border at that time but up at San Angelo. I had a connection with a Mexican on the other side who used to work for us at the ranch in Menard. I sent word over there and he came to see me. He kept me posted as to where the murderer was over in the little villages until I could get sufficient help.

Our government tried and tried to get him out legally and, of course, Mexico knew all about it. That's why I had to be so quiet.

Sheriff Jim Nance of Terrell County finally decided to help me. It was through his reputation and through his father's reputation before him that we managed to get the man. He really did more than I did. I said to Jim, "We'll work this out and get him delivered to us in the middle of the river." We swore to one another that we'd never tell how we did it. But he's dead now and I can tell it.

You've got to buy Mexicans, even the good ones. It's a reward. My two Mexicans had located the man and knew where he was. Jim said he had two men who might help us. He got an old Mexican to get hold of them and proposition them.

Jim Nance wanted those two Mexicans for minor crimes. He made a deal with them to catch the murderer and bring him out in exchange for not going after them.

It took a while to get my two Mexicans and his working together. His were afraid that men like Jim and me would arrest them or kill them.

You got to treat Mexicans rough. If you tell him you're gonna kick his ass or kill him, then you'd better do it.

People had made up a fifteen-hundred-dollar reward and John Sutton, the old district judge in Angelo, gave me the money and I said "I'll bring the man or the money."

He said, "Yes, I know you will."

Jim couldn't go out in the middle of the river 'cause he had a warrant for those two men. But he didn't want those two, just the murderer. I could go out in the middle of the river because I didn't have a warrant for their arrest, but only for the Yacqui Indian.

At midnight I went by myself on horseback out in the middle of the Rio Grande. Jim Nance was on the bank of the river with a rifle in case anything went wrong. If it hadn't been for him, I would never have gotten that Mexican out. He was sure a good man!

Our Mexicans came out to the middle of the river and turned

their prisoner over to me. They had smuggled him from thirty-five miles back on horseback. They gave me the lead rope and then I gave 'em the reward which I'd got from Judge Sutton.

As soon as I got back to the American shore, Jim Nance and me took the Mexican off the horse and turned it loose across the river.

The people back in them days was different than they are now. We had to slip that man into Schleicher County or there would have been an uprising.

The murderer wasn't really so much a Mexican as a Yacqui Indian. A very small fella. I and Jim Furnow took him out of jail to show us where the murder gun was.

The Indian had already been indicted when I caught him. The trial took about fifteen minutes.

The damn Mexicans found out about it and tried to get him extradited back to Mexico. So the man could not be executed until those proceedings were over.

We sent him to the electric chair. I took him over there and I know.

CANUTA MENDEZ YZAQUIRRE RAMIREZ: A SOUTH TEXAS WEDDING

Premont, TX

Born 1892

Canuta Ramirez grew up in South Texas before World War I. The Anglo presence was still so small that she never needed to speak much English until after her husband's death when she moved to San Antonio in 1942 and worked in a store. Canuta had never much wanted to speak English anyway because of the bad experiences her family and friends had had with the acquisitive, domineering gringos. Her father had arrived in South Texas from Mexico only a half-century after the fall of the Alamo and its legacy of bitterness was still fresh in people's minds. His own community in Duval County was entirely Spanish-speaking.

After Canuta's marriage to Ponciano Ramirez in 1921 she moved to Laredo, where she, Ponciano, and his three brothers ran a *tiendita,* a small general store, across the street from an elementary school. In her father's family of thirteen children she had been poor and in Laredo she was poor, too. "But we were the same as everybody else," she says.

Canuta has two boys and one girl. None of them are farmers. Her son David Ramirez is a space-program technician, son Ponciano is an offshore radio specialist, and daughter Bertha Barrera is an educator. Only a couple of Canuta's brothers, lacking education, continue as small farmers like their father before them.

Canuta has nine grandchildren and ten great-grandchildren, several of whom have married Anglos, a trend she approves.

Canuta Ramirez does not want to return to the old days, but she misses the best parts of that lost world.

Concepción was where they all came to town to get supplies. Every summer after the cotton was harvested, people would come to celebrate at the outdoor plaza. While the strings and trombones played, people strolled (dando la vuelta), *the girls toward the center of the plaza and the boys on the outside. Just walking, not dancing. There were many things to eat, many people laughing and gathering and playing* loteria, *a game like bingo but where the cards had pictures of things you could win. That was where my future husband Ponciano used to try to see me.*

Wedding photo, Ponciano Ramirez and Canuta Mendez, January 15, 1921.

BECAUSE I WAS BORN JANUARY 1, 1892, my father used to say I had "four beginnings." New year. New month. New week. And a new moon. But I was the first in the family, too, so I actually had *five* beginnings.

When he was a boy, my father settled just across the border from Ceralvo about 1870. He worked for the men with the sheep and the lambs. One day he and the other men had to run and hide from the Indians. He barely missed being hit by an Indian's arrow by jumping off a post into the big corral. Later he saw that arrow, plugged in the post where his hand had been.

When people had to go into town for supplies, they traveled together for protection.

My mother came from Ciudad Mier in lower Mexico in 1892. Her mother's name was Yzaquirre, early settlers in Mier. Her mother's house was a very large one-room house made of adobe. In one corner they stored dry corn so that it formed a wall.

My mother married at *el rancho de mi tío Manuel.* My mother was about fifteen years old; they said she was too young.

My parents settled along a stream in 1890 where Concepción first was in Duval County. Everyone settled along streams in those days because water was so scarce.

My mother had thirteen children and I was the oldest. I was three years old when I got lost because we went to "Grandpa" Hector, some good neighbors named Hector across the creek with whom we grew up together, sharing like a family. When we went to visit, my momma had a six-months or nine-months daughter with her, too. I was a three-year-old. Then when coming back, I feel tired and I had to jump a little fence to get into the yard of my little house. Then I feel so tired and my momma says, "Come on, come on, jump the wire to go into the house."

I say, "No, no, I am too mad. The sun is too hot."

Later my mother took my baby sister home and put her in her crib. When she came back for me, I was not there.

She was so worry because she didn't see me nowhere. There was big cactus. She say, "I left the baby in bed and it is going to fall down and I don't know what to do." Then my father comes into the house and she say, "You call everybody!"

Grandfather Hector, he goes to the neighbors. There was a deep-down creek and then many people come to look for me. The horse was gone. Then the time was nine o'clock in the morning.

They find me at three o'clock in the afternoon walking in and around the cactus and mesquite. I could walk in there because I was so small.

The house was full of ladies when my momma brought me back. Everyone was asking me, "You were lost, were you no afraid?"

I said, "I was not alone. There was with me a man, a lady, and a little boy. They were with me and I was not afraid."

I don't know. Momma say, "My God, this little girl. . . . I had prayed to the three sacred names—Joseph, Mary, and Jesus.

I was three years old. They find a little shoe there from me, because I have on just one. And they found the footprints of a man, a lady, and a child.

My father was a farmer who farmed with horses. He dug water wells for people and to this day there are old-timers that remember him or hear say of wells he dug. One of his brothers died and that family came to live with us and helped my father with his farming.

When I was growing up, there were those cousins plus my parents' thirteen children. It was such a big family that we had to take turns eating. All the girls helped prepare and serve the food. The boys and the men that worked for my father came first. Then the ladies and babies last because the ladies were always serving the boys and the men.

My mother's children were all born close together, one right after the other. So the older ones had to take care of the younger ones so that Momma wouldn't have so much work. I was the oldest. There was a big garden and my job was to take care of the irrigation ditches. We had cabbage, sweet potatoes, white potatoes, tomatoes, lettuce, onions, garlic. Everything in the garden. Orange trees, grapevines. There was too much and we gave a lot away to the neighbors.

We ate a lot of beans, hominy, sometimes meat from cows, goats, or sheep. A hog, they would kill him and cut up the meat and save it. Save the lard and make chorizo and chicharrones.

Chorizo is a spicy ground meat mixed with red chiles and vinegar. We stored this mixture in a cleaned and dried cow's intestine casing. Dried chorizo kept for a long time.

Chicharrones are pork skins which we fried in lard to make them crisp. They also lasted a long time.

We had other animals we also butchered.

Everybody worked hard. Every member of the family had a chore to do. One would feed hogs. Another would take care of goats and lambs. I milked cows because with so many babies we needed milk. Today is better than the old days because there was no powdered milk then!

The children went to a little country school and the boys farmed and helped with the well-drilling. But my father wanted the three oldest girls to learn something more. So when I was about fifteen, he sent us to Laredo to a school for girls. We learned a little more English there, talking with the English people.

Some of my cousins went to Mexico to live with their grandparents.

My husband came from a family of five boys and five girls. His mother was short and blue-eyed, the only one in the family with blue eyes. She was like a queen bee in her home. Everybody listened carefully to her words, whatever she said. She was so nice to all the family! If a child was not so good, she said, "No, no, niño. Don't do that. No, no." She didn't get mad like I did.

I first met my husband when he came to help somebody on our farm and he was also a student at our little country school in old Concepción. He later played the fiddle and his parents had a store in Realitos, which was about thirty miles north of Concepción.

All summer long there were birthday parties and dances. In Realitos there was a dance hall owned by my husband's grandfather. He and all his brothers were there every weekend.

So many boys were always looking for me. They say I'm so pretty. Because I was the oldest girl in our family.

Ponciano was always looking for me. But my father did not want him to come to the house to see us. He wanted to keep us home working. And he only wanted to see good people around, that's why. He never say anything bad about my husband because he knew he was a good man. He was a good man but no house and no place to live. So no good for me.

So Ponciano would try to see me at the plaza on weekends. All the family would go to the plaza on weekends. During the week we sent letters and made dates. At the plaza we spoke with each other while walking around the gazebo where the musicians were playing. Boys and girls were always meeting there.

Finally after two summers Ponciano sent a commission, two of my father's friends, to speak to head of the family. They came to our house and they said, "Well, we have this thing that we need to discuss. We want to ask the hand of the lady in marriage."

A father usually waits a week or two weeks to answer. Then he sends for the commission and asks them to return for the answer.

My momma talked to his family to make sure that everyone knew of the commission. This was a very delicate situation. I was the first to marry and my parents were not used to parting with their children.

My parents checked to see that Ponciano had a job and that he was a good man. And my momma and my father asked me and I said, "Yes, I do, I like him."

In a week my father said yes to the commission. Then it was all set.

It was a very exciting phase of my life! His family liked me and my family. They visited and planned a wedding.

Ooooh, the wedding! About fifty people attended at the church in Laredo.

I went to get my wedding dress at Laredo. It was just a dress. Ankle-length. White, high slippers—I didn't like them but one of my sisters-in-law-to-be said "This looks great on you."

Ponciano had lost his father when he was young, so his oldest brother Felipe was working like the man of the family. He and Ponciano's mother came to bring me the *donas*. What you call a dowry in English. They give me this money to buy my wedding gown, veil, and whatever I needed.

Some friends and all our families were at the church in Laredo. There was a reception in a separate room and Ponciano's brothers played music.

We were very happy. Ponciano had built a house and I looked forward to married life.

OCTAVIO GARCIA:

A PRIEST AND A

MULE NAMED CHULA

McAllen, TX

Born 1899

Octavio Garcia is as fine a Texan as you could ever meet. Not only did he doctor to Lower Rio Grande folks for a half century; but also he is a gifted memoirist and a man of great compassion and learning. And he has been a bicultural ambassador on both sides of the international border.

Dr. Garcia is the son of a large landowner of Mier, Tamaulipas, who fled during the Mexican Revolution to his twelve-thousand-acre ranch thirty-two miles from Falfurrias, Texas. Dr. Garcia attended medical school at St. Louis University and overcame Lower Valley prejudices against Spanish-surnamed citizens to practice medicine. He doctored all degrees and classes of patients from his office in McAllen, Texas, or from his vehicle anywhere in the Lower Rio Grande Valley on either side of the border.

Dr. Garcia has described the bigotry he encountered as not "an isolated experience directed toward me" but a widespread situation. "The Anglos obviously considered the Mexican an inferior race, thereby apparently justifying their premeditated or thoughtless practices. This discrimination permeated all levels of society—the educational field, housing, job procurement, health care, the market place, and most of all, in the administration of justice."

Amazingly, this learned and humane man was never embittered by the ugliness he encountered. I think he was saved from that by his deep sense of who he was and by his Spanish heritage of "faultless courage."

The following account of one of his lifelong mentors and friends is from *Otros Dias.* * It is about a Catholic priest named Father Janvier, and I include it as a tribute to all the religious folk who have served the Southwest's poor for three centuries.

ONE OF MY MOST ENDURING friendships with a man of God began while I was living on the family ranch in Texas. The Spanish colonists of the Oblate province now known as the Rio Grande Valley were the first to bring and spread the gospel. After the war with Mexico and the annexation of this vast territory to the United States, the Catholic atmosphere first brought to Texas by the Franciscans began to decline. The original settlers retained their faith, but it was difficult for the church to minister to their needs. Often, some families crossed the river into Mexico for weddings, baptisms, and other practices of their faith.

The situation did not improve until the arrival of missionaries of the Oblate order between 1849 and 1853. These were hardy pioneer priests, traveling from ranch to ranch and small communities undertaking the needed task.

My dear friend, Father Janvier, walked in the steps of these holy men. Father Missionary was small in stature, light in weight, slightly stooped due to his advanced age, with sparse yellowish hair, not white, and an oval face with large brown and honey-colored eyes that radiated kindness and inner peace.

Father Janvier spent his life as a missionary along the north side of the lower Rio Grande River, carrying on his mission on horseback. He was born in France, and soon after his ordination, was sent to this area by his religious order, the "Oblates of Mary Immaculate."

His ministry consisted of trying to reach those Christians living in remote areas that, due to difficulties of transportation, were unable to attend church services or send their children to Christian Doctrine classes. His visits were welcomed by all, even by the ranch owners who were not Catholic, since they were always glad to

---

*Octavio Garcia, *Otros Dias* (Westford, Mass.: Grey Home Press, 1984), pp. 159–163.

receive news and an occasional newspaper or book he carried. During the few days he would spend at a ranch, he baptized babies, married couples who had awaited his rounds, celebrated the mass, and visited and counseled those who sought his advice.

While he admired the simple faith of his scattered flock, he deplored the multiple superstitions that were rampant among them—their belief in the "evil eye," of "encantos" (enchantments), and their fear of ghosts—and their prayers to a medal or a picture without any clear conception that they must pray to God. Father Janvier emphasized the simple "Our Father" and "Hail Mary," and asked them to elevate their petitions in simple conversation with their Creator.

I first met him as a young man at my father's ranch, La Encantada, in Brooks County, Texas. At the time I paid little attention to him, as he usually spent most of his time with my elders on his not too frequent visits.

While visiting at the ranch, he had the opportunity of good quarters, good food, care for his horse and mule, and an opportunity for rest and conversation. He would talk at length with my father, sometimes in English interspersed with French phrases when he wished to emphasize a point.

I left the ranch to pursue my medical studies and for many years I did not see or even hear of the good Padre. Our paths crossed again at St. Peter's Novitiate, south of Mission, Texas, twenty-two years later, when I was doctor to the Oblates. He was very patient and entrusted his health to me.

At that time he was retired and lived at the monastery. He spent his time, after his early morning mass, in reading, meditation, and seeing after the welfare of his pet ducks and geese at a nearby pond on the extensive grounds of the monastery.

I enjoyed visiting at the seminary, taking time from my busy schedule usually late in the afternoon. We would pace up and down the long gallery, or he would sit on a reclining chair while I sat on a projection at the base of a supporting gallery arch. At other times, we walked to the pond to see his flocks of ducks and geese, where he would give me a natural history lesson. In the early spring, we would walk to the river with fishing poles and while away the time in conversation.

His speech was rapid and marked by pauses and expressive

gestures. He was equally at home conversing in his native French, in English, or in Spanish, preferring to speak in Spanish since few of us knew much French. We would talk of many things: Nature, history, politics, folklore, geography, philosophy (usually ethics), and rarely religion. His vast experience with human nature and his knowledge of the frontier enriched his anecdotes.

The only time he was not relating some of his adventures in the brush was while on his rounds, or when he would be really silent while fishing. If, after throwing the line into the water, he noticed a nibble, he turned all other thoughts aside and watched the movements of the cork with care. He had infinite patience, and observing him quietly, I tried not to disturb him. In my mind I tried to fathom his thoughts, only to be surprised when, after a long time, he returned to his seat and uttered, "It was only a turtle."

Late in the afternoon we would return to the monastery to continue our discussions and partake of chocolate and cookies that the nuns of the kitchen had prepared.

At other times, usually when he came to my house in McAllen for dinner, he entertained my wife, Cecile, and the children with stories of his rounds (trips) to the ranches to the north and west.

"Here, in this area, autumn simulates another spring. The rigors of summer have abated, and a harbinger of the coming winter is the migration of birds on their southward trek, which is particularly evident after the first norther. Whitewing doves, having raised their young, become native, feed heavily, and prepare for their migration south. Doves, as well as other birds, arrive from the north. But the most impressive are the late evening and night flights of geese. To be aware of their call while in flight and, better, to see their vee-shaped colony late in an evening sky, or outlined on a moonlit night, is to witness a symphony of sight and sound never to be forgotten.

"Often in my trips to minister and spread the Gospel, I could not reach my destination before dark, many times due to my cantankerous and difficult pack mule, 'Chula,' who refused to obey and be led if we neared a waterhole. She stubbornly refused to budge, in spite of my urging and pulling on the rope from my horse. So I would then camp for the night and resume my journey in the early morning, when I was again regaled by dawn gradually lighting the eastern sky and the cacophony of sound from the early birds.

"Chula, Chula, how can I forget you? You served me well, but you also tried my soul, my patience. I remember you well: small, from your father Jack. You also inherited his donkey disposition, and from your mother mare, nary a thing. Chula, I do not know who bestowed that name on you. Your looks and disposition betray it, but you taught me patience and tolerance even if, at times, I had to pray aloud, stay my whip, and end by laughing.

"I had fear of getting lost, since I had a poor sense of direction, which was another of my reasons for not wanting to travel during the night time. I know that many of your vaqueros have an uncanny sense of direction, that getting lost is the least of their worries, and that they often preferred night travel to the rigors of the daytime heat. However, I preferred to travel during the day on the old roads and trails that, at times, were only barely discerned paths, due to infrequent travel.

"I could always tell the approach of a watering place, first by the sight of a windmill in the distance, its fan slowly turning with the wind, or by the multiple narrow paths made by cattle as they went to water, or finally, by the sound of the pumping shaft of the windmill. I frequently stopped to rest my horse and mule, to eat a little jerky and hardtack, and sometimes, to rest and doze in a welcome siesta.

"Many were the times I enjoyed seeing the wildlife, such as the deer and turkeys, coming to water. I could tell the near arrival of a badger from the movements of the grass and weeds, since his short legs prevented a clear view of his squat and powerful body. Also, I remember birds slaking their thirst at the small pond formed by the surplus water from the tank.

"Often in the summertime, I would take the opportunity of a good bath, either in the tank or a shower emerging from the pipe as the mill turned. This was a must, as facilities for bathing were few and far between."

Children loved to gather around Father Janvier and listen to his stories of earlier times, like in his youth when he lived as a child in France, on a small farm near the Spanish border. There, his father had an olive grove that was ancient in the family, and he remembered laboring there and sharing with him the traditional midday repast of bread, wine, cheese, and olives.

Years would pass and our lives, mine and Father Janvier's, would still intertwine. When my wife suffered a cerebral vascular accident, it became imperative to confine her to a nursing home. After trial and error, I finally confided her care to the San Juan Nursing Home. Again, I was to see the Padre often, for he, too, was a patient there. He was able to conduct early morning services in the small chapel of the nursing home. While he rendered service to all the patients, he particularly looked after and cared for Cecile's welfare.

In time, he was confined to his room, because of a coronary attack. I visited him frequently when I made my visits to my wife. He recovered somewhat, and we were able to enjoy our accustomed drink of sherry during my visits.

One day he suffered a relapse and had to be hospitalized at McAllen, where I worked. His condition worsened, but he retained full consciousness. After my rounds I would visit him.

One evening he asked me to stay. I did, noting that his condition was terminal. He was quiet, in spite of his difficult breathing. He grasped my hand and started to pray the Rosary. There were intervals of quiet and intervals of prayer. He recited the Lord's Prayer, and I answered. Then he began the Hail Mary in English, reverted to French, and finally to Spanish. His voice failed, and when I said, "Pray for us now and at the hour of our death . . ." his hand relaxed. A few short breaths and he had gone to his eternal reward.

FILIBERTO NUÑEZ:

BOOTMAKER

San Antonio, TX

Born 1919

Cowboy boots have centuries of practical outdoor experience tied into their design, but this workaday ancestry may be overlooked when the pair in question is an exotic leather creation that will never get any closer to a cowpie than the dance floor of the local country club.

Filiberto Nuñez handsewed Western boots after his 1949 arrival in Texas from Mexico. For many years before retiring back south of the border he was an hourly wage "bottom man" at Dave Little Boots. Together with a specialty top man and a finishing man, he produced made-to-order boots of high quality. To construct the entire bottom of a boot is complex work, often involving as many as fifty separate operations. Filiberto Nuñez took a person's foot measurements through the whole process, adapting the contours of a foot to a standard last and molding the rich leathers to that shape.

But the shape of this craftsman's art was formed on the last of his own family history.

MY GODFATHER STARTED OFF WORKING as a shoemaker because *his* godfather was a shoemaker. If his godfather had been a plumber, he would probably have been a plumber.

In Mexico the godparents are very, very important. They are with you for life and you respect your godfather.

My godfather had a big shop. He said to me when I was a young boy, "You come and I'll give you a job." And that is the way I started, making women's shoes in Guadalajara.

When I moved from Guadalajara in 1949 to Laredo, Texas, they didn't have any shoe factories there so I had to learn the boot trade. There is a lot of difference in the construction of boots and ladies' shoes because the shoes are so lightweight. The lady's shoe is a very fine product if you hand-welt it. But most of the time the hand-welt in the Western boot is a lot better because it has heavier material.

When you are building the heel, you have to make sure to give it the right pitch to make the boot comfortable. If the boot-heel pitch is wrong, you have an arch problem with it because it will feel high on the bottom. I have to give it the pitch necessary to make it comfortable. I don't want the boot to feel unbalanced or like you have a pencil underneath your heel.

I am what we call a bottom man who does the mounting, lasting, hand-welt sewing, and putting the soles and heels on. I cut and sew the heavy leather insole, outsole, heel, and welt. I do that heavy construction until I get the boot topped. Then my biggest job is to mount that thing by hand correctly on the mold so that it will fit properly. If it is not mounted correctly, the boot will never fit properly.

Bootmaking has always provided me a livelihood. I have been very happy with my trade. My satisfaction has been to be recognized as a good craftsman.

WILLIE LEWIS BROWN, JR.:

"CONFIDENCE THAT

YOU COULD LEARN"

San Francisco, CA

Born 1934

Few subjects are as important to Texas's future as universal access to educational opportunity. Each child denied a chance to learn is a net loss for Texas and the nation. Even today this is not well enough appreciated at the local level but during the segregated 1940s and early 1950s things were even worse. That was when Fred McKenzie served as a small town school trustee. He reports in his fascinating memoir *Avinger, Texas USA* that:

Anytime any funding came into the white board's hand, . . . from whatever source, at least ninety percent of it was spent on the white school facilities and only what happened to be left over trickled down to the blacks. This was typified by an expression I heard over and over until it got to be somewhat of a joke with us. It usually came about this way—We'd get a sum of money to spend on improving school property. After spending it as just indicated, some board member would say "Well now, you know we ought to spend some of this on the coloreds" (only he usually used another word). Then the others would chime in and say, "That's right, we'll buy 'em some paint and let 'em paint their building, that should take care of them for a while." I used to think that old 1921 building must have paint an inch thick on it by this time. Maybe that's why it has lasted so long.*

---

*Avinger, Texas USA, Vol. 1. By Fred McKenzie. Privately printed, 1988.

That same denial of opportunity was faced a black teenager named Willie Brown in nearby Mineola. In 1951 when Willie escaped from Texas, his situation was that of a seemingly hopeless *outsider,* growing up in a one-room shack and shining white men's shoes to earn quarters he had to retrieve from a spittoon. But instead of continuing to work for the Man in Texas, he worked his way through San Francisco State (1955) and law school (1958) and into San Francisco politics. Today as California's Assembly Speaker, Willie Brown is one of America's consummate political *insiders.*

MINEOLA HAD NOTHING, ABSOLUTELY NOTHING, going for it. It was a small, very poor, very backward community, totally and completely racially segregated. It was run under the old high sheriff system, where the sheriff ran the town. The mayor was the elected official, but the law enforcement guy ran the town. Period. There was just no question about that.

My school was a very small black school. It had five or six classrooms. When I first started, there were only ten grades in the school. They added the eleventh and twelfth grades while I was attending. Before that, you had to travel eleven miles by bus up to Quitman for the high school. They also added a wing while I was there, but the wing was only for the lower grades—first through fifth—and in the wing they added inside rest rooms. Before that we didn't have inside rest rooms. There was no gymnasium for basketball. Everything was outside.

The white school, Mineola High, was located on the other side of town. They had a great football team, the Yellowjackets, and they had a great football stadium, in which we were allowed to play when we had a game. They had all the facilities; they had indoor bathrooms, they had indoor showers, they had all of that. They had a gymnasium in which they played basketball. They had a library; we didn't have a library. Not only that, but we only had used books, books that had already been used by the white students. All the way through school, I never touched a new book.

I had two uncles who left Mineola, one who went off to war and the other who worked in the defense industry in California. Mineola had one method by which people earned a living—a pea house that processed pinto beans and black-eyed peas—and that was the only thing that went on in that town. My mother also left Mineola and moved to Dallas. I was raised by my grandmother. My sisters and brothers and my two uncles and my mother supplied the resources for her to raise us. Every week money came back, and once or twice a year, those relatives would come back. This one particular uncle, Uncle Itsie, wanted desperately to get me out of Mineola.

I had always, apparently, shown some promise in terms of thinking ability, and as far back as I can remember I had had a lot of motivation. When I was nine and ten, I was shining shoes in Parker's barbershop and sweeping the floor for three dollars a week. By the time I was twelve I had also bought my own bicycle because I managed my money. Apparently those qualities said to my uncle, "This is a kid who could do something. He's got a shot." He kept insisting that I be allowed to come to California.

Everybody in my family had always insisted that the kids had to have an education. They absolutely beat that into us—that you had to go to college. But there was no place in Texas to go besides Prairie View A & M or Texas College down in Tyler, the black colleges. My sisters all went to Texas College down in Tyler and two of them became teachers.

I had decided I wanted to become a math teacher. I was good in math and somebody had told me that Stanford had the best math. I didn't have any counsel in that direction; there weren't any counselors at Mineola Colored High. So I came out to California with the intention of going to Stanford. When I got here, of course, I didn't have the appropriate credentials; I hadn't had the subject matter in high school. Instead I enrolled in San Francisco State College. I was not even able to pass their entrance exam because there were words and concepts I had not been exposed to. But the professor who was administering the tests said, "I really think you could do college-level work. Why don't we admit you as a special admittee?"

Within six weeks I was doing college work. I went on through and got a B.A. and a law degree with no trouble.

It is true that whatever training I had in high school and whatever discipline was instilled in me in Texas stood me in good stead in my post-Texas world. The one thing I know now about my experience in Mineola was that every black youngster in that town was required to graduate from high school. You could be twenty-three, and you'd still be in high school if you had not passed whatever minimal training they'd provided you with. No matter how inadequate it may have been, they insisted that you grasp it before you were allowed to move on. So there would be kids who stayed in the fifth grade three years; there would be kids who were twenty-three and still playing high school football—seven years they'd been playing football—but they had to complete the work.

And those teachers! I had a professor teaching geometry who knew *nothing* about geometry. Nothing. He was a coach; he'd never completed math himself. But what he did was make us memorize the entire geometry textbook. You learned every theorem. Theorem Ninety: I can cite Theorem Ninety in my sleep. Theorem Eighty-four. Theorem Three. Every day you had to memorize a new theorem. The examination was whether or not you wrote exactly what was in the book, and that's how you got your grade. Well, obviously, that taught you not one ounce of geometry. But it gave you discipline and made you believe in yourself. It gave you confidence that you could learn.

And that's what I learned in that black school. I didn't fully appreciate it, I suspect, at the time, but on reflection—especially now, as I see what kids are getting in California schools—I'm telling you that there is something to be said for those all-black schools. The black mothers and fathers and teachers might not have been qualified, but they knew they had to equip me to survive in this world. You learned that it was really awful to drop out. Period. We didn't have any dropouts in Mineola. It was ingrained in us that there was no such thing as people who were so totally stupid that they could not perform. That quality came from the heart and soul of the black community, and it's still there.

CECIL GILSTRAP: WILDCATTER OF THE FAR RIGHT

Big Spring, TX

Born 1930

I got quite a different slant on Texas's public schools from oilman Cecil Gilstrap of Big Spring.

The Gilstrap family has always believed in the constitution. We're independent and we're individuals. I'm one of the few individuals left in this town. I don't believe in taking a little five-year-old kid and start brainwashing him in kindergarten. And the first thing they do when you take your child to school now is that the teacher will take him by the hand and say, "Come here, Johnnie, let me introduce you to the group." Now if he doesn't conform to that group, if he's an individual, "Hey this kid's got problems. We need to send him to a psychiatrist."

Like his prize watermelons, West Texas wildcatter Cecil Gilstrap needs lots of space in which to flourish. Historically Texas was the sort of safety valve where such space was available. In the Old South "Gone to Texas" used to describe a certain type of personality as well as a destination.

Many people tell me that in the 1990s the wildcatter is about as extinct as an 1890s cowboy. Cecil Gilstrap has not gone extinct yet, but they aren't making many like him lately. "I've got a diamond-and-gold belt buckle," he told me, trying to peer over his ample midriff, "but I can't see it any more."

I suspect that the prospect of oil in the ground and freedom in the air will tantalize many more generations of Texans, though Cecil Gilstrap's idea of the good life probably would not suit most folks. His enormous yard looks like a tribe of hillbillies camped there and moved on, forgetting to take all their vehicles. There is a rusting landscape of oilfield equipment outside Cecil's door waiting for this tall wildcatter's next bonanza.

Big Spring district attorney Rick Hamby is a Gilstrap admirer, though often at odds with the conservative wildcatter on local issues. He appreciates what he calls Gilstrap's "commonsense West Texas grip on things."

I photographed Cecil Gilstrap at his house beside a mid-1920s Jumbo 4 spudder, an oil-well rig used in the famous Yates field but soon outmoded. The spudder looks about as mobile as a dinosaur, but for a man who grew up in the early boom fields this contraption must be very nostalgic.

I think that the proverbial man in the street would be perplexed by Big Spring's most famous conservative. After all, he shuns *both* Democrats and Republicans and says "It's a farce, the whole damn system."

Cecil Gilstrap equates Democrats with Socialism and Republicans with "lack of ideology."

MY FATHER WAS IN THE OIL business a long time ago. He used to move rigs with a team of mules. He was a muleskinner back during the old days during the Ranger and Desdemone booms. Back in Tyler down there in the East Texas field. Killgore.

We moved from town to town to town. Just moved all the time. That's all we ever done.

Well, that's all I ever knew, I guess. I worked in it when I was a kid. It was natural that when I got out of college I just stayed in the oil business.

I went down to the University of Texas. I'm what you call a tea sip. [Laughter] Oh, it don't bother me about what they call ya. Hell, they've called me everything in the world. That's a good name compared to what they've called me. [Laughter]

I'm so conservative that I make the John Birch Society look like a liberal group. I just believe in the constitution. Nothing else. I am not really a conservative. I believe in *individual rights.* Nothing else.

Cecil Gilstrap holding an oil dowsing rod.

I don't believe in the redistribution of wealth. None whatsoever. Not at all! I don't believe in helping the poor.

Or the old. That's how we've gotten away from the family! Because nowadays everybody says "Hell, give your old folks to the government. They'll take care of 'em."

Whereas when I was a kid we took care of our own people. My grandfather lived with us for twenty years before he died. We took care of him. He died at one hundred and seven. But we took care of that man. He didn't belong to the government. He was part of our family.

He was an engineer on the railroad. And he was awful conservative. He believed in free enterprise.

Our family has been a family of rebels. We don't believe in the things the government does today. We don't need and I don't want their services. In my grandfather's day there weren't any of these services and people lived good. A lot of people had to work hard and we didn't have much money, but everybody was the same way we were.

My dad was strictly an old dyed-in-the-wool Democrat. He and I had more verbal fights over politics. And he thought I was a radical. And that's probably what I am.

All my family has been kinda funny about the government. We just don't want the government tellin' us what we can do. Where we can live. How we can live. Lady Bird Johnson can beautify the streets but she can't come out here and beautify my land 'cause I'll kick her ass off it!

MISS CHARLES EMILY WILSON:

A NEGRO

SEMINOLE TEACHER

Bracketville, TX

Born 1910

"Teaching is just within you. That hasn't changed at all even though we have more bookwork now and more help than we had when I started teaching."

Charles E. Wilson is a woman, not a man. That's because each generation of her family always includes a Charles and she just happened to be it in 1910. More unusual than her name, however, is her relationship to a usually forgotten part of Texas history. Charles Emily Wilson's grandfather, Samson July and five of his sons, were part of the United States Army's Negro Seminole Indian Scouts. During the chaotic period after the Civil War, dispossession of the Indians moved forward to its inevitable conclusion. The last battle in North Texas took place in 1875 between twenty-seven Texas Rangers and one hundred Indians. The Indian Götterdämmerung came in 1881 when Ranger Captain George Baylor ambushed a group of Apaches in the Sierra Diablo.

At the end, the U.S. Army employed a group of mixed-race black/Seminole Indian scouts to follow the hapless Apaches into their last redoubts. This group, under Lt. John Bullis, was headquartered at Fort Clark at Bracketville, Texas. Many of the men's descendants, including Charles Emily Wilson, still live in the area.

The Negro Seminoles trace their origin to Florida's Seminole Indians who stole slaves from plantations, intermarried, and were forced to the Indian Territory after the Seminole War of 1850. Eventually one hundred fifty of them were employed by the Army as scouts.

Miss Charles Emily Wilson is a Bracketville elementary school teacher who had begun teaching locally in the late 1940s in a segregated four-teacher elementary school. I visited her at her classroom, where children of all races seemed to be getting along as peacefully as the Seminoles' past had been violent.

Many blacks in Texas celebrate their freedom on Emancipation Day, "June 'teenth." That's when the Seminole Indian Scout Cemetary Association puts on a "Freedom Day" celebration at the old Carver School where Miss Wilson got her start as a teacher. She is the descendant of slaves who escaped from their masters; she is a person who overcame segregation with dignity.

Miss Wilson's sure authority and her grandmotherly charm were a joy to behold for someone who believes that childhood education is the most important mission of any free society.

MY MOTHER'S DAD WAS A Seminole Indian of Florida. He had quite an influence on my mother, which she passed on to me.

As a kid the history of the Negro Seminole Scouts didn't have much influence on me, but as I grew older. . . . My mother always instilled in us that there was something to it. She made us feel like we were someone. That we were somebody. We were out here, a group apart from the rest of the Negroes. We were surely different in our ways. It has had quite an impact on me.

Maybe the closeness. We were more familylike. We had more community spirit. I'm sure that was handed down from my granddad.

Integration started here in 1961 or 1962. We were glad to see it happen. It has been very good, very good.

In Brackettville itself the blacks hadn't actually been segregated. We always intermingled. Not all the Anglos did, but most intermingled.

There were some places that we couldn't go in the front door, but that didn't bother us.

When the Ninth Cavalry came here in World War II, 1942, even that didn't make any difference to us, but it did to the Anglos. They weren't used to that many blacks. You take twenty-five hundred blacks coming to a little place like this, the Anglos were disturbed. It affected some of the people that had come from the South, like Georgia and Arkansas, and they were uptight about it.

But as a group we got along fine with the Anglos. We worked on their ranches. We worked together with them.

But we were segregated in schools and churches.

We had more freedom here, though, than black people did in other parts of Texas. We could get to where we wanted to go. If we had a dance, we could dance until two or three without too much turmoil or arguments. Some places, you couldn't do that; there was a curfew.

We are unique here between Del Rio and San Antonio.

We were just full of free spirit!

JOHN G. PRUDE:

THE ENDURING LURE

OF A RANCH CHILDHOOD

Fort Davis, TX

Born 1904

"One of our favorite sayings," said the horseman patriarch, "is 'Whip and ride.' Whip means to whip him and ride means to stay up there."

Nowadays only a relatively few Texans are able to grow up on a wide-open-spaces ranch. But don't worry! Even if a child is unlikely to ride anything more exciting than the family GMC Suburban, there is a way to grow up tall in the saddle. Meet John G. Prude of Fort Davis, Texas. For seventy years his Prude Ranch has been turning city kids into horse wranglers. "A lot of children come here," he says, "who have never been around horses, but the next summer those kids come back to our ranch just to ride the same old horse again."

At the four-thousand-acre Prude Ranch, John G.'s old-timey program of horsemanship has as much to do with developing kids' characters as it does with their love of Old Paint. "We tell everybody," he says, "that the outside of the horse is good for the inside of a kid. We have seen these old horses change a child from one type of person to another."

With all the emphasis on developing confidence and character, I asked John G. who had most influenced *him*. He immediately mentioned his parents, who "always stood for the best and usually saw that we did the best," but then he started telling me about his Aunt Jettie Pruett Smith. I later had the pleasure of meeting one-hundred-one-year-old Aunt Jettie. And I learned that she had been responsible for the Prude boys having the *best manners* in those parts when they were growing up.

Aunt Jettie helped raise her many nephews and nieces. Once when my mother and father went on an extended vacation, Aunt Jettie came to run the Prude house. We ate at a big family table, six Prudes and four cousins. Aunt Jettie insisted on good manners. We did not put our elbows on the table. We did not ride our chair and we did sit upright. We always had our grace and then our plates were served very orderly.

One of my biggest disappointments was when Aunt Jettie told Andy, my older brother, and me that she would give us something real nice if we would brush our hair neatly before our meal for one week. Andy and I were so excited by that idea that if we ever forgot to brush our hair, we jumped up to do it. So by the end of that week we had never missed brushing for a meal. But our big disappointment came when Aunt Jettie gave each of us a comb and brush!

YOU DIDN'T HAVE AIR CONDITIONING in Houston and Galveston in the twenties and early thirties and people would come to Fort Davis because at six thousand feet it was cool. After June was over with, you were sleeping under blankets!

My father's first paying guest was R. J. Calder of Galveston, on July 1, 1921. Later, the Depression didn't affect our business because instead of going to California or Colorado, what Texas people saw was West Texas!

Prude Ranch has always had the most desirable type of person, but in those early years people came for two weeks, a month, or maybe all summer—where now they come for only two days or a week.

I was born right here at the Prude Ranch February 27, 1904, and the room I was born in later became my classroom for my first four grades.

Folks used to ask my parents, "How long has he been ridin'?" My mother always said, "Well, he was riding before he could walk." So I'm sure my daddy took me everywhere he went.

I wouldn't name anyone as inspirations above my mother and father. However, my mother had a younger sister named Jettie

Pruett and Aunt Jettie was the one that if we didn't take our hat off when we come in the house, she would let us know about it!

She had four sisters including my mother and she helped raise all the children in those four families. The Pruetts were very prosperous and Aunt Jettie, the youngest one in the family, had everything she wanted. She had her own cattle, own steers, own herd, and sure enough Aunt Jettie had the fanciest automobile in Jeff Davis County when she was a young woman. We were always real careful to do what Aunt Jettie told us to do because if we didn't, we wouldn't get to ride in that beautiful automobile.

Aunt Jettie was a little bit younger than the other members of my mother's and father's family and she just kept us pretty much in line because she appreciated us and she was the right kind of a person to lead us. She and my mother and father were great examples to us as we grew up.

I don't suppose there ever was a better cowboy or ranchman than my father. He established a cattle outfit here in 1897. From 1900 to 1933 Prude Ranch occupied forty sections of land. About twenty-five thousand acres. At the present time we have only four thousand acres.

My mother and father operated just as a cattle ranch until 1921, and then they started taking in paying guests. In 1930 my mother and father both decided that they would rather be in the guest business than to be in the cattle business. I tell people today that if it hadn't been for the guest business, Prude Ranch might not even be here today. There have been many changes among the ranch people in this area, with the old-timers going broke or dying out and the new oil-money people buying in.

The only reason Prude Ranch is in the horse business is because the horses pay their way. We rent twenty, thirty, or fifty horses a day.

I didn't ride rodeo broncs because my mother wouldn't let me ride them. She thought it was too dangerous. We raised horses here and she knew what a bucking horse could do to a person.

I couldn't ride them and I couldn't ride bulls, but I could do anything else I wanted to do in West Texas rodeos.

I was a good roper and I made my way in roping. I was the champion roper of the Marfa, Texas, Fair in October 1933.

I think that I will always respect my mother and daddy greatly for what they did. They always stood for the best and they usually saw that we did the best. They encouraged us to work. They set the right example for us.

Let me tell you about how my parents met. Whit Keesey and his wife were friends to everybody around Fort Davis. They were much older than my mother's parents. Keesey Canyon was named for Mr. Keesey because his Mexican herdsmen used to run a big herd of goats up and down that canyon. Whit Keesey is a very important part of the early development of Fort Davis. He had a four-story home over where the McKnights live now. They even had a little chute that carried laundry all the way down to the basement. Can you imagine such a thing seventy-five years ago?

Well, the Keeseys and the Pruetts, my mother's family, were Odd Fellows, and their lodge had a big celebration once a year. The Keeseys lived on the south side of Fort Davis, and sure enough Mrs. Keesey invited my mother and her older sister Viola to come and spend the night with them. My father was an Odd Fellow, too, and he and my mother met at that Odd Fellows dance while my mother was staying with Mrs. Keesey. After the party was over with, my father asked my mother if he could walk her home. My mother said, "Let me go ask Mrs. Keesey. I have to get permission from her."

Mrs. Keesey gave my mother permission to walk home with my father and that was the first date they ever had! They courted for two years and were married January 13, 1897.

Ever since my parents' time, we at the Prude Ranch have been encouraging the children to ride like an old cowboy does because we figure we are a cowboy ranch and we want to teach the children to ride Western style.

Some children have never ridden a horse before so we teach them how to put their feet in the stirrups, how to hold the reins. One of our favorite sayings is "Whip and ride." Toes point gently toward the front and a little out with the heels pointing in, the ball of your foot in the stirrup, heel lower than your toe, and a lot of weight in your stirrups. We tell children to hold both reins in one hand and pull the reins in the direction they want the horse to turn. The old pony usually does what the child tells him to do. We prefer that the children hold their reins in their left hand because the right hand can be used for so many other purposes. The cowboy has to have his right hand free to rope a steer, rope a cow, rope a horse.

The children ride every day except Sunday. We do not touch the horses on Sunday.

We are set up on two-week sections. The first week the boys ride the horses in the morning. Our boys are divided in two groups, the Three Bar Ranch and the Triangle Bar Ranch. At eight-thirty the Triangle Bar boys get on the horses and ride for two hours. They come back at ten-thirty and the Three Bar boys get on the horses. In the afternoon the girls are divided into two tribes, the Apache Tribe and the Comanche Tribe. At two-thirty the Apache girls get on the horses and ride for two hours. They come back and the other tribe gets on and rides for two hours.

Every kid rides a horse every day during camp except on Sunday.

We have big summer rodeos. Every week we rodeo on Friday night and Saturday and the child rides the horse just as fast as he can get the horse to go.

By the end of their stay here, the children love the horses more than they love the Prudes!

We praise the Lord because we feel that we have changed many children's faces right here at Prude Ranch. Psychologically a kid can come. . . . He doesn't want to do what his parents want him to do. He doesn't do what the counselors want him to do. But he loves this old horse. So if he doesn't do what the counselors tell him to do, he just isn't permitted to ride his horse that day. So he starts thinking twice before he does something wrong again.

We have seen these old horses change these children from one type of person to another, always for the better. We think that when a child learns that he can get on a horse and make that old horse go, turn, and stop, that it gives the child a great deal of confidence to know that he can boss something, really have charge of something. We tell everybody that the outside of the horse is good for the inside of a kid.

RAE FILES STILL:
PAPPY AND
"THAT WOMAN"
Waxahachie, TX
Born 1907

In a state where political passions run very high and where the old "yellow dog Democrat" majority has been seriously eroded, Rae Files Still was a maverick.* In a state with a weak tradition of organized labor, she was a five-term friend of labor in the state House of Representatives. In a state with a historically poor record of public education, she (a high school history teacher) gave her own reluctant legislature a lesson in educational reform.

The Files family of Hill County's Files Valley dates back to the Texas Revolution and so Rae Files's liberal views cannot be attributed to some sort of Eastern poisoning. Instead, she was influenced by her cotton-planter father, Samuel M. Files, to root for the underdog.

We were the biggest cotton-growing county in the state at one time. Of course, when I was coming along, we picked cotton by hand and blacks were the ones that primarily picked it by hand. They would come into Waxahachie in a truck and they would pick cotton.

To tell you the truth, I don't think we ever thought about what the blacks did when it was not cotton-picking season. They did other things on the farm.

---

*Rae Files never had a Republican opponent during her five legislative terms, which began in 1941.

Life was extremely segregated in Hill and Ellis counties in those days. When I was small, my family moved to Itasca, Texas, because Itasca had a school. The part of Itasca in which the blacks lived was always known as Free Town because that's where the freed slaves had settled. I never called that side of town anything else but Free Town.

I ended my teaching career in Dallas, Texas. The last three years I had nothing but black students. Therefore I was quite familiar with the black people. The thing that gets me with a number of friends my age who were also brought up on cotton farms, they still will not use the term black. *They don't even say* Negro. *They just some of them come out with* nigger.

I cringe.

Representative Files's advanced views put her in disfavor with charismatic Governor W. Lee ("Pappy") O'Daniel, whose 1940 landslide produced the state's first million-vote tally. Pappy O'-Daniel had literally come out of thin air with his Light Crust Doughboys radio band, advertising flour. He was the first Texas beneficiary of the new mass media, but his heyday was still a time when a good stump speech counted for much more than telegenic looks, "spin control," and multimillion-dollar war chests. When in 1942 Pappy won a tight race for the U.S. Senate against Congressman Lyndon B. Johnson, he took his rural style of political showmanship to Washington, where it played much less well and where he only stayed one term.

Rae Files remained in Austin and was chairman of the House Education Committee in the fiftieth and fifty-first legislatures. A high school history teacher since 1934, she led the successful fight for the Gilmore–Aikin school reorganization bill, which in 1949 established state responsibility for funding a nine-month minimal program for every school in Texas* and required that black teachers be paid on the same basis as white teachers.

Rae Files Still is a reminder that one person with gumption can make a difference, no matter how unpopular his or her politics. But the Gilmer–Aikin effort exhausted her and she did not run for

---

*Until that point some schools had only been able to provide five months of schooling per year.

reelection in 1950. "I was so tired when I quit," she remembers, "that I said I was not even going back to the House to visit."

Why did this unassuming little daughter of a cotton planter take on Texas's most popular governor and the political establishment of her day? "I was concerned," she said, "with getting a better education for children."

MY MOTHER DIED WHEN I was five years old and I was reared by two sisters. My father was a fairly well-to-do farmer, but whenever we discussed politics in our family he was always on the side of the candidate that he thought was nearest to the common persons. Nine times out of ten the candidate my father wagered on lost!

I suppose my father was my hero.

He discussed politics a lot with us but he never engaged in politics at all. He loved the land. He loved farming. With his last breath he was telling us to hold onto the land.

He liked to speculate in land. That was his downfall. He had just sold land and bought land at a high price just before the Depression came. Eventually, after his death, we let the land go simply because he owed more on it than the land at that time was worth.

The Depression had quite an effect on my way of thinking. I believed in all of the Roosevelt New Deal policies, heart and soul. By that time my father had died and I had a National Youth Administration job at thirty-five cents an hour at the University of Texas in Austin. I worked my way through the university waiting on tables, cleaning up rooms, and working in the office of the dean of engineering, anything that I could find to do.

I began teaching high school history full-time in 1934 and soon became alarmed at the way the state was shortchanging the need of our kids for a good education. In those days primary and secondary education wasn't financed entirely at the local level because country schools could get appropriations from the legislature. But they never knew from one year to the next what that appropriation might be. They could make no plans ahead. The middle-sized schools had to depend on a tax base which wasn't very much. Only the city schools had enough tax base to carry on pretty well.

We had no state sales or income taxes and Texas generally had no industrial tax base. Our educational revenues were totally dependent on just the farming community. Yet Texas did have a great opportunity for education in its untaxed oil and gas resources.

By 1940 I had decided that the best place to do something about this was in the state legislature. That was also the year that Governor Pappy O'Daniel ran for his second term. Pappy's whole campaign was against the legislature. "Just give me a new legislature," he said, "and I'll get old-age pensions. The legislature was the only thing that kept me from getting the pensions during my first term."

He didn't tell the plan that he had for financing old-age pensions because, he said, the professional politicians would block it before he ever got elected. So he ran on the Ten Commandments. Yes, he put out his newspaper in everybody's mailbox with the Ten Commandments instead of telling what his tax bill was going to be to pay for the old-age pensions.

He was on the order of "Kissin' Jim" Folsom and some of the other politicians that we have had in the South. It was frustrating to have a fella like that as our governor!

Of course, big business was running him and they loved it. He had been an unknown, but they quickly stepped in and he came out on the ultra-right side against even a sales tax.

My heavens above, you can imagine how business loved that!

Anyway, in 1940 to have any chance at all of winning you had to put in your literature that you would support Governor O'Daniel. Without that you didn't have a chance of getting elected. So I carefully hedged my materials. I said, "I will support Governor O'Daniel as long as I think he is right"—knowin' to myself that I never was goin' to think that he was right.

I was running with three handicaps. In the first place I was a woman. In the second place, I was running against an incumbent. Third place, he was crippled. He only had one leg and that made people sympathetic to him when he got up to speak. We used to have to get up on trucks to make our talks in all these little country towns, some even without a post office. It would be at night and they would just back a flattop truck up there so you would be above the crowd and make your speech. We had our primary elections then in August. Oh, I walked through plowed ground right out there to where the men were working and gave them my cards and campaigned with them! In later years I'd see somebody and he'd say, "Oh, I remember you. You came out to my hay baler and campaigned with me."

Every night all the candidates went to one of these little towns to make their speeches. People sat around in their cars. It was hot and there was nuthin' to do at home so our political speeches were the big entertainment.

Fortunately I was able to make those speeches. Otherwise people wouldn't have known me except that I had taught in three towns in the county. Often I would meet some old man and he would say, "Oh, my grandson told me to vote for you. He said you had more sense than any of those men down there."

I campaigned over the Czech community in Ellis County, where they weren't too far removed from their native country. If you know anything about them, the whole family works hard. They get themselves a little bit of land and then they work hard and increase that land. They keep it in apple-pie order.

Anyhow, one day my opponent asked an old Czech farmer, "Are you gonna vote for that woman that's in the race?"

"No," the old man says, "I'm not gonna vote for that woman. Woman's place is not in the legislature. Woman's place is in the field."

I quickly became known as "that woman."

Early in the campaign I had a girl named Elizabeth Sewell campaigning with me. We went into a little secondhand store and I could tell that the woman who owned it was really against me. I had already learned that if somebody is against you, don't waste your time. Don't spend a minute. Just get away. Thank them and go. So I was almost to the front door but Elizabeth, who had never campaigned before. . . . I looked back and this old lady was standing there saying, "And furthermore, what would she want with that job with all them men smokin', drinkin', and a-womanin'?"

Later when I made my first speech to a service club, I told that story. "I'll bet that old lady knew more about the legislature than I did."

In August 1940 people just came out to listen to the political speeches. I suppose it was as near as possible to a true democracy. People really knew who was running and really knew what they stood for. It was a boon to an unknown candidate. What was most important in that type of rural campaigning was personal style. I feel sorry for the politicians now; they don't have any way to really meet the people very much because they are too unimportant to be on television. All they can do now is go around personally, send letters, and put up signs in yards. Ours was a far, far easier system.

It was hard, though. I lost fifteen pounds. I weighed ninety-nine pounds when that first campaign was over and I was so tired I looked like something the cats had drug in.

After the first primary, I had a lead over my three opponents of a thousand votes. Didn't quite make it without a runoff.

The incumbent went out to the country schools and got a country school teacher to work for him to convince voters that I was going to do away with all the country schools (which I had never even thought about). That was all done in the very last part of the campaign and I didn't know anything about it in time to counteract it. So election evening I suffered so, sitting down on the square in Waxahachie watching the ballot boxes come in. As the returns were added up from each box the numbers were posted on a big board at the courthouse. That was the most nervewracking thing!

Everybody gathered at this big board at the courthouse. Everybody set around, yelled and hollered if they felt like it when the votes were posted up there. It drove me stark raving crazy.

I had been a nervous wreck at the beginning of the second primary election day even though I had a thousand-vote lead. I was just. . . . I decided to get out of town and that I was not even a-goin' down there to the courthouse.

So I did.

When I thought all the votes were counted, it doesn't take long for a runoff, I called back. I said, "What happened in that race between Rae Files and Gerald Faulkner?"

They said, "Rae Files has an eight-vote lead."

I knew that I was going to lose. I had lost a campaign one time when I was down at the University of Texas. I had gone to bed thinking that I had won but I had lost by nineteen votes.

Now I thought, "History is going to repeat itself." I suffered that weekend. Just suffered.

On Monday they recounted the votes and found an error *in my* favor and I won by sixty votes!

Pappy O'Daniel had run against the legislature. There were a hundred and fifty members in the House of Representatives and when we met for that first session after I was elected, there were ninety-four *new* members. That's how popular Pappy was!

Of course, it was my first term and I didn't know very much about parliamentary procedure. We were having a big meeting one night of the whole legislature meeting as one huge committee, and people had been invited to come in and speak. It was about something that I felt strongly about so right in the middle of all that goin' on. . . . I wasn't on a committee or part of the proceedings but I went up to the Speaker and told him that I wanted to make a speech on that. He said, "Oh, Rae, we already have all the speakers listed here. You can't make a speech."

I knew that you could get quorum on personal privilege so I said, "If you are not going to let me make a speech, I want the floor on personal privilege."

He said, "You are not goin' to insist on that, are you?"

I said, "I certainly am!"

You know on personal privilege they stop everything. He stopped everything and I got up and started making my speech. You are not ever supposed to speak on personal privilege unless you have been personally hurt by some matter. So I was a representative talking completely about the bill and not about a personal wrong and one of the other representatives got up and he said, "Mr. Speaker, I protest. She can't speak on personal privilege."

I didn't give the speaker a chance to answer I said, "I certainly can. My feelings are hurt as a citizen of Texas and as a citizen of the United States and I have a right to speak."

He sat back down. After I had said a good deal he got up again and said, "Now Mr. Speaker, I protest. She can't speak on personal privilege."

I had nearly said everything that I wanted to so I didn't answer. The speaker looked up and he said, "I know she can't but I have been married too long to tell her she can't."

There was another woman who was elected in that 1940 election, too. During the Texas centennial celebrations in 1936 she had been elected the trail drivers' Sweetheart of the Centennial Wagon Train. She had ridden her white horse from Uvalde to San

Antonio and had rode into the lobby of the Gunter Hotel and signed the register from the horse's back.

Her one bill was about cattle brands. She ran us all crazy talkin' about those cattle brands all the time there in that legislature.

That was all she thought about and all she was interested in getting passed. One day there was a vote on the floor while she was out in the lobby talking on the phone. Remember that in those days we didn't have offices. Our desk on the House floor was our office. All the people who wanted to see us came down to our desks when we were not in session. There we were, sitting ducks!

I can't get over it now when I go down there and find offices in that capitol building.

Anyway, they had paged the trail drivers' Sweetheart to come out and answer the telephone and while she was there the vote bell sounded and she had to come back in and vote.

You voted from the back of the House. If you voted aye, you held up one finger. If you voted no, you held up two fingers. The Speaker would call your name to record your vote.

The Sweetheart was a tall, big woman, black hair piled high on top of her head. She bustled in from answering the telephone and got to that back rail to vote.

I had a seat at the front of the House. I could hear every aside that the Speaker made. He looked back there and saw her holdin' up one finger to vote. Before he called her name he whispered, "Here comes Mrs. Finley out of chute number three."

Then he said with a perfectly straight face, "Mrs. Finley votes aye."

There weren't many legislators who were liberals, and most of the members of the legislature thought that my votes were ridiculous. For instance, one representative, he came to me one day and said, "You are too smart to vote with labor. I can't understand that."

I said, "Oh, yeah. I vote with labor because I *am* labor. I vote for my interest and you vote for yours."

I was unusual, too, because I was a woman. There were only four women out of one hundred fifty House members.

But, no, I didn't think about their ever treating me like a woman. As a matter of fact, there were so few women that whenever I got to the microphone to talk, they listened because it was unusual to them. They just wanted to see what a woman was going to say. (By the time I had served my fifth term down there, they were ready to battle me just like they would any man.)

There was in 1941 no money to pay for the old-age pensions which Governor O'Daniel was always talking about. It needed some sort of tax to do it and the fight was over what sort of tax. Some of us were fighting to tax oil and gas and sulfur. That eventually did pass in the Omnibus Tax Bill of 1941, but Pappy gave us no help on it. Instead he was pushing a constitutional amendment to get a sales tax to support old-age pensions. Now, a sales tax does not belong in a constitution and there was no chance that it would ever pass. I finally decided that Pappy was not actually in favor of old-age pensions and that his sales tax amendment to the constitution was just a way of getting around the issue. And he was certainly not in favor of educational reform and for raising revenues to ensure that every community in Texas could provide a *minimum* nine-month level of schooling.

But every Sunday morning Pappy had this "Light Crust Doughboys" hillbilly program from the governor's mansion. Every Sunday morning after he had his musical program, he would then say, "I want to call the roll of the legislators who were against the old people of Texas." Because we had voted against his bill. Then he would start reading and my name was always on the list. Then I would get the letters!

I finally got me a form letter, sent it back, and told them that if we passed the governor's bill, "You will get nothing but a hot check because there is no money there to pay." I said that we were working night and day to get a tax bill passed to put the money there so that people would be sure to get the old-age pensions.

Well, eventually *our* Omnibus Tax Bill on oil, gas, and sulfur passed and it has brought in the money since that time to run the state of Texas. But Pappy never gave us one bit of help. We passed it in spite of him.

We were frustrated to the nth degree on the educational reform bill. You can't imagine the things they thought up to keep that bill from passing. Finally I wrote a famous letter against Pappy in the Dallas *Morning News*. There was one of the columnists in the Dallas

Morning News that had really been taking Pappy to task. So I called him up one day and said, "I have written an open letter to the people of Texas. I am just furious about Pappy. You can't use my name but I think maybe there are parts of that that you can use in your column because I point to specific things that the governor has done."

He said, "Well, you send it to me and I'll see."

So I sent it and in a few days I got a telegram from the managing editor of the Dallas *Morning News* and he said, "Used anonymously this won't be of benefit. Used with your name over it it will be a great thing for the state of Texas."

I knew that to be against Pappy O'Daniel was political suicide. So I told some of my friends about it and they all said the same thing. They would love to see it published but it would really ruin me politically.

Then Pappy made another speech that made me furious.

I thought, "I didn't run for this legislature as a career. I just thought it would help me in my teaching government."

So I okayed publishing the letter.

They called me and told me that I had mentioned several things that had happened between the governor and the legislature and that I had to give an absolute guarantee that if Pappy ever questioned any of those things that the paper could verify that they had actually happened.

So I went around to each representative individually and checked my stories.

We had one young representative who had not been old enough to take office when he ran but he was old enough just after the election. He was young and quite idealistic and very much an admirer of O'Daniel. His was the best story of all because he had gone in to see the governor and he had said, "Governor O'Daniel, I have always supported you but I can't support this appropriation bill that you have introduced. I am enough of an economist to know that would just ruin the state of Texas."

The governor looked at him and he said, "You are right. It's a bad bill but it's good politics and you vote for it."

This young fella would never let me use that in my letter at all, but the other things were all there.

The Dallas *Morning News* waited until Sunday. On the front page they had "See page such-and-such: Representative Rae Files Still tells all about the governor." I turned over to page such-and-such and there is my picture, my biography, and there's the letter. You couldn't have missed it!

Then, lo and behold, I turned over to the editorial page and the first editorial and the cartoon were based on the letter. I was nearly sick. I thought they would run me out of town on a pole when I would get back to Ellis County.

The Monday after that letter appeared on Sunday, I walked into the legislature and representatives all came up, "Well, Rae it has been nice knowin' you, but you are blowed."

Blowed is a Texas expression that you are gone. You are just out of it. You are blowed, like the wind blowed you out.

So, lo and behold, my post office box was just full of letters. I couldn't stand to open them. I couldn't stand to read those things that folks were going to say.

I started pulling them out and they were all praise! There were people that all felt the same way. Nobody had ever questioned Pappy before. They were all scared to. If he could get ninety-four new members elected. . . . Jiminy, nobody had ever done that before. That was the biggest turnover they had ever had.

When I ran for a second term in 1942, that's when my new opponent got a hillbilly band and was going to give them politics in the tried-and-true Texas manner. But even though I had fought O'Daniel, I won that time by a whole lot more votes than the first time because again people voted for individuals rather than party. He carried Ellis County, Pappy did, but I carried it, too.

GORDON WOOD:
HIGH SCHOOL
FOOTBALL COACH
Brownwood, TX
Born 1914

If Gordon Wood were a politician, he would be an old-time West Texas populist. America's winningest high school football coach says that sport is the only part of life's competition in which everyone is equal regardless of looks, wealth, brains, or connections. No matter who you are, he says, you still "have to make ten yards for a first down."

During forty-three football seasons, coach Wood won nine state championships (all with the Brownwood Lions, 1960–1986) for a total record of 391–81–11. That he came so far from his cotton-chopping beginnings near Abilene is a testament to his fight-to-win style. As the authoritative 1985 *Texas High School Football* puts it, "Brownwood has never been a haven for college recruiters . . . for the most part Wood has accomplished his exceptional feat with 150-pound or so running backs and 180-pound linemen." Just as he used to beat his older brothers in day-long, broiling-sun cotton-picking contests, Gordon Wood won at football through gumption and self-discipline.

One might argue that school is primarily for academic, not sports, achievements and that Texas high schools (*and* colleges) have stressed the latter at the expense of the former. That was the case made by defeated governor Mark White and educational reformers such as H. Ross Perot. Under their controversial 1984 no-pass/no-play rule any high school athlete who failed even one

Gordon Wood
with student
Keith Cook
(Credit: David
Branch,
Brownwood
Bulletin)

course in any six-week period would be ineligible to play during the next six-week period.

Coach Wood responded that it was not the athletes who were most likely to "stub their toes" but those students who were uninvolved in anything. He denied Governor White's unpatriotic slander that Texas high schools ranked fourth from the bottom nationally. No-pass/no-play, he said, was "just political football."

In fact, opposition from the influential high school coaches association helped defeat governor Mark White for reelection in 1986.

Contrary to the stereotype, this coach values education. He went from chopping and picking cotton to a master's degree and says he never wants to go back to the farm. In fact, even lawn work is repugnant to him. He hires a yard boy. "The fact is, I prayed to get off the farm," he says. "But I really believe that I picked more cotton than anybody in Brown County. There's very few people that could or would pick as much as I did. Or stayed on it as many years as I did."

Coaches are by definition father figures and Coach Wood has kept up with his boys' success in life. He tells of this or that one's fame in business, science, or politics. He brings out a photo of one of his state championship teams on which thirty-one out of thirty-five students graduated from college.

Mindful of his own difficult start in life, Coach Wood says that "You can't separate education from economics" when many families in the Brownwood area "just have a hard time." But if a coach can inspire disadvantaged kids with confidence, "The sports team is the one place where there isn't any class difference."

DURING MY FIRST SIX OR seven grades I didn't even go to school except the days that it rained.

We'd go the first day, draw our books, and go back when it rained. Until after Christmas.

I lived on a farm. My dad was a super, super man and had the best farm in Taylor County. But he really didn't think that if you could read and write there was any purpose in going on in school. He said, "Well, you'll end up a schoolteacher or a preacher. And they're both starving to death."

He was partially right and he really didn't believe in education.

But my mother was a red-headed Irish lady and she encouraged me a great deal. "Just keep goin'." And she helped me. But nobody ever talked to me about makin' better grades.

I had a preacher in seventh grade during the Depression years. And I knew that he hired a McMurray boy to come out and work with us in basketball. That preacher paid for it out of his own little old meager check. His name was Parmenter and he was a tremendous influence to me. I always thought about the things he did for me and I hoped that I could do some of them for somebody else.

When I was a freshman, Dr. Comer Clay got me started debating. And I got interested in other things besides chopping cotton. Reading and studying. I know that I got more out of debating than I did any subject matter. It was one of the bigger factors in me going on and becoming a coach.

Up until we got into this mess [no-pass/no-play] one of the very few people that pushed students to make better grades was the coach. We've made 'em pass forever.

In the state of Texas the problem with education is not now and never has been extracurriculars. The problem is for somebody to get ahold of these kids that have given up on themselves.

It makes a great theory to say no-pass/no-play. But it's the most ridiculous rule in the world.

Governor White appointed a committee headed by Ross Perot, and Ross Perot is an egotistical person and just doesn't have any compassion for those that don't have everything. In other words, we're judged on brains and beauty and money but most of us are not in that category. People need something to give themselves a good self-image. If they can excel in extracurriculars, they feel good about themselves and they can do well in every other subject. But no-pass/no-play would take that away from them. It doesn't help 'em. It discourages 'em.

There wasn't anybody that wasn't paid that did more to get Mark White elected than me. And there were not many people working any harder to see that he got out of there, either.

I know full well that there's lots of values in athletics if the program's run properly. In the Navy I was a chief petty officer and a company commander. I pushed thirteen companies through San Diego Naval Training Station. Why, I could pick out the people who had been in athletics real quick because they knew how to take orders and how to become a team.

Right now at Brownwood High School we've got a couple of young coaches and they handle the cafeteria. The minute they go eat, you'll see a drove of boys gather around 'em. Why? Because for a lot of those kids that's the only male role model that they see. And they want to talk and they want to visit. So many kids today are in one-parent 'homes—and that's a mother—that it's more important today that we have coaches than ever before.

I don't care what anybody else thinks or says. I *know* what its meant. We've got a fella that lives here that teaches at Trinity University. Dr. Gerald Pitts will tell you that he was a one-hundred-forty-five-pound guard and quarterback. He played first string on a state championship team. And he found out that if he could do that, he could do anything in the world that he set his mind to do. And he was one of the computer scientists instrumental in putting the first men on the moon.

The students' accomplishments are much more important than winning. The finished product: what he is.

In sports you learn discipline. That's one of the few places in school where there is any discipline any more. Students learn how to work extremely hard.

There are so many valuable lessons to be learned out there that it's unreal! Like learning to be part of a team. For instance, if I were going into the Army today and I were in a foxhole, I would want some of those football kids right alongside of me there because I could depend on 'em. I'd know that they're competitive and that they believed in their country.

We worry now that people don't believe in America any more, but if you go to a football game everybody is standing with their hats off and their hands on their hearts and they're singing the national anthem. A lot of people don't think that's important but it is.

There is no doubt that there is a lot of interest in football in Texas. But it is a ridiculous thing to make little old kids think they're failures because they fail one subject. The real problem with education is simply that they're not teaching students to read and write during those first six years.

If they ever get 'em to reading and writing down there, well, we won't have any problems making 'em pass in high school.*

---

*In 1990 Texas outpassed and outran fewer than half the fifty states in SAT scores. Its math (461) and verbal (413) standings were below even the depressingly mediocre national average.

FRIEDA WILLIAMSON AND MARY OLDHAM: GENERATIONS OF TEXAS WOMEN

Lampasas and Marble Falls, TX

Born 1909 and 1922

Both Frieda Williamson and Mary Oldham are quilters whose designs were handed down both within families and among friends. "New neighbors," says Frieda, "were greeted with joy in the early days because they were likely to bring new and exciting patterns."

Quilting was originally a means to convert discarded material into insulated coverings for icy beds. Early-day Texas quilts, if inspected closely, display this heritage of frugality in their humble battings and their remnants of flour sacks, feed sacks, tobacco bags, and old clothes.

Quilts are either appliquéd or pieced and come in many forms. Friendship quilts were joint efforts by groups of friends, each of whom signed her name on her square. Quilting bees were social occasions, often to create a quilt for a bride, and each woman had to be careful not to prick a finger because that would be bad luck for the bride. Quilt patterns have colorful names such as "Grandma's flower garden" or "double wedding ring." "Log cabin" is one of the most popular. Its center square was always red to symbolize the fire and hearth at the center of the cabin. Other nineteenth-century patterns are turkey track, birds in air, bearpaw, rose of Sharon, drunkard's path, pine tree, and Dresden plate.

What interests me is not so much the patterns or the artistry of quilting but its personal meaning for individuals. I asked Frieda Williamson and Mary Oldham about how the daily act of quilting ties them to earlier generations of Texas women.

Frieda Williamson

GOODNESS KNOWS HOW MANY QUILTS I have made! I have dozens of them now to be quilted. I love to make them as well as quilt them. Quiltmaking is addictive; you can't make just one.

Believe it or not, Mrs. Frank James helped me design a quilt. You know, Jesse and Frank James, the wife of Frank James. I was just a youngster when she came to West Texas as a very elderly lady to visit the mother of my sister-in-law. They were very good friends. She came to Texas and I was piecing a quilt out there and she was very interested with me being so young. She wanted to show me a design that she had. This whole day she came down and had dinner at my brother's place. We were vacationing out there. My mother, father, and my twin brother. Mrs. James hated all those paperback books that blamed the James boys for everything.

That was in El Dorado, Texas, in the early 1920s. It was a Dresden-plate quilt.

Quilting is a lot of our history. These quilts were kept and prized and handed down from generation to generation.

They had a lot more work on them a long time ago. At that time when women started making the quilts, they batted their own cotton. They probably went out and picked the cotton and took the seeds out and put that cotton batting inside the quilt. They had to quilt it real fine, close together, to keep the cotton from matting inside when they washed it. Nowadays you just go down and buy, probably a synthetic now. It just rolls out and you don't have to put as much quilting into it any more unless you are going to put it in a show.

My mother was born in sixty-six and my father was born in

sixty-four while his father was away from Tennessee in the Confederate Army. My mother's father, Herman Ludwig Hensel, came to Travis County from Germany by way of the California gold fields. He lived way off down in that country by Travis Peak, really way back in the hills, in a beautiful rock home he built. He was quite a lady's man, they say, in his time. He made his own wine and was evidently quite a character. He was forty years old when he married a nineteen-year-old girl from Germany. They had six girls.

My father, Eric Mathews, moved here from Travis County in the latter part of the 1800s. His cattle brand was the TZ bar.

In 1987 I went to the Lampasas courthouse and searched for my husband's grandfather's brand. I found out that he had had four different brands, because when you bought out somebody you sometimes bought his brand, too. He also had what they called a road brand for whenever he moved his cattle and threw them in with everybody else's on the trail to Abilene, Kansas.

So I decided to make a quilt of Texas cattle brands for my son. I appliquéd different Texas animals—longhorn steers, jackrabbits, armadillos, robins, and roadrunners—onto squares and in each corner of each square I put a brand. There were over a hundred brands on that quilt when I was through.

I was the baby of a big family. My mother quilted and I bothered her to death and she had to let me try. She started me darning socks when I was five.

I made my first quilt before I was ten years old. My mother gave me a design and she let me cut it out and she gave me a shoebox to put my things in. "Nine patch" was just nine patches to each square, of whatever color the quilter wanted to make and you set it together later with strips or you could set it together just like it was.

Why, of course, my mother inspired me! Of course. She did a lot of handwork. I never did see her sit down unless she had something to do with her hands. Either crocheting, or mendin', or doing something. She was always doing something with her hands.

I love that today, too. I keep something going all the time. Happiness to a quilter is a needle, thread, thimble, and a box of scraps.

I've got a lot of nervous energy! I'm just. . . . It takes me a month to make a quilt and then a little bit more than a month to quilt it. You figure that up, how much that is for an hour. I quilt six to eight hours a time in a day. I have to have my colors like I like them. If they don't come out right, I'll tear it up and redo it. I have umpteen quilts that are unfinished but I can't finish them because I find another design I want to get into. Then I've got to go ahead and do that new one.

Mary Oldham

You didn't just sit. You always had something in your hand to work on. I inherited boxes and boxes of little blocks that were made to go into quilts that never got finished up.

My grandmother Mattie* was born and raised in San Saba County. She designed this prickle-pear quilt herself. I have never seen one anywhere else. It is all appliquéd and quilted. It is a real jewel of fine quilting.

To go to Grandma and Grandpa Taylor's nearly every Sunday was like a family reunion. I can't remember how old I was before they let me quilt. My mother† taught me to embroider, crochet, and knit when I was ten years old. When she passed away, she had the blocks already done for some quilts and I put them together and did the quilting to save some of my mother's and grandmother's handwork.

Because they always had so many children in those days, mothers didn't have room to leave anything down. So quilting frames were always hung from the ceiling. I can remember all the grandmothers and aunts coming to Mother's dining room. The quilting frame was over the dining room table on pulleys. When Mother let it down, as many as wanted to could quilt.

There was always a quilt in progress on the ceiling and you rolled each one up as you moved along with the quilting. A frame would hold a 120-by-95 piece.

Here is the first embroidery I did as a little girl. It is a huge quilt with a big collection of butterfly squares. I started these butterflies

---

*Martha Terry Taylor, 1863–1944.
†Gladys Ione Perry Taylor, 1894–1954.

Mary Oldham
with her cactus
quilt.

in 1934 and I have just finished it now. Recently I made some new blocks so I would have enough to finish a quilt big enough for my oversized beds. So I drew all of these flowers and embroidered them to put them in with the butterflies.

My grandmother and mother and I never threw a piece of fabric away. I want to show you this "double wedding ring" quilt of blocks that are all postage-stamp size. I had these tiny squares because I never threw anything away. When I cut pieces for one quilt pattern, I saved the scraps in a basket. As the scraps got littler I put them in other baskets according to size.

This "double wedding ring" has four generations of all-female fabric scraps from my grandmother, mother, me, and my daughters.

Or take feed sacks! I'm talking about flour and sugar and horse feed, chicken feed. All the stuff for the ranches came in this flour sackin' fabric. I still have the old Bull Durham tobacco sacks. Roll your own cigarettes. My mother and grandmother saved their husbands', brothers', and everybody's little ole tobacco sacks. I still have a bunch of them. They would rip them apart, wash them, and then dye them to whatever color they wanted to go into the quilt.

Would you think about saving a little piece like that?

I have several friends that we quilt with. Quilting is more popular than ever now and is still a social occasion. There are lots of civic clubs and just neighbors who get together to quilt. Like every once in a while I'll call four or five and say, "Well, bring something to work on and I'll have lunch for everybody. We'll have a day."

I quilt very much the same as my mother and grandmother except when they didn't have reinforced thread but had to use beeswax to strengthen their thread.

My mother always was doing quilting or some kind of handwork. Of course, she taught me from the time I was big enough to hold a needle. I didn't appreciate it until after I was married. Of course, when you got married you got a quilt from Grandma, a quilt from Auntie, a quilt from. . . .

My family's quilts are symbols of the generations. I've got quilts from my grandmother, from my mother. My daughters have quilts. My granddaughters have quilts and they appreciate them.

The grandsons don't have the beautiful quilts. They've got the most usable ones that don't have as much work. For a boy it has to be something other than the "flower garden" or "Dutch dolls" or. . . . Boys are different, you know. They appreciate them and they don't abuse them and they know that there is a lot of work that has gone into it.

My daughters have always appreciated our family quilts and I think they will go right on down in my generations of children and grandchildren. I think they will pass it on to theirs. My great-grandkids will be talkin' to someone like you, Ron, telling them the same thing about what Grandma Mary Oldham did or Great Grandma.

I had that butterfly quilt in here over Easter. My seventeen-year-old grandson came down to spend his spring break with us for a week. One morning I was settin' there quiltin' and he came in and he sat down on this stool and was watching me. He said, "Grandma, what are you going to do with your quilts?"

I said, "Well, one of these days you are going to get married and have children and I hope that your grandchildren appreciate these. I will be long gone and you can say, 'I watched my grandma do that.' "

He sat there I don't know how long that morning wanting to talk about it.

Of course, thirty minutes after that he said, "Come on, Grandma, let's go tee off. It's time to hit the golf course."

So we went and teed off.

Will he appreciate these quilts? I think before I let him have them I will have to put a little more impact on it. Like as threaten to kill him if he ever lets anybody sit on them!

RICHARD E. PEARSON:

CIVIC PRIDE

El Paso, TX

Born 1938

I often hear it said that the city of El Paso is not really Texan. It is too distant and too Mexican.

Richard Pearson is an El Paso native going back seven generations on his mother's side. He does not take kindly to being ranked as a second-class Texan. Recently I found him and other El Pasoans crowing over their city's economic stability while the rest of Texas faltered in a series of oil, farm, banking, and real estate slumps.

Richard Pearson is the general manager of TV Channel 7, and his outspoken editorials are one of the more lively features of El Paso's airwaves. He is likely to take on anything or anybody, from a flamboyant city councilman he compares to Muammar Qaddaffi to local drug traffickers, whom he described as bloodsuckers. But his biggest peeve is the Dallas–Houston way of downplaying El Paso. "I'm a native and I don't talk funny," he says, broadly splaying a Dallas accent. "You talk to other Texans and they have that little twangy bullshit thing. But all of us here at the station are El Paso natives and *we* don't talk that way!"

DID YOU KNOW THAT EL PASO is farther west than Denver? Did you know that El Paso is the only city in Texas on a different time zone? We're on the mountain time zone. We are closer to San Diego than we are to Dallas. We are closer to Denver than we are to Dallas. We are closer to Los Angeles than we are to Houston. Think about that.

That's why that central corridor in Texas—Dallas, Fort Worth,

San Antonio, Austin—they could care less about us. We are so far away. It takes over an hour and a half to fly to Dallas. *Fly!* Nonstop. That's why Texas has always ignored us and why we haven't had any clout in this state.

Right now we're pushing six hundred fifty thousand people. Juarez is one-point-two million. If you add into our metro viewing area southern New Mexico, over eight hundred thousand people are watching this TV station. That's bigger than San Antonio, but Texas ignores us because we are so far away and because we are surrounded by a foreign country and by a state line.

I worked here for twenty-three years in sales but when I became general manager eight years ago, I finally had a chance to do something back for my city. We put a personality on this station which we call "7-together," which means we're together with the community. And I've hired people that are either natives or long-term residents. We don't bring people in from out of town to read the news and then leave. They care. I care. The station cares.

I care about the community because I go back generations in this town. I went to grade school up in the valley here. I went to El Paso High School. And I graduated from the University of Texas at El Paso.

I get letters from all over the place thanking me for doing this and doing that. The station sponsors all kind of events. I think that makes a real difference. We have a caring personality as opposed to a cold, television business personality. If you cast a little bread on the water, it comes back a loaf.

Here's a letter from a lady today about my editorial against one of our councilmen. He's a very flamboyant man and kind of a jerk. In my editorial I likened him to Muammar Qaddaffi. Well, the lady writes me, "Thank you *very much.*" And at the end of her letter she says, "Please don't use my name on the air because I am afraid of him."

I get letters like that all the time. I answer them all back.

I'm the only manager in El Paso who does editorials like that. Our CBS competitor, Channel 4, they do commentary but it has no balls. I get out there and I get very emotional.

And it works. I have created a niche for this station which nobody else had. We found a need and filled it. Nobody else has had the courage to do that.

There is a radio broadcaster here that I respect immensely and that I have patterned myself a little bit after. Jim Phillips. His AM–FM station has a philosophy like our TV station. That if you care about a community, the community will care about you and you will get the money back.

I speak out about everything. Pro-life and pro-choice protestors. I spoke out against this councilman who used some money the city council hadn't approved. Anything. I have freedom to speak about whatever I want. I try not to step over the bounds. . . . It's an extremely powerful medium. I try to control that power and not damage someone or something.

I think my opinions have swayed people, and I'm proud of the fact that this community has a voice through this television station. No one else has been able to do that.

In El Paso we like the fact that we're independent and that the state of Texas is finally beginning to recognize that we're pretty damn big!

The El Paso–Juarez area is majority Hispanic. I'm half Hispanic. My mother's family were originally Spanish land-grant settlers. My mother was the twelfth child of Juan Amador, and by tradition the last daughter was supposed to be the nun. But my father came here during the Depression from a small town in Arkansas where there was no work. He met my mother while he was working as a bellboy at the Del Norte Hotel downtown. They met at some party and they eloped. [Laughter]

And my grandfather Juan Amador didn't speak to 'em until my sister was born because he had planned that my mother was going to be the nun, by God!

ROSA R. GUERRERO: DANCING UP FROM THE BARRIO

El Paso, TX

Born 1934

From a life of poverty to a high profile position in the El Paso community, Rosa Guerrero is a symbol of the magic which hard work, luck, and the American dream can perform on the U.S. side of the border. Rosa is a former public school teacher who was greatly influenced by her grandmother's Mexican dance traditions. As a cross-cultural ambassador and as the founder of her own folkloric group, she is a forceful voice for the power of education to transform El Pasoans' lives for the better.*

The best tribute any of us can receive is from those we have inspired. Carol Viescas was a student at Austin High School in the 1960s when she fell under the sway of Rosa Guerrero. Carol remembers often hearing Rosa say, "Before being black, brown, or white you are a human being. Pride begins in yourself." Carol says that Mrs. G instilled such a strong belief in self that her message "stayed with me throughout my years."

She taught modern dance and gym classes and was adviser to the modern dance troupes. But she truly was adviser—meaning counselor—to any student. Sure, her classes were for young women. But many young men soon found she was a fountain of wisdom on growing up and learning about yourself.

---

*A 1983 interview by Paulina Aldrete was the seed for my more recent work with Sra. Guerrero.

MY GRANDMOTHER WAS BORN IN San Juan near Jalisco and she always worked very, very much as a young girl, as an adult, and as a *viejita*. Her household responsibilities were unlimited. She just went on and on. I never saw her sick until I found out that she was dead. She used to cure herself like my mother does with *hierbas,* home remedies. She never saw a doctor. She never in her life stepped into a beauty shop. She never saw most of what we call "civilization" because she was very, very much at heart a traditional Indian and was afraid of escalators and airplanes.

My grandmother followed Pancho Villa during the Revolution. She wanted to really follow the footsteps of what he believed in, and she was a cook and nurse for him. Later on, in the forties, she evolved to be the cook for the president, Manuel Avila Camacho.

The *mole* that my grandmother made was the most authentic *mole* I have ever tasted because she used to get on her hands and knees and start from scratch. There was no Doña María, no jars at that time. There was the *ajonjolí,* and different types of chiles: chile chipotle, chile colorado, and chile *de esto y el otro.* And *cacahuate,* chocolate—mix it all up. I remember doing it. When I tried, I used to smash my fingers with the *metate,* but what a beautiful experience. I was so proud!

I wanted to imitate Grandmother. I remember wanting to make
tortillas de maíz and they used to come out crazy, longer or fatter,
funny or whatever. But at least I said *"Yo quiero aprender, abuelita.
Yo quiero aprender."*

I always wanted to learn. Whether it was the kitchen or whether
it was history or language, I was always wanting to learn. More than
anybody in my family.

I am still seeking that. I guess I will die learning.

Mí abuelita because she was such a good cook also worked outside the home in restaurants. And that's how she was elevated to
be the cook for presidente Avila Camacho in the forties. President
Camacho used to call her Doña Rosa. My dad also used to call *me*
Doña Rosa.

Since my father worked for the railroad, we could go to Mexico
every summer and be with the family over there.* It was a very
beautiful treat to go to Mexico City and be with my grandmother,
and go to Jalapa, Veracruz, and be with my grandfather where he
had a *sombrerería,* a hat factory. I remember my grandmother getting up at five in the morning and watering the patio and the *hierbas*
and all the *plantas* and starting her soups and *frijolitos* and tortillas
and the *comal* being ready by six!

I was born in El Paso, Texas, and my mother says I was about
eight months old when she first took me to Mexico, so that was
about 1935. My relatives still live in Mexico City and Veracruz and
Aguascalientes and Torreon, where some of my husband's family
are now.

What I liked to do with my mother and father was fiesta. Always,
always fiestas. It was a way of life. So much poverty yet so much
happiness, too! I can't remember our family ever not going to
Juárez every Sunday. Ciudad Juarez was our life. We would go to
the bullfights. I remember seeing the greatest of toreros. I saw
Manolete. I saw Silverio Perez. I saw David Liciaga. I saw the

---

*My childhood was very exciting because we would go to Mexico and immerse
immediately in the culture every summer. Sometimes Mother would even take us
out of school during Lent because in Aguascalientes were the *Ferías de las flores.*
We *had* to go to the *Ferías de las flores.* The heck with school! Ours was an
education that was different. What we learned out of school was as important as
what we learned in school.

beautiful Carlos Arruza. On and on and on. I even saw Cantinflas three or four times. I saw Conchita Cintrón, *la Regionadora,* beautiful bullfighter, on horseback.

Whenever they killed a bull, I turned around and hid my eyes. But I loved the art and the *olé* and the music and *tan tara ta tan,* when the *clarín* came out and announced that the bull was going to be dedicated to the mayor or to whomever. That was exciting, though I love animals too much now to attend bullfights any more.

But that period was when I was starting to get confused inside 'cause I didn't know if I was Spanish or Indian or Mexican because I liked all types of music. The Indian in me would come out when the Matachines would dance. The Spanish would come out when the pasos dobles would play. And the Mexican would come out when the Jarabes would play.

In my childhood, I remember my mother telling me all these stories when she used to get our *piojitos* out, looking for lice in our hair—which is part of the culture, too, whether we like it or not. She used to tell us stories about La Llorona and *cuentos de Pedro de Urdimalcas y las historias de diferentes fantasías románticas de bellas artes.* Things like Cinderella, Sleeping Beauty, the Seven Dwarfs, the beautiful Snow White, *La Blancanieves.* I immediately started stereotyping white as being very beautiful at that time and I wanted to be white like the *Americanas* and like Snow White. Also like Betty Grable and Ginger Rogers—how wonderful it would have been to have been very blond and white! But I had *piojitos* and I did not remember Snow White having them. She was too beautiful to have lice.

I thought I had very poor but very exciting parents. That was a kind of beautiful pride because the school would teach us everything about American history and the Pilgrim colonists and all the time I asked myself about my own ancestry. I would do a comparison in my mind between American history and where my grandparents came from and what they had done. What my grandmother had done in the Revolution and about how she had suffered and how people had died and about how she had come to Juarez and then eventually to El Paso.

So I was confused. I said, "What am I?" I remembered the great newspaper writer Ruben Salazar's words, "A stranger in our own land." And here I was in the United States, Lord have mercy! Confusion and schizophrenia. I tell my students now that when God made a Mexican, He got an Indian and a Spaniard and mixed them and made delicious guacamole.

But as a kid I loved all music and nobody was going to tell me what was right or wrong. I loved going with my mother and father to *la fiesta taurina,* the bullfights. From there we would go out and eat. I remember my father eating the *huachinango, un pescadote riquísimo.* A huge fish and my father would just leave the skeleton. I thought then that eating a *pescado* in such a beautiful way was an art in itself.

From the *restaurante* we used to go to exclusive nightclubs like the Lobby, the Tivoli, or the Casanova. The Casanova was one of the most elegant places in Juarez. My parents would take me because I loved the dancing and because at that time Juarez was very culturally known. It had the greatest musicians and concert pianists and opera singers and zarzuelas and operettas. I saw Veloz and Yolanda do the beautiful ballroom dancing—tango and paso dobles. I saw the greatest flamenco dancers in the world, Carmen Amaya and Antonio Triana. I loved them! They danced with all that Spanish glory! I wanted to be just like Carmen Amaya—with fire, feeling, and spirit.

During the Second World War our whole life-style changed because my four brothers were taken to war. Juarez and El Paso were full of American soldiers and the Red Cross invited adults and us little children to give *danzas regionales de México* to make them happy, like the Bob Hope caravan.

My mother was still very much a *fiestera.*

She still is one today! She's going to be eighty-nine on March the nineteenth and she is so alive. She's like an eighteen-year-old. She feels like one and she acts like one. She's Indian, *pata rajada,* strong and determined and that will never change. I adore her for it. I think that the more years that pass, the more I adore her. There were times in high school when I was ashamed of my mom because she didn't know English and was so uneducated. I saw so many faults in her. How stupid I was!

My mother had to work as domestic help because she didn't know English and she didn't have an education as such. She met my father here in El Paso and married him. Consequently all of us seven children grew up and were educated in the United States.

My father was unique. From him I learned about the culture, the dance, the music, and the language (*el Castellano, el Español* was my father's pride and joy). The *escuelita* he gave me at home. We would sit and conjugate verbs in Spanish just for the love of it. We would go over geography, history, dances, opera. Just a beautiful Socratic man. He would just ask me questions and I loved it.

None of my family was like me. I loved relating with my dad because I thought he was the smartest man in the world. Even though my dad drank a lot, I didn't judge him for that. I loved him. When you love somebody, you don't judge. You love and you forget and you forgive.

My mother had been a *hierbera* and a *curandera* and a *cartomanciana,* a fortune-teller. Later on in life I was very confused with that because being brought up a Catholic, I always thought magic was a no-no. That fortune-telling was the Devil's doing. I talked to a priest several years back at a retreat and he said, "You do not judge your mother. God will judge if she is helping people. Let her be!"

So I'm letting her be. She's a beautiful person. She has a different gift from God, to psychoanalyze people, to question them, and through her cards and her way she helps them. That's what she has been doing for a long time. She brought us up and she gave us food from that. I cannot judge and I cannot condemn. She is my mother and she is a very gifted lady. Very gifted.

She worked outside the home. For a dollar a week, I remember she used to boil and scrub all the linen. After Mother got married, she continued working because the Depression came and then my dad didn't have a job. She was the one that worked and my father stayed at home. He was the one that made us *sopita* and *frijolitos* and *arrocito,* and gave us delicious *capirotada,* and played El Papalote and *valero con nosotros. Nos enlazaba; sacaba la soga de Aguascalientes,* the *Lasso y nos enlazaba como si fuéramos los animalitos en el rancho, las canicas, el Juan Pirulero; a todos los jueguitos. ¡Pero iqué padre! Tan hermoso.* He was the first Mr. Mom, because he had to take the part of the woman 'cause there were no jobs during the Depression. Everybody in the neighborhood of Santa Fe Street wore these relief-type striped overalls. Everybody. It looked like the whole prison was there.

We lived at 620 North Santa Fe twenty years. Right in front of the old Providence Memorial Hospital. It's about three blocks from the Civic Center. We used to walk downtown to the library and to the Colon Theater to dance lessons. I started teaching dance at ten, tutoring little four- and five-year-olds. I was a born teacher!

The movies had taught me how to dance, speak, communicate, learn the good and the bad—'cause we saw some filthy movies, too! I remember seeing *Fiesta* twenty-five times with Ricardo Montalbán and Cyd Charisse because they were such great dancers.

We grew up with those movies. We saw some funny ones with Cantinflas the idol, Tin-Tan, and the beautiful movie stars. That was our growing-up time at the Colon Theater, where they used to have *variedades,* musicians and actors and singers, beautiful cultural programs Saturdays and Sundays. They had three shows, at three o'clock, at six o'clock, and at nine o'clock. And we *had* to go see one of those shows or go see Cisco Kid and Flash Gordon episodes for five cents a movie at El Alcazar. That theater smelled like an old sock and its rats and bugs were part of the show, too!

Mi mamá trabajó con una viejita que se llamaba Elizabeth Lee Griswald, who was our granny. She was my godmother and a very wealthy woman that lived in Sunset Heights in one of the old colonial homes on Upson. From her my mother learned everything of social amenities: how to set the table, the different ways to dress, the entire fashion. And even though Mama was a domestic, working with her, she was treated as part of the family. Mrs. Griswald was related to General Robert E. Lee. She was from Kentucky and had lost all her plantation home with the slaves in her grandparents' time during the Civil War. In Texas her husband lost everything in the Depression. I remember her saying how she hated the Yankees!

I still have heirlooms of her Early American linens, crystal, and china. They go well with my *metate* and my *molcajete* and are very traditional and very beautiful. But why didn't our history books tell us that our pre-Hispanic heirlooms are *older* than those "Early American" things?

Mi Mamá learned so much with Granny Griswald that to this day she still communicates with the sons and grandsons of the lady! They love my mother. Josefina, they call her.

She used to live in an apartment in the basement on Upson. Later on she moved to north El Paso Street and then I was born on 620 North Santa Fe. (Everybody was born at home because we didn't even know what a hospital was like.) There were seven of us. I don't remember really having a lot of chores as a child 'cause I was my father's favorite. My brother Bill and my brother George used to wash the dishes and used to do this and used to do that. I loved to clean and to volunteer to do things. To this day I love to help people. I love to please people, please my students, please my educators, my colleagues, my parents, my friends.

My four older brothers didn't have an easier time than I at all because they were given more responsibilities than I 'cause I was the first girl after the four boys. I was *la consentida de mi papá y de mis hermanos.* And I learned how to play all the boys' games and I enjoyed it. I loved my family!

We were very poor materially, though. We had only one bathroom and we had to share it with about thirty people and everybody was constipated!

I used to think anything with tile was Hollywood! I do not take a bathroom for granted. I just thank the Lord for my bathroom now. I thank the Lord for hot water. I thank the Lord for detergents to wash the dishes. I don't mind washing them because I remember not even having soap. And hot water! What a luxury. And a shower! Oh Lord have mercy, to have a shower and tile is like a movie star!

So I think I'm very rich. Rich in many, many things because I never had those wonderful things that I thought were really for *gente rica,* rich people.

Yeah, there were arguments in the family, especially when my father drank.

I used to take care of my father when he was drunk, *pobrecito.* I used to sing to him and take care of him. And I was the only one who could guide him. Mother would get mad with him because he would spend the whole check.

It is a very sad thing in *la cultura Méxicana* that the machismo element is there and is so evident *en la borrachera* (which I hated with a passion!). I can still see it around me today, the cycle of poverty, the borracheras, the machismo. It's terrible but it's still here with us today. The only way out of this cycle of poverty, ignorance, illiteracy, and oppression of our women is education. I try to instill this idea in our Hispanic women everywhere I go.

Yeah, my family was different from our neighbors. Very much so because my mother was a fortuneteller and people used to look at her. And so my home was not a regular home. It used to be like Grand Central Station, everybody visiting my mother. And all her friends, patients, *clientas* to see her. It was never really a home that I could see. Just a. . . . I never had my own room. Never, never until I got married because I had to wait until the *clientas* left and then the sofa was made into a bed. It was kind of sad because we didn't have the right studying facilities or anything like that. How we made it in school I don't know. By the help of the Lord, I guess, and a lot of hard work and desire.

I remember that one of my friends, Carmen Rodríguez, said to me, "My mother doesn't want me to play with you."

"Why not?" I said.

"Because your mother's a witch. A fortune-teller and a witch."

"No," I said. I had just seen *The Wizard of Oz*. "My mother's not a witch and if she's a witch, she's a good witch. She's a beautiful lady and she's my mother and she won't hurt you."

So that was sad. I remember those little things that people would say. Now I cry about it and can't imagine how we all survived. The system and cruel humanity was so bad!

My favorite childhood memory, of course, is my father and dancing with him, getting on his feet, dancing the corridos, dancing the pasos dobles, dancing the mazurkas, the varsovianas, waltzes, and schottisches.

I used to get on his feet and dance and I thought I was tremendously great. What a cultural education before kindergarten! And they used to call me culturally deprived!

And then seeing my mother and father dance, that was such a joy. Everyone used to make a circle around them. No one could dance the pasos dobles like *Pedro y Josefina Ramirez,* my parents!

At the very beginning I was kind of fearful of school. Speaking Spanish was a no-no! How we were punished for speaking that "dirty language"! So I became determined to know both English and Spanish so that no one could step on me.

Unfortunately, we didn't have any Spanish at all in grammar school, but my dear Spanish teacher Marie Stamps in high school was so great in Spanish that I used to wonder how she could speak Spanish better than I could and still be an Anglo.

I liked reading even though I knew I had an accent and my *ch*s were horrible. Twenty-five years ago I started trying to get a better articulation of my English language, but it was still horrible. My own kids correct me now, especially in writing. How I wish I could have learned how to write well!

There were many, many teachers that I liked. Miss Robinson, the art teacher, was gorgeous and wonderful and funny. And Miss Hignett, my gosh, I learned English with that beautiful Mary Hignett in my homeroom class in the sixth and seventh grades. My gosh, what a teacher! She used to teach every part of speech in English. She was just drilling it to us. And that's why I learned good English grammar, because of her.

Some of the teachers, Miss Eason, I didn't like her. She used to hit me with a ruler for speaking Spanish and hide me behind the closet. And I know she hated Mexicans 'cause I used to see her talking to Miss Hanna and other teachers, "These typical Mexican girls, they stink, blah, blah, blah." You know, we didn't dare say anything back because whatever the teacher said was right, whatever it was. I wish they could see this "dirty Mexican" now!

Nowadays the kids don't have any respect for themselves or for each other, and that's hard for me as an educator and as a person who struggled for so long to get an education.

My parents did not push any of us to graduate from high school because survival was first to them. Yet my dream from when I was a little girl was to graduate from *college.*

My little sister and I were the only ones in the family that did graduate from college. I just wanted to prove to myself and to my family that I could do it. At college in the 1950s in Denton, hundreds of miles away from El Paso, I used to cry sometimes because of the racism but I was determined to prove myself to the world. One of my counselors told me that I was too bossy; I temporarily went into a shell after that, because the kids from East Texas did not like bossy girls.

Some of my classmates had the same background as me. Unfortunately, I don't see them any more. A lot of them became immediately assimilated. Too assimilated in the American way. They don't dare speak Spanish any more. Some of them changed their names. Many were Anglo-white Hispanic. We just don't have any values, any ideas, anything in common any more. It's very sad because they mistake money for God and I don't care for materialism. I'm a very down-to-earth person.

I never have stopped going to school. I want to go back and I want to study this and I want to study that. I want to take languages and I want to take. . . . I always wanted to get my doctoral degree but I never wanted to be more educated than my husband. My husband is a very beautiful man. Very intelligent. He could have gotten any Ph.D., I'm sure. But he was never guided into that and he's not one of these opportunist guys. He's a very beautiful man: a teacher and a coach and a wonderful, respectable guy.

I got married in 1954 and continued at the university till I graduated in fifty-seven. I got pregnant in my senior year and had to practice-teach and even referee and play basketball while I was pregnant and nursing the baby. I don't want to remember some of those hard experiences, but hard work taught me a lot. I think that to sacrifice and to suffer a little bit, you appreciate life more.

People in El Paso have a tendency to forget their roots of poverty. And for a long time I forgot, too. You know why? Because I felt that everybody had probably gotten out with me, struggling through hard work.

Eventually I forgot that I had lived at the Alamito Projects in the forties with my sister-in-law Minnie when my brother was overseas in France. I forgot that I had thought that the projects were Hollywood because they had had tiles and running water and hot water. God, the first time I had seen hot water! You surely forget very soon. Once you're comfortable you don't want to be reminded how poor you were.

I don't want to be reminded that they have called me every label under the book. They have called me Chicana-honky. They have called me Tía Taco. They have called me Coconut. They have called me radical, militant, anti-American. From both the conservative and the liberal, I have had it.

And I went through a period of horrible, horrible depression and suffering and I even was saying, "Hey, I don't think there's a God. He's not listening to me." But there *was* a God. I was just too impatient with Him. I was not really devout in my faith, so God was testing me. Since then I have learned a lot from some students of mine. For instance, I had four older ladies from the barrio that didn't know how to read or write. They come and apologize to me. *"Señora Guerrero, no sé escribir*—I don't know how to write."

I say, *"Qué le hace, señora.* But look at your children and learn with them."

One has had twenty-three children. I call her my rabbit. *Mi coneja.* [Laughter] But now she is trying to learn. She just lost her husband last year and she's trying to get herself together. This is the first time in her life she can take classes in human relations, English, citizenship, even *folklórico.* I had my *viejitas* dancing *folklórico* down there. And so I made them feel good.

I told them, "It doesn't matter if you don't know how to read and write. It's not a sin. But here is the opportunity that we're teaching. Now take it by the horns and do it. I laugh and say that it is a sin *not* to do something about learning to read and write."

Soon I heard some of them saying *"Ay, Señora Guerrero, Usted habla tan bonito."*

They thought I was so intelligent, but I said "No, you are inspiring me. I don't talk pretty."

They felt that I'm such a scholar. "I'm nothing," I say. "I don't care how many degrees I may have acquired. I am down here trying to help you."

And that's the thing. I don't want to forget my poverty. I don't want to forget where I came from. I don't want to forget my ethnicity. Being proud of my heritage has made me a stronger human being. It helps me to tell others that they are all terrific, too!

I don't want to forget that there is a potential renaissance in all of us, whoever we are.

ALAN BEAN:
FROM FORT WORTH
TO THE MOON
Houston, TX
Born 1932

Alan Bean became the fourth man to walk on the moon as lunar module pilot for Apollo 12 in 1969. In 1974 he began to document America's space program with paintings based upon his own lunar experiences. "I have always been interested in art," he said recently. "I began painting when I was a Navy test pilot in 1960." Alan's favorite painters were Claude Monet and Old West masters Charles Russell and Frederic Remington. In 1981 he resigned as chief of NASA's astronaut training to become a full-time artist.

One writer referred to Alan Bean's Texas accent as "thick as crude oil," a tribute to his youth in Temple and Fort Worth.

Alan Bean attributes his success to his mother because she pushed him to persevere when he would have preferred an easier path. This astronaut hero says, "I was never the smartest person in the class, but I was always there when I said I was going to be. They could always count on me." He feels the same sense of responsibility about his current mission of recording the beauty and drama of space flight.

These stories won't get recorded unless I do it. All of us that walked on the moon in Apollo will be dead and gone in twenty or thirty years. My dream is that one or two hundred years from now we will be on Mars and going no telling where. People will look on my paintings as factual, beautiful capsule pieces of space his-

tory. How it really was! If there is any person to record it artistically that had actually been there, it is going to have to be me!

ONE SUNDAY IN 1974 I didn't have anything to paint and I said to myself, "Maybe I will paint the moon just for the heck of it." After I had been painting it for about three or four hours, I began to realize this is what I ought to be doing with the rest of my life.

I know everything about the moon, space suits, lunar modules, and all the Apollo equipment. With the flowers I used to paint, I knew leaf, stem, petal, and root; that was about it. When you talk about space flight, the moon, I know *all* the stuff. For eighteen years I learned it and loved it.

Painting the moon was a natural, but it didn't dawn on me for a while because the moon is gray, the sky black, the suits white— kind of boring! Then after a number of years of doing it I realized that it was up to me to make this lunar environment beautiful. It was up to me to take a white suit and make it beautiful. As I progressed in my profession, I saw my role change. I began to realize that it wasn't Nature's job to make the moon beautiful. It was my job as the artist to see the beauty that was there and enhance it, idealize it. Just like Monet did. We never see real water lilies like his beautifully painted water lilies.

Being on the moon was not all that science-fictionlike. We trained a lot in West Texas, Iceland, and other places that we thought were good analogs for what the moon might be like. West Texas turned out to be one of the most useful because of its desert varnish effect. Sometimes all the rocks look the same color at first glance because the way they have been exposed to the elements, they all get a surface coating that gives them a certain similarity even though they are different kinds of rocks. In this situation I had to learn to pick out the different types of rocks without using the most useful clue, color. I had to take samples by angularity, by shape, by edges, or by other factors about the rocks besides just color.

The moon was like that, too, because of the extreme lighting and because of the dust all around.

I was in elementary school in Temple, Texas, when World War II began. In 1941 I was nine years old. Going to war movies and having Camp Hood, a large Army base, nearby made me relate to the military and made me want to fly the same kind of airplanes that I saw in the movies. If John Wayne could fly, so could I! It looked like a lot of fun!

So I began to want to be an aviator.

One of the advantages of living in Fort Worth was the fact that there was a Naval Air Reserve Unit between Dallas and Fort Worth at Grand Prairie. I went over there when I was a junior in high school. I wasn't old enough to join, but I went over there just to be around military airplanes. I got my father to sign a release so I could join the Naval Air Reserve. I joined on my seventeenth birthday. I loved it. I got to help work on airplanes and got to fly in the back of TBNs, which was a single-engine World War II torpedo bomber.

When I got to be a senior in high school, I wanted to go away and fly for the Navy. By then I had decided that it would be fun to land on aircraft carriers. The Navy awarded Naval ROTC scholarships like they still do, but my grades had not been all that good in high school. I just didn't study that hard.

One of the days that changed my life completely was a Saturday morning that I was supposed to go and take the Naval ROTC exam. I didn't want to get out of bed and I decided "What the heck, I probably wouldn't pass it anyway."

I decided to sleep in.

My mother came in and woke me up and told me to get out of bed and she would drive me downtown. I told her that I wouldn't pass anyway. She would not take no for an answer. She got me up and took me downtown and I took the test.

Lo and behold, I did pass!

I was selected, I think, largely because during the interview they said "Would you like to be in the Navy?" I said I was already in the Navy as a reservist trying to learn all I could about airplanes.

This was just before the beginning of the Korean War, and when that war began, my reserve unit was sent to Korea. They discharged me and sent me to the University of Texas because I had been awarded a NROTC scholarship. I would serve later!

I didn't know what to study, but I knew I wanted to be a pilot so I decided to study aeronautical engineering.

I didn't really want to be an engineer. I just wanted to be a pilot, but I got my degree and my commission in 1955.

After I got my wings in 1956, I was assigned to a flying squadron at Jacksonville. I was really loving it. It was better even than I had imagined it as a kid. I loved the guys that I was working with. We were always thinking about the same thing.

One of the funny things was that for the first time in my life I was around a bunch of men that were interested in the same things I was. In high school and college, I was interested in airplanes and the rest of my friends weren't. But in the Navy squadron we were all thinking about landing on carriers and all the fun things we did.

Then I began to realize that it would be good to be a test pilot, because test pilots got to newer airplanes that flew faster and higher. I had the background and I was selected for Navy test pilot school.

After about a year or so, I turned on the TV and saw Al Shepard go into space on a rocket. I said, "Boy, that looks more fun than what I am doing." He is going higher and faster than what I am doing (which I thought was the most fun you could have). So I began to want to become an astronaut.

Once again, I was standing around with the right background and at the best age and in excellent health. My life has been lived doing things that were fun. As soon as I began a job, I saw another one that looked more enticing. But it wasn't all easy. It was a lot of work, too. My mother was on my case ever since I can remember, always *making* me have jobs, *making* me work around the house. . . . You notice the words I use. I didn't see it as inspiration, I saw it as "Why do I have to work, why do I have to take naps in the afternoon when the other kids don't, why do I have to have a job when other kids don't?" I would have to clean the kitchen woodwork or something, it had better be clean or she would just keep me there to do it. I wanted to be out playing.

None of the other kids had to do that. It taught me what doing a good job was. She always wanted me to be working and productive. She thought that was the right thing to do and I wasn't interested in doing it that way. Of course, I had to respond to her. Now, I credit her with ninety percent of my success. That is really what life is, how you relate to work, how you can handle frustrations, and what you consider a job well done.

She must have learned it from her parents. She was very methodical and she was very energetic. I didn't know it at the time, but she was very entrepreneurial also. For example, my father joined the Army at the beginning of World War II and was sent to Europe and then to the Pacific. My mother was there as a housewife in Temple, Texas, with me and my sister Paula to care for. Mom was restless. She didn't want to just stay home and read so she started up a grocery store. She named it Alpa for Alan and Paula, my sister. That was the good news. The bad news was that *I* had to work in it. That's how I saw it, of course.

All during the war my mother worked harder than my sister and I combined in that grocery store.

When the war was over, we moved to Fort Worth when my father resumed working for the Soil Conservation Service, Department of Agriculture. He was a flood control specialist, so when a river project was completed, they sent him to some other river.

My mother and sister and I lived in Fort Worth and Mom decided that she would like a nicer house, so she up and started an ice cream store. I *had* to work there along with my sister.

My mom wanted something better for our family so she figured out how to get it. She bought some land, had someone build a store, got the ice cream, and sold it. She worked very hard. So did my dad, sister, and I.

I realize now how lucky I was. But I didn't see it that way then. From my point of view, I was always working, and much more than my friends had to do. Life was not all that much fun.

One of the nicest things about being an astronaut was the effect that it had on my family. It labeled them as successful parents. And they were.

I tried to include my mom and dad in anything that occurred around Fort Worth when I got back from the moon. We had a huge parade in Fort Worth and, of course, Mom was included. I took her to Washington when I got my Navy astronaut wings. There is a little picture in my study of the Secretary of the Navy giving her a kiss on the cheek. She had this picture up in her house until she died about three years ago. By the way, she would paint a slightly different picture than I did about the morning of that NROTC test. She used to say that I had had the flu and couldn't get out of bed.

I don't remember it that way, but that's how mothers are. They don't always take the credit that they deserve. She was a wonderful mother and I miss her a lot.

MICHAEL DELL:
SCHOOL DROPOUT
Austin, TX
Born 1965

"When I told people in other states I was from Texas, they expected an accent, cowboy hat, and boots," says computer mogul Michael Dell. "But that wasn't at all what Texas was about for me."

Michael Dell is a living representative of America's transformation from extractive industries to a high-tech, information-based economy. As founder of a half-billion-dollar-a-year computer company, Michael at age twenty-six *is* the new Texas. His first childhood memory is of a man landing on the moon! He grew up in a Houston where "every other week another building would pop up." He and Houston grew up together.

"All my life my parents had said 'Be a doctor; be a doctor.' " Michael left for a pre-med biology major at the University of Texas at Austin just as Houston went into its 1980s recession. "It started to decline just as I was getting out of town," he laughs. His upward spiral with Dell Computer was about to begin.

Michael Dell is a native Texan whose parents, an orthodontist and a stockbroker, grew up in New York. Michael is bullish on Austin's prospects for the 1990s because of its powerful university and large pool of technical talent. Yet the state's creaky secondary system worries him. "We have had to watch that some of our job applicants don't have other people fill out their forms because they can't read and write well enough," says CEO Dell. "That's pretty bad!"

Only a couple of years ago this horn-rimmed, owlish fellow began his business with an inventory that literally fit into a bathtub. Despite being a college dropout, he turned his measly thousand-dollar capital into a megacompany through sheer competitiveness. He says modestly that "in any business there's always opportunity to do things." His idols are Microsoft founder Bill Gates and Apple's Steve Jobs and Steve Wozniak: "anyone who's done something which has never been done before in a creative or unique way."

(Credit: Courtesy, Dell Computer)

I WOULD NOT HAVE PLACED myself totally over into the nerd spectrum in high school, but I certainly leaned in that direction. I was fortunate enough to go to a very fine public high school in Houston. There were a lot of students at Memorial who were very ambitious and conscientious.

Among the teachers who inspired me, there was a Mr. Saatoff, my physics teacher. It was really a joy learning from him because he made complex topics fun and exciting.

In junior high school I had been in an advanced math class where we had access to a computer terminal. I started playing with that terminal and became very fascinated with it. I started to learn everything I could about computers. I earned enough money to be able to buy my own computer by selling just about everything I could sell. I had a long history of strings of businesses: stamps, coins, ball cards, stocks, bonds. You name it, I was sellin' it. Newspapers. I sold all kinds of stuff.

I graduated from Memorial High School in 1983 and came to the University of Texas. Why? Let me see if I can give you a good analogy about growing up in Texas and going to the University of Texas. You know how little kids wake up every Saturday morning and go watch cartoons? It's just something you do. Probably sixty percent of the people from my high school went to the University of Texas.

When you're in the tenth grade, if you get over a certain score on your pre-SAT tests, they send you a little post card which says "Sign here to enroll in the University Of Texas." I sent it in and fully two and a half years before I even set foot on the campus I was enrolled! It was kind of like subscribing to *Time* magazine. [Laughter]

Besides being a very good university and Austin being a nice place to live, I also had a brother that was here.

I had gotten into computers and become fascinated with the technology, and somewhere along the way the fascination with the product and the technology merged with my business interests and I found this opportunity which was irresistible to start this company in my freshman dorm room in Austin.

So in 1983–1984 I was going to school and selling computer add-on parts: RAM chips, hard drives, kits, things like that. The IBM PC had just come out in eighty-one and by eighty-three to eighty-four it had taken control of the market. But what disturbed me was that there was a discontinuity between the price that a customer paid for a computer and the value that they received. That phenomenon is still out there today in the retail computer channels. The reason for that is not because Compaq makes their computers for too high of a price down in Houston but that they provide a margin to the dealer which is inconsistent with the value that the dealer delivers to you. So I decided to sell directly to the customer through mail order and pass along the savings. Was I lucky? I entered the market at the right time with a good strategy. How much of that was luck and how much of it was market savvy no one will ever know.

My closest brush with trouble was the time that my parents got a rumor that I was selling computers instead of going to school. They were, of course, very upset about this because in the Houston neighborhood I come from it's not considered to be the right thing to do to drop out of school. So they hopped on a plane and called from the Austin airport and said "This is your mother speaking! [Laughter] We'll be there in fifteen minutes." Sunday morning kind of thing!

I was still selling out of my dorm. So I quickly woke up and convinced my roommate to put all the computers and associated paraphernalia in his bathtub. So in about a thirteen-and-a-half-minute period we put a dorm room of computers in one bathtub. Put a sheet over it. Because I deduced that my mother, while she would inspect every piece of the apartment, she would not inspect my roommate's bathtub. For some reason I concluded that that territory was off limits.

We were able to hide all the equipment in time and when she came, she couldn't find anything. They did, however, ask where my books were. And in typical quick-thinking style I told them that they were at the library.

I think they got the idea that something was up, but they still hadn't quite figured it out.

After their visit, I finished my freshman year in May of eighty-four. Then I decided to move the business into an official office to give a real go at it and see if it would really take off. I decided that I would wait until the end of August to see what happened.

Anyway, the business went from $80,000 a month in my dorm in April to $360,000 in August, so I knew I was onto something.

I didn't go back to school in the fall. I kept running the business. I did six million dollars' worth of revenue in that first nine months. The year after we did thirty-three million. Then sixty-nine million—169 million, 258 million, 388 million. So I never did go back to school!

GLOSSARY

AGGIE Student at or graduate of Texas A & M University.

BAR DITCH A barrow pit on either side of a road.

BITE DOWN ON AN EAR To distract someone (as to distract a wild horse while trying to mount it).

BLOWED Gone; blown away with the wind.

BORDERBLASTER A very powerful radio station broadcasting from Mexico.

BRUSH ARBOR A shade shelter made of brush.

BUFFALO Carp.

CARRY To take (as to take a girl to a movie).

CHOPS Whiskey sour mash.

CHUCK Food.

CUTTER A thin slaughter cow to be cut up into processed meat such as bologna; a card, a cut-up, a showman ("Ain't he a cutter?").

DOGTROT A hill country house of two separate sections connected by a covered breezeway or dogtrot.

FLATHEAD A man with a saw in a logging crew. Originally there was a flathead at each end of a crosscut saw.

FLOOR The main deck of an oil rig.

JOHNSON BAR Reverse lever of a steam locomotive.

LINE CAMP An outlying cabin away from a ranch's headquarters.

LONGNECK A beer bottle with an elongated neck.

PITCHING HORSE Bucking horse.

RAWHIDING A WINDMILL Using strips of green or wet cowhide for attaching wooden blades to windmills.

SHINY Good.

SHITKICKER A good old boy.

SHOTGUN HOUSE Dilapidated shack.

SLACK A period when rodeo contestants compete away from the public show.

STRIPPER An oil well that produces fewer than ten barrels a day.

SPUDDER An early-day oil-drilling rig.

SUCKER RODS Vertical pipes that convey the energy of a windmill to a pump in a water well.

TANK A farm pond in which seasonal rain is stored for livestock.

TALL BOY A twenty-four-ounce beer.

TEASIP Student at or graduate of the University of Texas.

TUSH HOG Bull of the woods; a big shot.

VEGA Sandbar or bottomland.

WILDCAT An exploratory, highly speculative oil well.

YELLOW DOG DEMOCRAT A voter so partisan that he or she would vote for the Democratic candidate even if that candidate were a yellow dog.

YONDER Over there; an indeterminate distance away.

INDEX

ABOUT THE AUTHOR

Ron Strickland is portraying America through the voices of its citizens in a series of regional self-portraits. For more than a dozen years he has been traveling widely in search of the "real America." After receiving his Ph.D. from Georgetown University in 1976, Dr. Strickland set out to create an eleven-hundred-mile foot and horse trail from Glacier National Park in Montana to the Pacific Ocean. An oral-history book called *River Pigs and Cayuses* (1984) grew out of his encounters along the Pacific Northwest Trail. *Vermonters* (1986) is about the people of Dr. Strickland's native New England. Subsequent interviewing tours in New England, the Southwest, and California finally led him back to his home state of Washington for another look at Northwest lore and life-styles. *Whistlepunks and Geoducks* (1990) is his second look at the Pacific Northwest. *Texans* is the fourth book in the *American* series. *Alaskans* (1992) will be the fifth.

Ron Strickland is currently at work on an oral-history portrait of the American South. He lives in Seattle.